English Compass

A1

Vanessa Clark

Gaynor Ramsey

Lynda Hübner

Langenscheidt

Berlin · München · Wien · Zürich · New York

English Compass A1

Autorinnen:
Vanessa Clark, Abingdon: In class, Task, Game
Gaynor Ramsey, Zürich: Your turn, Test yourself
Lynda Hübner, München: Reading

Beratung:
Vanessa Clark, Abingdon
Roswitha Fenes, Bergisch-Gladbach
Gaynor Ramsey, Zürich
Dörthe Zingel, Hamburg

Redaktion:
Helge Sturmfels (Projektleitung)
Lynda Hübner
Carola Jeschke, München
Hannah Windbichler, Wien

Grafik und Layout:
Design Im Kontor – Iris Steiner, München: Umschlag, Gestaltungskonzept und Layout
kaltnermedia, Bobingen: Satz und Layout

Lehrwerkskomponenten:

Kursbuch mit Beiheft *Out and About* und Learner CD/CD-ROMs	51251
Teacher Audio CDs	51252
Teaching Compass	51253

www.langenscheidt.de/englishcompass

Der Innenteil dieses Buches wurde auf chlorfrei gebleichtem Papier gedruckt.

1. Auflage 2008

Druck: Vorarlberger Verlagsanstalt GmbH, Dornbirn
Printed in Austria

ISBN-13: 978-3-526-51251-6

1 2 3 4 5 * 2012 11 10 09 08

Welcome to English Compass A1

Willkommen zu Ihrem Englischkurs mit *English Compass A1*. Ein Kompass hilft bei der Orientierung in unbekanntem Gelände und führt sicher ans Ziel. Ein solches Instrument soll Ihnen dieses Lernpaket auch sein: *English Compass A1* führt Sie zum erfolgreichen Abschluss der Niveaustufe A1 des *Gemeinsamen europäischen Referenzrahmens für Sprachen* (GER).

Bevor der Kurs beginnt, möchten wir kurz ein paar Fragen zu Aufbau und Inhalt des Lernpakets beantworten.

Was enthält das Lernpaket *English Compass A1*?

- das ***Lehr- und Arbeitsbuch*** mit 12 Lerneinheiten (**Units**), 4 Testeinheiten (**Test yourself**) und dem umfangreichen Anhang,
- das Begleitheft ***Out and About*** mit ebenfalls 12 Units, die den Themen des Lehr- und Arbeitsbuches entsprechen,
- die beiden ***Learner CD/CD-ROMs*** mit den Hörtexten der Arbeitsbuchteile und den Recap-CD-ROMs
- und ein umfangreiches ***Internetangebot*** mit vielen interaktiven Übungen.

Wie ist eine Unit aufgebaut?

- Jede Unit widmet sich einem Thema, das in zwei Teile (**Part A** und **Part B**) aufgeteilt ist.
- Part A enthält zunächst drei Seiten für den **Unterricht**. Am Ende der dritten Seite befindet sich die sog. **Flexizone** mit zwei flexibel einsetzbaren Übungen. Danach folgen zwei Seiten **Your turn** für die Nacharbeit des Unterrichtsstoffes zu Hause.
- Part B enthält vier Seiten für den **Unterricht**. Die vierte Seite ist immer ein flexibel einsetzbares, unterhaltsames **Spiel** oder eine **kommunikative Aktivität**. Danach folgen wieder zwei Seiten **Your turn**.
- Am Ende einer jeden Unit finden Sie eine Seite mit dem Titel **Reading**, auf der sich ein unterhaltsamer Lesetext und ein kleines Rätsel zum vergnüglichen Lesen außerhalb des Unterrichts befinden.

Was genau gibt es auf den Seiten für den Unterricht?

- **Lernziele** am Anfang der Unit, damit Sie wissen, worum es in der Unit geht,
- der **Kompass-Starter** als kommunikative Übung, um in das Thema der Unit einzuleiten,
- **Word focus**-Kästen mit den wichtigsten Vokablen der Lerneinheit,
- **How to …**-Kästen mit den Redemitteln der Unit,
- **Grammar focus**-Kästen mit einer übersichtlichen Darstellung der Grammatik,
- **Info**-Felder mit sprachlich-kulturellen Tipps,
- **First aid**-Felder mit Strategien, wie Sie sich bei sprachlichen Problemen selbst helfen können,
- **Say it like this** mit Ausspracheübungen,
- Kennzeichnung **berufsrelevanter** Sprache,
- und natürlich viele abwechslungsreiche, kommunikative **Übungen und Aktivitäten**.

Und was enthalten die Arbeitsbuchseiten mit dem Titel Your turn?

- Vertiefende Übungen zu **Redemitteln**, **Hörverständnis**, **Wortschatz** und **Grammatik**. Schließlich eine Übung **Round up**, in der die Lerninhalte kombiniert geübt werden,
- Say it like this: Eine Übung zu **Aussprache** und **Intonation**, die Sie mit geschlossenem Buch machen sollten,
- einen Verweis auf **zusätzliche Übungen im Internet**,
- **Jetzt kann ich …**: Hier können Sie Ihr sprachliches Können einschätzen und entscheiden, wie sicher Sie sich in bestimmten sprachlichen Bereichen fühlen. Wenn Sie noch Hilfe brauchen, dann erfahren Sie hier, wo Sie weitere Übungen finden.

Welche Materialien finde ich im Anhang des Buches?

- **A/B Files:** Informationen für die entsprechenden Übungen im Buch,
- **Grammar:** Referenzgrammatik zum Nachschlagen,
- **Key:** Lösungsschlüssel für alle Übungen der Your turn- und Test yourself-Seiten,
- **Audio scripts:** Transkripte der Hörtexte der Your turn- und Test yourself-Seiten,
- **Words and Phrases:** Lernwortschatz und Redewendungen aus den einzelnen Units,
- **Word list:** Alphabetische Wortliste aller Wörter im Buch,
- **Can do list A1:** Checkliste für die Stufe A1 des GER.

Was mache ich, wenn ich etwas noch nicht so gut kann?

Im Element **Jetzt kann ich …** am Ende der **Your turn**-Seiten können Sie entscheiden, ob Sie zusätzlich zu den **Your turn**-Übungen noch weitere Aufgaben machen wollen:

- Zu allen Kannbeschreibungen gibt es interaktive Übungen im **Internet**. Ein Verweis mit Code zeigt Ihnen, wie Sie die Übung finden. Im Beispiel **www: U1A3** gehen Sie auf die Seite www.langenscheidt.de/englishcompass und geben Sie dort den Code **U1A3** in das Eingabefeld ein. Sie kommen dann direkt zu der gewünschten Übung. Auf der Website finden Sie auch weitere Übungen zu Grammatik und Wortschatz.
- Zu ausgewählten Kannbeschreibungen gibt es Hörübungen im Recap-Teil Ihrer ***Learner CD/CD-ROMs***. Ein Verweis mit Tracknummer zeigt Ihnen, wie Sie die Übung finden. Im Beispiel **CD-R 1: 14** starten Sie die ***Learner CD/CD-ROM 1*** in Ihrem Computer und geben Sie die Tracknummer **14** in das Eingabefeld ein. Sie kommen dann direkt zur gewünschten Übung.

Wie kann ich auch außerhalb des Unterrichts mein Englisch anwenden und vertiefen?

Sprechen, hören, lesen und schreiben Sie so viel Englisch wie möglich. Um Sie dabei zu unterstützen, bietet Ihr Lernpaket folgende Möglichkeiten:

- ***Out and About:*** In diesem Begleitheft finden Sie für jede Unit des Kursbuches eine Reihe von abwechslungsreichen Aufgaben und Aktivitäten, die Sie dazu ermuntern, Englisch auch außerhalb des Unterrichts anzuwenden. Sehen Sie sich die Einleitung und das Inhaltsverzeichnis von *Out and About* an. Sie werden erstaunt sein, wie viel Sie nach ein paar Units schon können.
- ***Recap-CD-ROM:*** Sie wollen den Unterrichtsstoff noch einmal wiederholen oder haben eine Stunde verpasst? Kein Problem! Mit der *Recap-CD-ROM* auf der *Learner-CD/CD-ROM* können Sie die wichtigsten Inhalte aller Unitteile in kurzweiligen Hörübungen wiederholen und nachholen.

Was bedeuten die Symbole im Buch?

= kommunikative Starter-Übung am Anfang eines Unitteils

L1:10 / L2:10 = Verweis auf die Tracknummer einer Tonaufnahme auf der beigelegten *Learner CD/CD-ROM 1* oder *2*

T1:10 / T2:10 = Verweis auf die Tracknummer einer Tonaufnahme auf den separat erhältlichen *Teacher CDs 1* oder *2*

= Grammatikbereiche im Buch

= interessante und wichtige sprachlich-kulturelle Informationen und Lerntipps

= Strategien, wie Sie sich bei sprachlichen Problemen selbst helfen können

= berufsrelevante Redewendungen etc.

= flexibel einsetzbare Übungen und Aufgaben

→ www = zusätzliche interaktive Übungen im Internet unter www.langenscheidt.de/englishcompass

→ G2 (S. 70) = Seitenverweis auf die Nachschlagegrammatik im Buchanhang

S. 180 = Seitenverweis auf den Lösungsschlüssel im Buchanhang

OOO = Einschätzung des eigenen sprachlichen Könnens:
O = kann ich gut
O = kann ich so einigermaßen
O = kann ich noch nicht

www: U1A1 = Verweis auf eine interaktive Übung im Internet mit Eingabecode

CD-R 1: 10
CD-R 2: 10 = Verweis auf die Tracknummer einer Hörübung der Recap-CD-ROM auf der *Learner-CD/CD-ROM 1* oder *2*

↺ U1A = Rückverweis in die entsprechende Unit aus der Nachschlagegrammatik im Buchanhang

Viel Spaß und viel Erfolg wünschen Vanessa Clark Gaynor Ramsey Lynda Hübner

Contents

Contents

Unit 4 Daily life

Unit 5 Active and healthy

Unit 6 Food and drink

Unit 7 On holiday

Unit 8 Entertainment

Unit 9 Doing things your way

Contents

Making contact

Part A Nice to meet you

Hello and *goodbye* | Introductions | Countries and nationalities | Present of *to be* (1), singular | *my, your, his, her*

Make a name card.
Machen Sie ein Namensschild.
Say hello to the person next to you.
Begrüßen Sie die Person neben Ihnen.

Hello. I'm Bettina.

Christian Weik

Margarethe Schneider

Bettina Hey

Hello. How are you?

1a T1:2 Listen to the dialogues. Match the dialogues to the photos. Write the numbers 1–3 in the boxes.
Hören Sie die Gespräche. Ordnen Sie die Gespräche den Fotos zu. Schreiben Sie die Zahlen 1–3 in die Kästchen.

1b T1:3 Read these phrases. Then listen to the dialogues again and tick (✓) the phrases you hear.
Lesen Sie diese Sätze. Hören Sie die Dialoge noch einmal und haken Sie die Sätze ab, die Sie hören.

Dialogue 1
- ☐ Hello. I'm Jill.
- ☐ Hi. I'm Jill.
- ☐ Nice to meet you, Jill.
- ☐ What's your name?
- ☐ My name's Richard.

Dialogue 2
- ☐ Hi.
- ☐ How are you?
- ☐ Fine, thanks. And you?
- ☐ I'm very well, thank you.
- ☐ I'm OK, thanks.

Dialogue 3
- ☐ David, this is Emma Stevens.
- ☐ I'm Emma Stevens.
- ☐ Hello, Emma.
- ☐ Nice to meet you.
- ☐ Nice to meet you, too.

T1:4 **Say it like this.** Listen and repeat the sentences.
Hören Sie und wiederholen Sie die Sätze.

1c Look at the photos again. In groups of three, read the dialogues.
Sehen Sie sich die Fotos noch einmal an. Lesen Sie die Gespräche zu dritt.

English speakers normally use first names.

2 How to say hello
Wie Sie jemanden begrüßen.

Hello. / Hi.
I'm (name). / My name's …
Nice to meet you.
How are you?
Fine, thanks. / I'm OK, thanks. / I'm very well, thank you.
And you?

2a Walk around the class. Shake hands and say hello to the other students.
Gehen Sie in Ihrem Kursraum umher und begrüßen Sie die anderen Teilnehmer.

3 How to introduce a person
Wie Sie jemanden vorstellen.

This is (name).
Nice to meet you.
Nice to meet you, too.

3a Work in pairs. Walk around the classroom and introduce your partner to the other students.
Arbeiten Sie zu zweit. Gehen Sie im Kursraum umher und stellen Sie Ihren Partner / Ihre Partnerin den anderen Teilnehmern vor.

Where are you from?

4a Look at the two pictures and write in the missing words.
Sehen Sie die beiden Bilder an und schreiben Sie die fehlenden Wörter in die Lücken.

Hi. I'm ________________.
I'm from Hallein. It's near ________________,
in ________________.

Salzburg | Katja | Austria.

Hello. ________________ name's Dieter.
I'm ________________ Erding.
It's near Munich, ________________ Germany.

in | from | My

I (ich) is always a capital letter.

T1:5 Listen and check your answers.
Hören Sie und überprüfen Sie Ihre Antworten.

4b Look at the photos again. Talk to a partner.
Sehen Sie sich die Fotos noch einmal an. Sprechen Sie zu zweit.

Her name's …
She's …

His name's …
He's …

What's **your** name?
My name's … .
His name's Dieter.
Her name's Katja.

5a Put these words in the right order to make questions.
Ordnen Sie die Wörter so an, dass Fragesätze entstehen.

1 name / What's / your / ?
2 from / are / you / Where / ?
3 that / Where's / ?

5b Talk to a new partner and ask your questions. Write a profile of him/her. Read your profiles to another pair of students.
Sprechen Sie mit einem neuen Partner / einer neuen Partnerin. Schreiben Sie ein Profil von ihm/ihr. Lesen Sie Ihre Profile einer anderen Zweiergruppe vor.

6 Word focus Countries and nationalities

6a Look at these stamps. Where are they from? Write in the missing words.
Sehen Sie sich diese Briefmarken an. Woher kommen sie? Schreiben Sie die fehlenden Wörter in die Lücken.

1 It's a ______________ stamp.   2 It's an ______________ stamp.

It's **a** German stamp.
It's **an** English stamp.
Use *an* with words starting with a, e, i, o, u.

6b Now look at these stamps with your partner. Where are they from? Match a country and a nationality to each stamp.
Sehen Sie sich jetzt diese Briefmarken zu zweit an. Woher kommen sie? Ordnen Sie jeder Briefmarke ein Land und eine Nationalität zu.

Country: Switzerland | Italy | Australia | France | Ireland | Turkey | Greece | Austria
Nationality: Australian | Turkish | French | Irish | Italian | Austrian | Greek | Swiss

1 *I think it's from France. It's a French stamp.*

1 2 3 4 5 6 7 8

7 Grammar focus

Present of *to be* (1)

I'm English.
Are you from London?
Yes, **I am**. / No, **I'm not**.
He's (she's, it's) French.
Is he (she, it) from Paris?
Yes, **he (she, it) is**. / No, **he (she, it) isn't**.

'm = **am**   **'s** = **is**   **isn't** = **is not**

7a Choose the right word.
Wählen Sie das richtige Wort.

1 Is / Are you Greek?
2 Is / Are your teacher American?
3 Is / Are Salzburg in Switzerland?
4 Is / Are you Austrian?
5 Is / Are Munich in Germany?
6 Is / Are you from Hamburg?

7b Work with a partner. Ask the questions in Exercise 7a and give a short answer, e.g. *Yes, I am. / No, I'm not.*
Yes, he/she/it is. / No, he/she/it isn't.
Arbeiten Sie zu zweit. Stellen Sie die Fragen aus Übung 7a und geben Sie Kurzantworten.

Flexizone

A Interview people in your class. Write the information on a piece of paper. Then report one piece of information to the class.
Sprechen Sie mit anderen Teilnehmern. Schreiben Sie die Information auf ein Blatt Papier. Berichten Sie Ihrer Kursgruppe.
Name (What …?)   From (Where …?)   In / Near (Where …?)

B Think of a famous person and ask the class: *Where's (name) from?* Now think of a town and ask the class: *Where's (town)?*
Denken Sie an eine berühmte Person und fragen Sie: *Where's (name) from?* Denken Sie nun an eine Stadt und fragen Sie: *Where's (town)?*

Goodbye

8 Say goodbye to your teacher and to the other students in your class.
Verabschieden Sie sich von Ihrem Kursleiter / Ihrer Kursleiterin und von den anderen Kursteilnehmern.

Goodbye!
Bye!
See you next week!

Your turn Nice to meet you (→ www)

1 How to …

Schreiben Sie die Wörter in die Lücken.

a Wie Sie jemanden begrüßen und sich vorstellen.

Hi | I'm | meet you | my | Nice to | too

Karl: Hello, ________ Karl.

Laura: ________, ________ name's Laura.

Karl: Nice to ________ ________, Laura.

Laura: ________ ________ meet you, ________.

b Wie Sie andere Personen vorstellen.

meet you | meet you | nice to | nice to | this is | too

Laura: Karl, ________ ________ Astrid.

Karl: Hello Astrid, ________ ________

________ ________.

Astrid: Hello Karl, ________ ________ ________

________, ________.

c Wie Sie nach persönlichen Informationen fragen und Auskunft geben.

are you | in | I'm from | My | name's | near | Where's | that | your

Astrid: I'm Astrid. What's ________ name?

Mark: ________ ________ Mark.

Where ________ ________ from, Astrid?

Astrid: ________ ________ Baden.

Mark: ________ ________?

Astrid: It's ________ Switzerland, ________ Zurich.

d Wie Sie sich verabschieden.

Bye | next | See | week | you

Karl: Goodbye, Laura.

Laura: ________, Karl. ________

________ ________ ________.

L1:2 Hören Sie und überprüfen Sie Ihre Dialoge.

L1:3 **Say it like this** Hören Sie und sprechen Sie nach.

2 Word focus Countries and nationalities

Schreiben Sie die Nationalitäten der Personen aus diesen Ländern:

~~Australia~~ | Austria | England | ~~France~~ | Germany | Greece | Italy | ~~Ireland~~ | Turkey | Switzerland | USA

with *–ian* at the end Australian, ________

____

with *–ish* at the end Irish, ________

____

other French, ________

____

3 Grammar focus

3.1 Present of *to be* → G1 (S. 170)

Are you from Austria?	No, **I'm not**.	**I'm not** Austrian.
Are you German?	Yes, **I am**.	**I'm** from Berlin.
Is she from England?	No, **she isn't**.	**She isn't** English.
Is she Irish?	Yes, **she is**.	**She's** from Dublin.
Is he from Italy?	No, **he isn't**.	**He isn't** Italian.
Is he French?	Yes, **he is**.	**He's** from Paris.
Is it from Greece?	No, **it isn't**.	
Where **is it** from?	**It's** from Turkey.	

Kurzantworten (*Yes, I am. / No, it isn't.* usw.) werden im Englischen häufig verwendet. Es kann unhöflich klingen, wenn Sie nur mit *Yes* oder *No* antworten.

a Sehen Sie sich die Sätze in der Grammatiktabelle an. Beantworten Sie diese Fragen:

1 Where's the man from?

________ ________ ________.

2 Where's the woman from?

________ ________ ________.

3 Is the man French?

________, ________ ________.

4 Where's the stamp from?

________ ________ ________.

b Schreiben Sie diese Sätze. Verwenden Sie die Kurzform.

1 It is an Italian film, it is not French.

It's an Italian film, it isn't French.

2 She is from Ulm, she is not from Bonn.

______

3 He is not German, he is Austrian.

______

4 I am not English, I am Irish.

______

c Schreiben Sie die fehlenden Wörter in die Lücken.

1 She's English. ______

from London? – No, ______ .

She ______ from Liverpool.

2 ______ Australian. ______

from Sydney? – No, ______ .

______ from Melbourne.

3.2 *My, his* and *her*

→ G3 (S. 171)

a Schreiben Sie *Anna* und *Karl* in die Lücken.

I'm from England.	**My** name's Tom.
He's from Germany.	**His** name's ______ .
She's from Switzerland.	**Her** name's ______ .

b Streichen Sie die falschen Wörter.

1 This is Christian. *My / His / Her* surname is Weik.
2 This is Bettina. *My / His / Her* surname is Hey.
3 Hello, I'm Jill. *My / His / Her* surname is Carr.

3.3 *A* and *an*

→ G2 (S. 170)

It's **a** It's **an**	**G**erman, **F**rench **A**merican, **I**rish	book.

a steht vor einem Mitlaut: b, c, d usw.
an steht vor einem Selbstlaut: a, e, i, o, u.

Schreiben Sie *a* oder *an* in die Lücken.

1 ______ Italian book.
2 ______ Swiss stamp.
3 ______ English car.
4 ______ Austrian town.
5 ______ Turkish stamp.

4 Round up

Wenn Sie etwas hören, machen Sie sich keine Sorgen, wenn Sie nicht alles verstehen. Versuchen Sie nur, genug zu verstehen, um die Aufgabe lösen zu können.

a L1:4 Hören Sie ein Gespräch von zwei Personen und haken Sie die korrekte Information ab.

	♀	♂
first name: Donna	✓	
first name: Simon		✓
surname: Smith		
surname: Jones		
nationality: American		
nationality: Australian		
from New York		
from Chicago		
from Sydney		
from Melbourne		

b Vervollständigen Sie die Informationen über Donna.

Donna is ______ . ______ from ______ .
______ surname ______ .

c Schreiben Sie nun über Simon.

Simon ______

d Schreiben Sie nun über sich selbst.

I ______

S. 180

Jetzt kann ich ...

mich und andere vorstellen.	www: U1A1 CD-R 1: 1+2
andere nach persönlichen Informationen fragen.	www: U1A2
andere begrüßen und mich verabschieden.	www: U1A3 CD-R 1: 3
über Länder und Nationalitäten sprechen.	www: U1A4 CD-R 1: 4+6

Part B More about you

Alphabet I Numbers 0–9 I Giving and asking for contact details I Form filling I Present of *to be* (2), plural I *our, their*

Which one of these is *not a* television channel?
Welches Logo steht *nicht* für einen Fernsehsender?

BBC	CNN
MTV MUSIC TELEVISION	SMS

Contact details

1a T1:6 Listen to the alphabet. Underline the letters that you find a bit difficult.
Hören Sie das Alphabet. Unterstreichen Sie die Buchstaben, die Sie eher schwierig finden.

a b c d e f g h i j k l m n o p q r s t u v w x y z

Now say the alphabet round the class.
Sprechen Sie das Alphabet der Reihe nach in Ihrer Kursgruppe.

1b Look at this chart. Work with a partner.
Student A: Hold the book at a distance.
Student B: Say the letters you can see.
And then change roles.
Sehen Sie sich diese Tafel an. Arbeiten Sie zu zweit.
A: Halten Sie das Kursbuch in einiger Entfernung hoch.
B: Sprechen Sie die Buchstaben, die Sie erkennen können.
Wechseln Sie danach die Rollen.

E
A D
H M J
Z R P T
Y J F V X
W U K C B I

2 How to give your name

Wie Sie Ihren Namen sagen.

What's your name? / Can I have your name, please?
It's Louise Hanley.
Can you spell your first name for me, please?
Yes, it's L-O-U-I-S-E.
Can you spell your surname for me, please?
Yes, it's H-A-N-L-E-Y.

2a Ask three people in your class for their names and write down the information.
Fragen Sie drei Personen in Ihrer Kursgruppe nach dem Namen und schreiben Sie die Informationen auf.

First name: ______________________

Surname: ______________________

First name: ______________________

Surname: ______________________

First name: ______________________

Surname: ______________________

3 Word focus Numbers 0–9

Match the words to the pictures
Ordnen Sie die Wörter den Bildern zu.

seven | three | nine | five | eight | four | two | one | six

a ________ b ________ c ________

d ________ e ________ f ________

g ________ h ________ i ________

T1:7 Listen and check your answers.
Hören Sie und überprüfen Sie Ihre Antworten.

4 How to say a phone number

Wie Sie Telefonnummern sagen.

What's your phone number?
Can I have your phone number, please?
563071 – It's five six three oh seven one.

What's your mobile number?
Can I have your mobile number, please?

0 in phone numbers: GB: *oh* US: *zero*
GB: *mobile phone* US: *cell phone* (**not** *handy*)

4a T1:8 Listen and write the phone numbers.

Hören Sie und schreiben Sie die Telefonnummern.

1 ________
2 ________
3 ________

When you don't understand someone, say:
Wenn Sie jemanden nicht verstanden haben, sagen Sie:
Can you repeat that, please?

5 How to say an email address.

Wie Sie eine E-Mail-Adresse sagen.

What's your email address?
Can I have your email address, please?
jennycohen@bookworld.com – *It's Jenny Cohen* ***at*** *book world* ***dot com***.
khartmann@berlin.de – *It's K Hartmann* ***at*** *Berlin* ***dot D E***.

Can you spell that for me, please?

5a Look at these three email addresses.

Lesen Sie die drei E-Mail-Adressen.

1 ☐ mariab@work.house.at
2 ☐ mariab@workhouse.ch
3 ☐ mariac@workhouse.at

T1:9 Now listen and tick the email address you hear.
Hören Sie nun und haken Sie die richtige Adresse ab.

5b Work with a partner and practise saying these email addresses.

Arbeiten Sie zu zweit und üben Sie folgende E-Mail-Adressen.

1 alison.baker@cybertron.com
2 info@hotelsearch.net
3 jpmartin@swissweb.ch
4 inge29@sportnet.at

Welcome

6 T1:10 Listen to two couples in a hotel. Write down the missing information.
Hören Sie zwei Paaren in einem Hotel zu. Notieren Sie die fehlenden Informationen.

Our surname is Roberts.
Their surname is Jones.

1

My first name is ______________________.

Our surname is ______________________.
We're from ______________________.
We're in room number ____________.

My first name is ______________________.

2

Their surname is ______________________.
His first name is ______________________.
Her first name is ______________________.
They're from ______________________.
They're in room number ____________.

7 Grammar focus

Present of *to be* (2)

We're in room 149.
Are you in room 148?
Yes, **we are**. / No, **we aren't**.
They're in room 102.
Are they in room 103?
Yes, **they are**. / No, **they aren't**.

're = are **aren't = are not**

7a Match two words from the list to make sentences.
Kombinieren Sie zwei Wörter aus der Liste zu Sätzen.
He's | They're | We're | She's | They're |
American | English | Turkish | Austrian | Australian

1 James and Laura are from Liverpool.
They're English
2 Kate's from Canberra. ______________________
3 Gabi and I are from Vienna. ______________________
4 Ekrem and Bahar are from Ankara.
____
5 Steve's from Boston. ______________________

7b Student A: Look at page 161. Student B: Look at page 162.
A: Gehen Sie zu Seite 161. B: Gehen Sie zu Seite 162.

8 Talk to a partner. Fill in the form with your partner's information. (You can give false information if you want.)
Arbeiten Sie zu zweit. Tragen Sie die Angaben Ihres Partners / Ihrer Partnerin ein. (Sie können falsche Angaben machen, wenn Sie das möchten.)

Riverside Language School
Cambridge

Surname	
First name	
Nationality	
Phone number	
Mobile	
Email	

Flexizone

Game My name is my product

Play this game with a partner. Use one book.
Tear a piece of paper into 16 small pieces and use them to cover the 16 squares.
Spielen Sie zu zweit. Verwenden Sie nur ein Buch.
Teilen Sie ein Blatt Papier in 16 kleine Stücke und decken Sie damit die 16 Felder ab.

Player A:
Lift two pieces of paper.
If you don't find a pair (e.g. a person and his/her product), put the pieces of paper back.
But if you find a pair, you can keep the two papers. But first you must say some things in English about your pair.
Spieler A:
Decken Sie zwei Felder auf. Wenn Sie kein passendes Paar entdecken (also eine Person und ihr Produkt), legen Sie die Papierstücke wieder zurück.
Wenn Sie ein passendes Paar finden, haben Sie diese Runde gewonnen und dürfen auf Englisch etwas zu dieser Person sagen.

His/Her first name's … (and spell it).
His/Her surname's … (and spell it).
He's/She's from … .
This is his/her product. It's … .

Player B: Now it's your turn.
Spieler B: Jetzt sind Sie an der Reihe.

The winner is the player with the most pieces of paper at the end of the game.
Gewinner ist, wer am Ende des Spiels die meisten richtigen Paare gefunden hat.

Friedhelm Steiff

pasta

Alfred Ritter

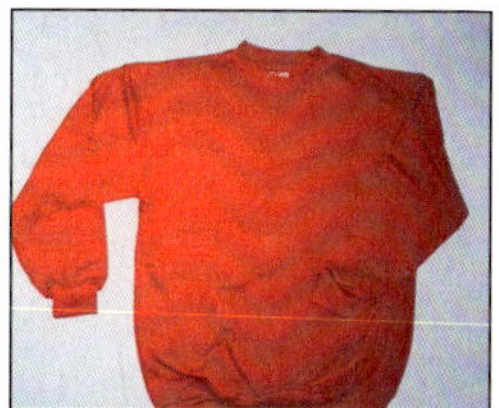
a pullover

baby food

Giuliana Benetton

a car

Wolfgang Porsche

chocolate

Andreas Langenscheidt

August Oetker

a pizza

Claus Hipp

a book

a teddy bear

Guido Barilla

Your turn More about you (→ www)

1 How to …

a Wie Sie Ihren Namen sagen.
Schreiben Sie diese Wörter in die Lücken.
can | first | have | me | name | please | spell | surname | your

1 Hello. What's ________ ________?
2 Can I ________ your name, ________?
3 ________ you ________ your ________ name, please?
4 Can you spell your ________ for ________, please?

Ordnen Sie diese Antworten den Fragen 1–4 zu.
☐ Yes, it's M – A – R – T – Y – N.
☐ It's Martyn Gurnett.
☐ Yes, of course, it's G – U – R – N – E – T – T.
☐ Yes, it's Martyn Gurnett.

b Wie Sie nach persönlichen Informationen fragen und sie geben. Vervollständigen Sie die Wörter.

1 What's your p________ n________?
It's 044, that's for Zurich, 307395.

2 What's your m________ n________?
It's 079 422368.

3 What's your a________?
It's 8 Marktgasse, 8001 Zurich.

4 What's your e________ a________?
It's gurnett1@hotmail.com.

c Wie Sie das Alphabet sprechen.
Sprechen Sie das Alphabet laut. Schreiben Sie die Buchstaben neben den Buchstaben, der ähnlich klingt.

a [h] [ ] [ ]
b [ ] [ ] [ ] [ ] [ ] [ ] [ ]
f [ ] [ ] [ ] [ ] [ ] [ ]
i [ ]   o   q [ ] [ ]   r

L1:5 Hören Sie und überprüfen Sie Ihre Antworten. Sagen Sie die Buchstaben in 1c laut, während Sie sie überprüfen.

L1:6 **Say it like this** Hören Sie und sprechen Sie nach.

2 Word focus Numbers

Schreiben Sie die Zahlen 1–9 als Wörter in die Kästchen.

n _ _ _ | _ _ o | _ _ _ _ _ t | _ n _
_ e _ _ _ | _ _ _ | _ _ _ e
_ _ _ _ _ | _ _ _ _

Überprüfen Sie nun diese Rechenaufgaben. Sind die Lösungen richtig (✓) oder falsch (✗)?

1 ▢ – ▢ = ▢ ✓ ________
2 ▢ + ▢ = ▢ ________
3 ▢ – ▢ = ▢ ________
4 ▢ + ▢ = ▢ ________
5 ▢ + ▢ = ▢ ________
6 ▢ – ▢ = ▢ ________
7 ▢ – ▢ = ▢ ________

Fünf Lösungen sind falsch! Schreiben Sie die richtigen Antworten als Wörter auf die Linien.

3 Grammar focus

3.1 Present of *to be*

→ G1 (S. 170)

Zunächst ein Blick auf die Grammatik in Unit 1 Part A:

Are you …?	Yes, I am. / No, I'm not.	I'm … / I'm not …
Is she …?	Yes, she is. / No, she isn't.	She's … / She isn't …
Is he …?	Yes, he is. / No, he isn't.	He's … / He isn't …
Is it …?	Yes, it is. / No, she isn't.	It's … / It isn't …

Und nun:

Are you in room 306?	No, **we aren't**.	**We aren't** in room 306.
Are you in room 304?	Yes, **we are**.	**We're** in room 304.
Are they in this hotel?	No, **they aren't**.	**They aren't** in this hotel.
Are they in the Ritz?	Yes, **they are**.	**They're** in the Ritz.

a Ergänzen Sie das Gespräch an einer Hotelrezeption.

are | aren't | I'm | is | They're | We're

■ Hello, __________ you John and Pat Smith from London?

◆ __________ from London, but we __________ John and Pat Smith. This __________ Anna Smith, and __________ Jack Smith … not John Smith.

■ Oh, sorry. __________ in room 204 and you're in 304.

b Geben Sie Kurzantworten auf diese Fragen:

1 Are Jack and Anna from London? __________

2 Are Jack and Anna in room 204? __________

3 Is your teacher English? __________

4 Are you and the people in your class English?

____

3.2 *Our* and *their*

→ G3 (S. 171)

Zunächst ein Blick auf die Grammatik in Unit 1 Part A:

I'm from England – my name's Tom.
He's from Germany – his name's Karl.
She's from Switzerland – her name's Anna.

Und nun:

We're from Germany.	**Our** surname is Schrandt.
They're from England.	**Their** surname is Smith.

Schreiben Sie die Wörter in die Lücken.

Her | His | My | Our | Their

__________ surname's Smith.

__________ name's Anna.

__________ name's Jack. __________ name's Anna.

__________ surname's Smith.

4 Round up

a L1:7 Hören Sie die Information, die ein Gast am Empfang eines Hotels gibt. Ergänzen Sie:

Surname __________

First name __________

Address __________

____

Phone number __________

Mobile number __________

Email address __________

Wenn Sie sich nicht sicher sind, ob Sie in einem Gespräch einen Namen oder eine Nummer richtig verstanden haben, vergewissern Sie sich, indem Sie die Information wiederholen – genauso wie es die Empfangsmitarbeiterin getan hat.

b Ergänzen Sie nun Ihre persönlichen Angaben.

My personal info

My first name:

My surname:

My address:

My phone number:

My mobile number:

My email address:

S. 180

Jetzt kann ich …

meinen Namen sagen und buchstabieren.	○○○	www: U1B1 CD-R 1: 8+9
jemanden bitten, ein Wort zu buchstabieren.	○○○	www: U1B2 CD-R 1: 10
nach persönlichen Informationen fragen und antworten.	○○○	www: U1B3 CD-R 1: 14
von 1 bis 9 zählen.	○○○	www: U1B4 CD-R 1: 11

Reading The Henry Convention

In Sydney, Australia, 120 men named Henry meet at the 'My name's Henry' convention.

Henry Pantie, from Canberra and Henry Pop, from Sydney start to fight.

Henry Jones and Henry Dyer try to stop the fight – but more Henrys start to fight! One Henry phones the police.

A policeman stops the fight. What's the policeman's name? Shane!

Out and About

Handshake puzzle

Six Henrys meet at the convention and they all shake hands. How many handshakes are there?
Sechs Henrys treffen sich auf einer Versammlung und reichen sich die Hand. Wie viele Handschläge sind es?

Find the solution in *Out and About*, page 7.
Die Lösung finden Sie in *Out and About*, S. 7.

Towns and cities

Part A In town

Talking about towns | Saying where things are | *There's a / an*

Name a town or city beginning with each letter of the alphabet.
Nennen Sie Städte, die mit den Buchstaben des Alphabets beginnen.

Aberdeen

Boston

C...

What's in your town?

1a What is there in Wantage?
Was gibt es in Wantage?
There's a bookshop.

1b T1:11 Listen to a radio interview with David. Tick (✓) the signs when David talks about the places. Which place does he *not* talk about?
Hören Sie ein Radio-Interview mit David zu und machen Sie bei den Schildern ein Häkchen (✓), über die er spricht. Wovon spricht er *nicht*?

2 Word focus Things in a town

Work with a partner. Write these words in the gaps:
Arbeiten Sie zu zweit und schreiben Sie diese Wörter in die Lücken:
centre | office | park | place | pool | restaurant | shop | station | store

1 leisure ______ 4 swimming ______ 7 train ______
2 sandwich ______ 5 post ______ 8 Italian ______
3 car ______ 6 market ______ 9 department ______

3 T1:12 Listen to David again and complete these sentences.

Hören Sie David noch einmal und vervollständigen Sie die Sätze.

There isn't a ______. There isn't a ______.

4 Grammar focus

There's a / an ...

There's a post office in Wantage.
There isn't a department store in Wantage.
Is there an Italian restaurant here? **Yes, there is. / No, there isn't.**

In English we don't use *the* before the names of people or the names of streets:
David's from Wantage.
His house is in Willow Lane.

4a Work with a partner. Ask and answer the questions about your town or your part of town.

Arbeiten Sie zu zweit. Fragen Sie und beantworten Sie die Fragen zu Ihrer Stadt oder Ihrem Stadtteil.

Is there ...
1 a good bookshop?
2 a very nice Italian restaurant?
3 a big post office?
4 an Irish pub?
5 a department store?
6 an ice cream shop?
7 a Chinese restaurant?
8 a small cinema?

Is there a good bookshop in your part of town?

Yes, there is. There's a good bookshop in Leonrodstraße. It's called Colibris.

Is there a bank near here?

5a Number these lines 1–8 to make a dialogue.

Nummerieren Sie folgende Zeilen von 1–8, sodass ein Dialog entsteht.

- [ ] *Where in West Street?*
- [ ] *Yes, there's a bank in West Street.*
- [1] *Excuse me.*
- [ ] *Thank you.*
- [ ] *Is there a bank near here?*
- [ ] *You're welcome.*
- [ ] *Yes, can I help you?*
- [ ] *It's next to the post office.*

5b T1:13 Listen and check your answers. Then read the dialogue with a partner.

Hören Sie und überprüfen Sie. Lesen die dann den Dialog zu zweit.

The answer to *Thank you* is *You're welcome* or a smile!

6a Look at this street plan.
Sehen Sie sich den Stadtplan an.

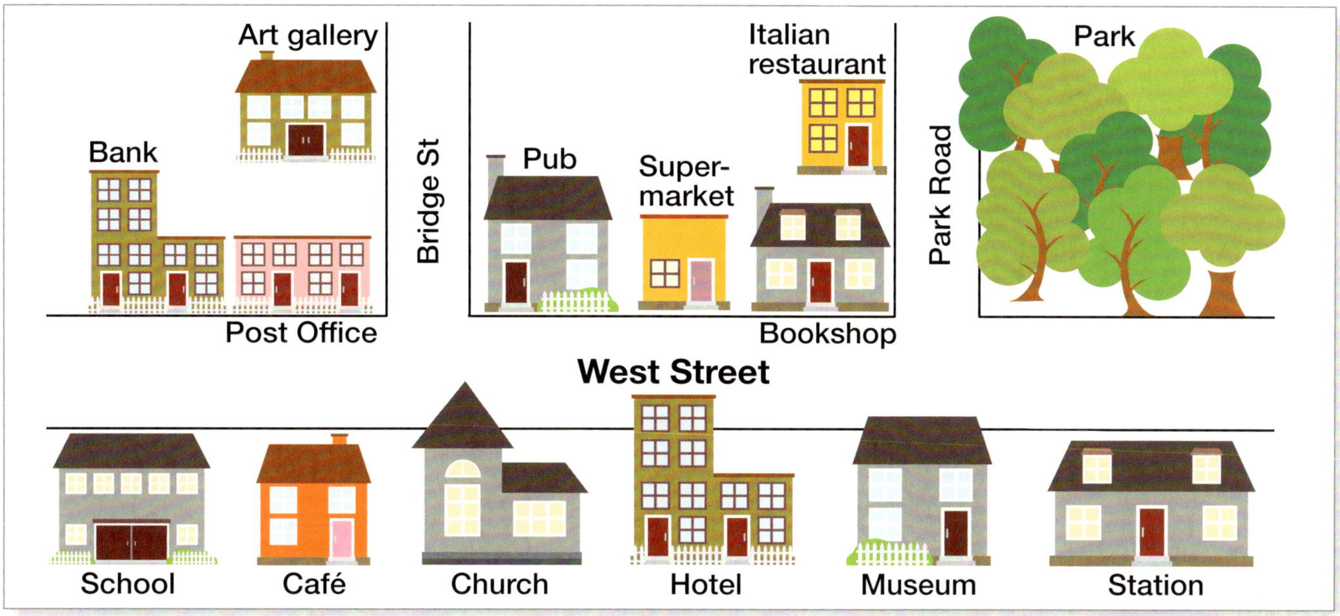

6b Which sentence is true? Tick (✓) the correct answer.
Welcher Satz ist richtig? Machen Sie ein Häkchen.

1 a ☐ The bank's in Park Road. *or* b ☐ The bank's in West Street.
2 a ☐ The bank's next to the post office. *or* b ☐ The bank's next to the station.
3 a ☐ The supermarket's next to the hotel. *or* b ☐ The supermarket's opposite the hotel.
4 a ☐ The museum's near the park. *or* b ☐ The museum's next to the park.
5 a ☐ The park's on the corner. *or* b ☐ The church is on the corner.

7 How to ask and say where things are in a town

Wie Sie nach etwas in der Stadt fragen und antworten.

Excuse me. Is there a bank near here?
Yes, there's a bank in West Street.
Where in West Street?
It's near / next to / opposite the post office.
It's on the corner.

7a Make a dialogue with your partner. Ask for different places on the street plan above.
Erstellen Sie zu zweit einen Dialog. Fragen Sie nach unterschiedlichen Orten auf dem Stadtplan oben.

Flexizone

A Think of a person in the classroom. Tell your partner where he or she is. Who is it? Use the words below.
Denken Sie an eine Person im Kurs. Sagen Sie Ihrem Partner / Ihrer Partnerin, wo er / sie sich befindet. Ihr Partner / Ihre Partnerin errät, um wen es sich handelt. Verwenden Sie folgende Wörter:
near | next to | opposite
This person is opposite Klaus.

B Make a plan of your ideal street in a town centre. What is there? Then tell other students about your street.
Erstellen Sie den Plan Ihrer idealen Straße in der Stadtmitte. Was gibt es dort? Erzählen Sie dann anderen Kursteilnehmern von Ihrer Straße.
In my street there's a very big bookshop and a small Italian restaurant.

Your turn In town (→ www)

1 How to …

Schreiben Sie die Wörter in die Lücken.

a Wie Sie jemanden fragen, was es in einer Stadt gibt.

a | an | is | Is there | Where

1 ______ ______ ______ French or ______ Italian restaurant in your town?

2 ______ ______ the French restaurant?

b Wie Sie herausfinden, wo es etwas in einer Stadt gibt.

can | Excuse | help | Thank | welcome | you | You're

A: ______ me.

B: Yes, ______ I ______ you?

A: Is there a post office near here?

B: Yes, there is. It's opposite the station.

A: ______ ______.

B: ______ ______.

c Wie Sie anderen Menschen sagen, wo es etwas in der Stadt gibt.

in | near | next to | on | opposite

Where is it?

1 It's ______ George Street.

2 It's ______ the corner of George Street.

3 It's very ______ the station.

4 It's ______ ______ the station.

5 It's ______ the station.

Amerikaner sagen ***on*** *George Street*, Briten dagegen ***in*** *George Street*.

L1:8 Hören Sie und überprüfen Sie Ihre Antworten.

L1:9 **Say it like this** Hören Sie und wiederholen Sie.

2 Word focus Places in a town

Wohin müssen Sie gehen, wenn Sie folgende Dinge kaufen oder sehen wollen?

1 p ___ o _____

2 b _______

3 c _____

4 s __________

5 c _____

6 b ___

7 a __ g ______

8 m _____

9 s _______ p ___

10 r _________

11 p __

12 c ___

13 s _____

14 p ___

15 t ____ s ______

16 d _________ s ____

3 Grammar focus

There's a / an → G4 (S. 171)

Is there a cinema in your town? **Is there an** art gallery in your town?	Yes, **there is**. No, **there isn't**.
There's a cinema in my town. **There isn't an** art gallery in my town.	

There is wird verwendet, um zu sagen, ob es bestimmte Dinge gibt oder nicht gibt.

a Schreiben Sie die Wörter in der richtigen Reihenfolge und antworten Sie mit *Yes, …* oder *No, …* .

1 near | Is there | park | your school | a | ?

2 Italian restaurant | in your town | Is | an | there | ?

3 café | there | near | school | Is | a | your | ?

b Lesen Sie, was es in der Stadt dieses Mannes gibt.

I'm from a small town near London. There's a good supermarket in my town and there's a big market, too. There's a leisure centre but there isn't a swimming pool.

Schreiben Sie einen Paralleltext über die Stadt, in der Freunde des Mannes leben. Ändern Sie die hinterlegten Wörter.

town near Bristol | department store (big) | bookshop (good) | museum ✓ | art gallery ✗

They're

4 Round up

Wenn Sie mit jemandem reden und Sie etwas nicht verstehen, dann sagen Sie bitte: *Sorry, can you say that again, please?* Wenn Sie einer Tonaufnahme zuhören und Sie etwas nicht mitbekommen, können Sie sie noch einmal anhören.

a L1:10 Hören Sie, was der Mann über seine Stadt sagt. Schreiben Sie die ersten beiden Buchstaben der Wörter für die Gebäude in den Stadtplan. Sie beginnen bei *Sc* für *school*.

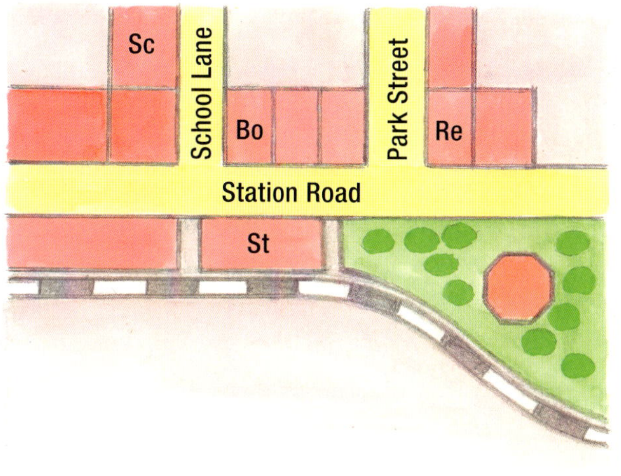

b L1:11 Hören Sie jetzt die Fragen und beantworten Sie sie. Halten Sie die Aufnahme an, um die Antworten zu schreiben.

1
2
3
4
5
6
7

S. 180

Jetzt kann ich …

über Dinge reden, die es in einer Stadt gibt.	www: U2A1 CD-R 1: 17
herausfinden, wo es etwas in einer Stadt gibt.	www: U2A2 CD-R 1: 15+18
anderen Leuten sagen, wo es etwas in einer Stadt gibt.	www: U2A3 CD-R 1: 16+19

Part B A city break

Talking about cities | Numbers 10–99 | *There are some/There aren't any*

Ask and answer the questions.
Stellen Sie Fragen und beantworten Sie sie.
Where's ...?
the Semper Opera House | the Golden Gate Bridge | the River Thames | Charles de Gaulle Airport | Bondi Beach

Cities of the world

1a T1:14 A lot of people take city breaks – a short holiday to a different city. Listen to three tourists talking about their favourite cities. Which cities are they?
Viele Menschen unternehmen Städtereisen – einen kurzen Urlaub in eine andere Stadt. Hören Sie drei Touristen, die über ihre Lieblingsstädte sprechen. Um welche Städte handelt es sich?

1b T1:15 Listen again and tick (✓) the things you hear.
Hören Sie noch einmal und machen Sie ein Häkchen bei den Dingen, die Sie hören.

- ☐ restaurants
- ☐ shops
- ☐ an opera house
- ☐ a bridge / bridges
- ☐ a beach
- ☐ old buildings
- ☐ churches
- ☐ pubs
- ☐ an airport
- ☐ a river
- ☐ museums
- ☐ art galleries
- ☐ a café / cafés
- ☐ a park / parks
- ☐ tourists

shop → shop**s**, pub → pub**s**, museum → museum**s**
chur**ch** → church**es**, bea**ch** → beach**es**
cit**y** → cit**ies**, art galler**y** → art galler**ies**

2 **How to** talk about a town or city
Wie Sie über eine Stadt sprechen.

***It's** big / small / old / modern / beautiful / nice / international / romantic / quiet / busy.*
***There's a** big river.*
***There are some** beautiful churches.*
***There are a lot of** tourists.*
***You can see** the Mona Lisa.*

When you want to know a word, ask:
What's ... in English?

2a Talk to a partner. Use the phrases to talk about a capital city you know. You and your partner can each choose a different city.
Arbeiten Sie zu zweit. Verwenden Sie die Sätze, um über eine Ihnen bekannte Hauptstadt zu sprechen. Sie und Ihr Partner / Ihre Partnerin können unterschiedliche Hauptstädte wählen.

3 Grammar focus

There are some … / There aren't any …

There are some churches.
There aren't any American restaurants.
Are there any old buildings? **Yes, there are. / No, there aren't.**

3a Cross out the incorrect word in each sentence.
Streichen Sie in jedem Satz das falsche Wort.

1 There are *some / any* nice restaurants near the river.
2 Are there *some / any* good hotels near the airport?
3 There aren't *some / any* old buildings in the city centre.
4 Are there *some / any* good shops near our hotel?
5 There are *some / any* beautiful buildings in the city centre.
6 There aren't *some / any* English restaurants in Paris!

3b Work with a partner. Tell him/her the name of your favourite city. He/she will ask you the questions below. Give short answers e.g. *Yes there is. / No, there isn't. / Yes, there are. / No, there aren't. / I don't know.* Then change roles.
Arbeiten Sie zu zweit. Nennen Sie Ihre Lieblingsstadt. Ihr Partner / Ihre Partnerin stellt Ihnen die folgenden Fragen. Geben Sie Kurzantworten wie *Yes there is. / No, there isn't. / Yes, there are. / No, there aren't. / I don't know.* Wechseln Sie dann die Rollen.

1 Is there a river in this city?
2 Are there any very old buildings?
3 Is there a famous bridge?
4 Are there any famous churches?
5 Is there an airport in (or near) this city?
6 Are there any American fast food restaurants?

Numbers

4 Word focus Numbers 10–99

4a Write in the numbers 10–20.
Schreiben Sie die Zahlen 10–20 in die Kästchen.

☐ sixteen
☐ thirteen
☐ nineteen
☐ twelve
☐ seventeen
☐ ten
☐ twenty
☐ eighteen
☐ eleven
☐ fourteen
☐ fifteen

4b With a partner, say these numbers. To make each number, use one word from each box below.
Arbeiten Sie zu zweit. Sagen Sie folgende Zahlen. Verwenden Sie dabei jeweils ein Wort aus jedem Kasten.

31 | 92 | 67 | 78 | 26 | 54 | 89 | 73 | 45 | 91 | 23 | 46 | 52 | 87 | 74 | 35 | 68

twenty-	one
thirty-	two
forty-	three
fifty-	four
sixty-	five
seventy-	six
eighty-	seven
ninety-	eight
	nine

5 T1:16 Listen. Which number is it? Tick (✓) the right number.
Hören Sie. Welche Zahl ist es? Haken Sie (✓) die richtige Zahl ab.

1	13	☐	30	☐
2	19	☐	90	☐
3	17	☐	70	☐
4	14	☐	40	☐
5	18	☐	80	☐

T1:17 **Say it like this** Listen and repeat the numbers above.
Hören Sie und wiederholen Sie die Zahlen oben.

6a Number practice. Dictate three numbers to your partner.
Übungen mit Zahlen. Diktieren Sie einem Partner / einer Partnerin drei Zahlen.

6b Count round the class in threes. 3 – 6 – 9 …
Zählen Sie reihum in Dreierschritten. 3 – 6 – 9 …

6c Open your book (but don't show your partner the page). Say the page number. Ask your partner to turn to that page.
Öffnen Sie Ihr Buch (ohne Ihrem Partner / Ihrer Partnerin die Seite zu zeigen). Sagen Sie die Seitenzahl. Bitten Sie Ihren Partner / Ihre Partnerin, diese Seite aufzuschlagen.

7a Read this tourist information about Oxford.
Lesen Sie folgendes Informationsblatt für Touristen über Oxford.

Oxford *Facts and figures*

- Distance from London: 57 miles (90 km)
- Colleges: 39 (some are open to the public in the university holidays)
- Bookshops: Over 20
- Museums: 7 (including the Ashmolean, Britain's oldest museum)
- Theatres and cinemas: 11
- Twin cities: 6 (including Bonn)

Christchurch College, Oxford University

7b Work with a partner. Take turns to read the facts to each other.
Arbeiten Sie zu zweit. Lesen Sie sich abwechselnd die Informationen vor.
The distance from London is fifty-seven miles, or ninety kilometres.

Flexizone

Task Marketing a town

Work in small groups. Read the emails below. What ideas can your group think of to market your town? Talk about them and write down the best ideas.

Arbeiten Sie in kleinen Gruppen. Lesen Sie die E-Mails. Welche Vorschläge fallen Ihnen ein, um Ihre Stadt zu bewerben? Sprechen Sie darüber und schreiben Sie die besten Ideen auf.

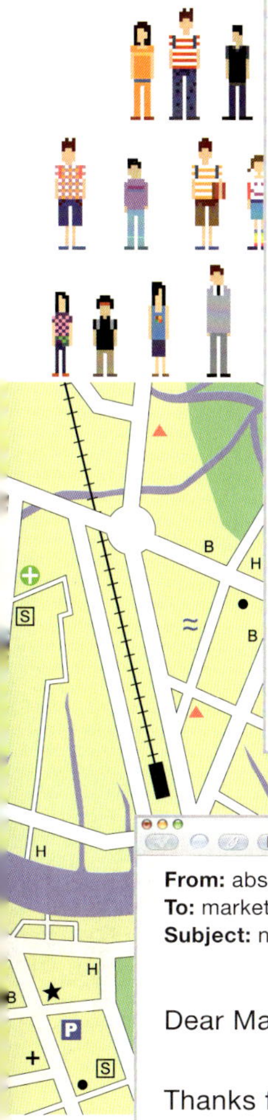

From: absaxon@town.co.uk
To: marketing@town.co.uk
Subject: new image

Dear Marketing

We need a new image for our town – a positive image for visitors (tourists, families, business people, …).

First, we need a photo for a new poster. A famous building? A park or sports centre? People in town?

Please talk together in your creative team and send me your ideas.

Thanks!

Alice Saxon

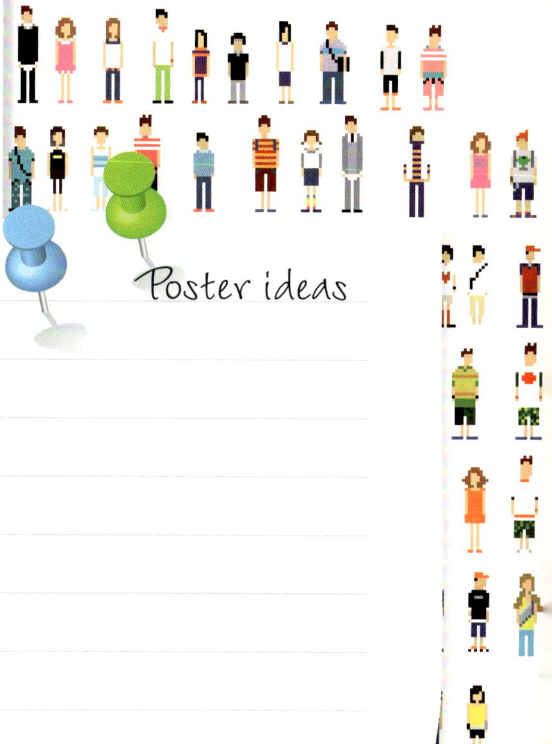

Poster ideas

From: absaxon@town.co.uk
To: marketing@town.co.uk
Subject: new image

Dear Marketing

Thanks for your ideas. Now we need a new slogan for our town – some words or a sentence to say the most important thing about it. Here are some ideas:

A town with …
A town for …
The home of …

Can you think of a good slogan?

Alice

Slogan idea

Now show your ideas to the other groups and choose the ideas you all like best.

Zeigen Sie nun Ihre Ideen den anderen Gruppen und wählen Sie die Vorschläge aus, die allen am besten gefallen.

Your turn A city break (➔ www)

1 How to …

a Wie Sie nach Dingen in einer Stadt fragen. Schreiben Sie die Wörter in die Lücken.

Are there any | Is there a | Where is

1 ________ ________ ________ parks in your town?

2 ________ ________ ________ beach in your town?

3 ________ ________ the park?

b Wie Sie eine Stadt beschreiben. Schreiben Sie die Wörter in die Lücken.

There are | There aren't | There isn't | There's | You can

1 ________ a small river.

2 ________ ________ an international airport.

3 ________ ________ see a lot of churches.

4 ________ ________ some beautiful parks.

5 ________ ________ any famous old buildings.

c Wie Sie über den Ort sprechen, aus dem Sie stammen. Schreiben Sie den Mini-Dialog, indem Sie Fragen und Antworten in die richtige Reihenfolge bringen.

Where's that? Yes, there is – but it's very small.

Hello. Where are you from? I'm from Bristol.

It's about 100 miles from London.

Is there an airport near Bristol?

■ ________

◆ ________

■ ________

◆ ________

■ ________

◆ ________

L1:12 Hören Sie und überprüfen Sie Ihre Antworten.

L1:13 **Say it like this** Hören Sie und sprechen Sie nach.

2 Word focus

a Places in a town or city

Suchen Sie die Wörter und ordnen Sie sie den richtigen Kategorien zu.

ARTGALLERYBARBEACHBOOKSHOPBRI
DGECAFÉCHURCHDEPARTMENTSTORE
MARKETMUSEUMOPERAHOUSEPARKPUB
RESTAURANTRIVERSUPERMARKET

Essen und Trinken	Einkaufen

Im Freien	Geschichte/Kunst/Kultur

b Opposites

Verbinden Sie die Adjektive mit gegenteiliger Bedeutung.

○ big ○ modern ○ quiet
○ busy ○ old ○ small

c Numbers

Schreiben Sie die fehlenden Zahlen und Wörter.

11	
12	
	fourteen
15	
	twenty
24	

	thirty-one
40	
55	
	sixty-seven
82	
90	

3 Grammar focus

3.1 *There are some / There aren't any*

→ G4 (S. 171)

Zunächst ein Blick auf die Grammatik in Unit 2 Part A:

Is there a/an … in your town?	Yes, there is. There's a … No, there isn't. There isn't a …

Und nun:

Are there any nice pubs in your town?	Yes, **there are**.
Are there any 5-star hotels in your town?	No, **there aren't**.

There are some nice pubs in my town.
There aren't any 5-star hotels in my town.

Some wird in positiven Aussagesätzen verwendet, *any* in Fragen und verneinten Sätzen.

a Ergänzen Sie die fehlenden Wörter.

1 ■ ______________ parks in your town?
◆ Yes, ______________ very nice parks.

2 ■ ______________ Japanese restaurants in your town?
◆ No, ______________. ______________ Thai restaurants, but ______________ Japanese restaurants.

b Streichen Sie die falschen Wörter.

1 *Is / Are* there *some / any / an* Italian students in your class?
2 There *isn't / aren't a / an / any* opera house near here.
3 There *is / are a / an / any / some* old churches in our town.
4 There *is / are a / an* art gallery, but there *isn't / aren't a / some / any* museums.

3.2 Plural nouns

→ G6 (S. 172)

one tourist / twenty tourist**s** (+ s)

one church / two church**es** (+ es)

a city = a lot of cit**ies** (y → i + es)

Setzen Sie folgende Wörter in die Mehrzahl.

1 hotel ______________
2 baby ______________
3 match ______________
4 bush ______________
5 party ______________
6 town ______________

4 Round up

In verschiedenen Ländern können Sie die unterschiedlichsten Arten von Englisch hören. Deshalb ist es gut, sich an verschiedene Dialekte zu gewöhnen. In der Höraufgabe hören Sie einen New Yorker.

a L1:14 Dan ist Fremdenführer in New York. Hören Sie Erläuterungen, die er während einer Sightseeingtour mit einem Bus gibt. Haken Sie die Orte ab, die er zeigt.

- ☐ a famous street
- ☐ a famous department store
- ☐ a park
- ☐ an opera house
- ☐ a famous restaurant
- ☐ a museum
- ☐ a famous station
- ☐ a church
- ☐ a famous hotel
- ☐ a famous bookshop

L1:15 Hören Sie noch einmal. Was hat Dan gesagt? Streichen Sie die falschen Wörter.

1 This part of New York is very *busy / quiet*.
2 *There are a lot of / There aren't any* small bars near here.
3 *There's one / There are 6 / There are 16* Barnes and Noble shops in New York.

b Schreiben Sie jetzt über New York.

Central Park: There's a famous park in New York called Central Park.

Grand Central: ______________

The Met: ______________

S. 181

Jetzt kann ich …

nach Dingen in einer Stadt fragen.	○○○	www: U2B1 CD-R 1: 22
eine Stadt beschreiben.	○○○	www: U2B2 CD-R 1: 24
über den Ort sprechen, aus dem ich stamme.	○○○	www: U2B3 CD-R 1: 23

Reading Wantage

David is from Wantage, a small town near Oxford.

There are some beautiful churches and a lot of old houses, nice pubs and interesting shops in Wantage.

There's a busy market place in Wantage. It's very old. Wantage was a market town in Roman times.

Wantage is the twin town of Seesen in Lower Saxony.

King Alfred was born in Wantage in 849.

You can learn more about the history of Wantage in the town's museum.

Glossary

busy belebt | was war | Roman times Zeiten der Römer | was born wurde geboren | history Geschichte

Out and About

Place names

In the information about Wantage above, you can see: *Lower Saxony* – this is *Niedersachsen*.
A lot of place names are written the same in English and in German, e.g. Berlin, Salzburg, Bern. But some place names are not the same, e.g. Munich *(München)*, Vienna *(Wien)*, Geneva *(Genf)*.
Can you name these states?
In dem Text oben über Wantage finden Sie: *Lower Saxony* – Niedersachsen. Geografische Namen werden im Deutschen und Englischen oft gleich geschrieben, z.B. Berlin, Salzburg, Bern, aber manchmal unterscheiden sie sich, z.B. Munich *(München)*, Vienna *(Wien)*, Geneva *(Genf)*.
Wie heißen folgende Bundesländer auf Deutsch?

Bavaria | Hesse | Lower Saxony | Mecklenburg-West Pomerania | North Rhine-Westphalia | Rhineland-Palatinate | Saxony | Saxony-Anhalt | Thuringia

Carinthia | Lower Austria | Upper Austria | Styria

Find the solution in *Out and About*, page 11.
Die Lösung finden Sie in *Out and About*, S. 11.

People

Part A The family

The family | *have got / has got* | possessive *'s*

Here are some things that people say about families.
Which is your favourite?
Hier sehen Sie einige Aussagen über Familien.
Welche gefällt Ihnen am besten?

YOU CAN CHOOSE YOUR FRIENDS, BUT YOU CAN'T CHOOSE YOUR FAMILY.

IN TIME OF TEST, FAMILY IS BEST.

THE BEST SORT OF FAMILY IS A WARM, LOVING FAMILY... IN ANOTHER TOWN.

Family

1 **Word focus** Family members

Match the pairs.
Finden Sie die richtigen Paare.

male	father	brother			grandson	husband		nephew	cousin
female			daughter	grandmother			aunt		

cousin | granddaughter | grandfather | mother | niece | sister | son | uncle | wife

2 Look at Jill's family tree.

Are these sentences true (T) or false (F)?
Sehen Sie sich diesen Familienstammbaum an.
Sind die Aussagen richtig (T) oder falsch (F)?

a ☐ Jill's got a brother and a sister.
b ☐ She's got a son and a daughter.
c ☐ She's got three grandchildren.
d ☐ She hasn't got any nephews.
e ☐ She hasn't got any nieces.

Hello. I'm Jill Carr.

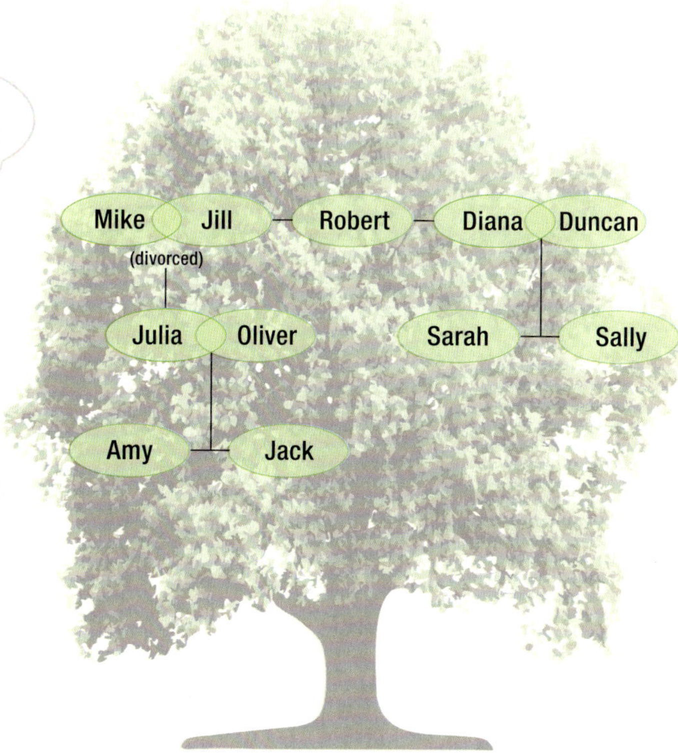

3 Draw your family tree. Underline your name. Your teacher will collect the papers and give them out to different people. Give the class two pieces of information about the new family tree.

Zeichnen Sie Ihren eigenen Familienstammbaum. Unterstreichen Sie Ihren Namen. Ihr Kursleiter / Ihre Kursleiterin wird die Blätter einsammeln und sie an andere Kursteilnehmer verteilen. Geben Sie Ihrer Kursgruppe zwei Informationen zu dem neuen Familienstammbaum.

Ulrich's got two sisters.
He hasn't got any children.

4a

T1:18 Listen to Jill's boss, David, talking about his family. Cross out the wrong word.
Hören Sie Jill's Boss David, der von seiner Familie erzählt. Streichen Sie das falsche Wort.

1 David's from a *small* / *big* family.
2 David's wife is from a *small* / *big* family.

4b

T1:19 Listen again. Are these sentences true (T) or false (F)?
Hören Sie noch einmal. Sind die Aussagen richtig (T) oder falsch (F)?

3 ☐ David's parents are both dead.
4 ☐ David's married.
5 ☐ David's wife hasn't got any sisters.
6 ☐ David and Mel haven't got any children.
7 ☐ David and Mel have got a lot of nephews and nieces.

Mel is David**'s** wife.

David and Mel

5 Grammar focus

have got

I've got two daughters but **I haven't got** any grandchildren.
He's got an uncle in Brighton but **he hasn't got** any brothers or sisters.
She's got three sisters but **she hasn't got** any brothers.
They've got a lot of nephews and nieces but **they haven't got** any sons or daughters.

Have you got any grandchildren? **Yes I have. / No, I haven't.**

Has he got an uncle? **Yes, he has. / No, he hasn't.**

've got = have got
haven't got = have not got
's got = has got
hasn't got = has not got

5a

Write *have / haven't / has / hasn't* in the gaps.
Schreiben Sie *have / haven't / has / hasn't* in die Lücken.

1 ________ David got an uncle?
2 Mel ____________ got any brothers.
3 David and Mel ____________ got a lot of nephews and nieces.
4 ________ David and Mel got any children?
5 ________ you got a brother?
6 I ____________ got any uncles or aunts.

5b

Ask your partner questions with *Are you* or *Have you got.*
Stellen Sie Ihrem Partner / Ihrer Partnerin Fragen mit *Are you* oder *Have you got.*

1 … from a big family?
2 … any children?
3 … any nephews or nieces?
4 … an only child?
5 … any grandchildren?

5c

Find a new partner. Tell your new partner some information about your first partner.
Suchen Sie sich einen neuen Partner / eine neue Partnerin. Erzählen Sie ihm/ihr von Ihrem ersten Partner / Ihrer ersten Partnerin.

A new member of the family

6 Read this advert.
Lesen Sie diese Anzeige.

Which is correct?
Welche Aussage ist richtig?

a This scheme helps old people to adopt babies.
b This scheme brings children and old people together.

7a T1:20 Listen to a radio interview. A mother of three boys is talking about a new member of her family. Cross out the wrong words in the sentences below.
Hören Sie ein Interview im Radio. Eine Mutter von drei Jungen spricht über ein neues Familienmitglied. Streichen Sie die falschen Wörter in den Aussagen.

1 The new member of the family is an adopted *grandfather / grandmother*.
2 They *are / aren't* all happy with the new member of the family.

7b T1:21 Listen again. Now match the beginnings and ends of sentences about the people in this story. Write the letters in the boxes.
Hören Sie noch einmal. Ordnen Sie nun die Satzanfänge den Satzenden zu. Schreiben Sie die Buchstaben in die Kästchen.

a	The boys haven't got any	☐	he's very fit.
b	The boys have got a	☐	and energy for the boys
c	The boys are	☐	grandparents near their home.
d	Harry is over 70 but	☐	near their house.
e	Harry's got time	☐	new adopted grandfather.
f	There's a park	☐	problems in Harry's family.
g	There are some	☐	happy with their new adopted grandfather.

Flexizone

A Walk round the class and ask different people questions with *Have you got …?*
Gehen Sie im Unterrichtsraum umher und stellen Sie verschiedenen Personen Fragen mit *Have you got …?*, z. B.
a dog, a cat, a German car, a nice job, a good boss, an assistant, a best friend, a baby.

B Have you got a photo (in your wallet or on your mobile phone) of a friend or someone in your family? Show your photo to another student and give some information about this person. No photo? – Just write the name or make a sketch.
Haben Sie ein Foto eines Freundes / einer Freundin oder von jemandem aus Ihrer Familie bei sich (in Ihrem Geldbeutel oder Handy)? Zeigen Sie das Foto jemandem aus Ihrer Kursgruppe und erzählen Sie ein wenig von dieser Person. Sie haben kein Foto? – Schreiben Sie einfach den Namen auf oder zeichnen Sie die Person.
This is my best friend. His/Her name's… . He's/She's … . He's/She's got … .

Your turn The family (→ www)

1 How to …

Schreiben Sie die Wörter in die Lücken.

a Wie Sie jemanden nach der Familie fragen.

a | an | any | Are | Are | got | got | Have | Have

1 ______ you from a big family?

2 ______ you ______ ______ brother or a sister?

3 Are you ______ only child?

4 ______ you married?

5 ______ you ______ ______ children?

b Wie Sie jemandem von Ihrer Familie erzählen.

any | from | got | got | haven't | He's | I'm | I've | My

1 I'm ______ a big family. ______ ______ four sisters.

2 ______ married but we ______ ______ ______ children.

3 ______ husband is from a very small family. ______ an only child.

c Wie Sie über die Anzahl Ihrer Familienmitglieder sprechen.

a | a lot of | any | His | Their | two

1 I've got ______ son. ______ name's Tom.

2 I've got ______ daughters. ______ names are Sophie and Kate.

I haven't got ______ grandchildren.

3 I've got ______ cousins in Australia.

L1:16 Hören Sie und überprüfen Sie Ihre Antworten.

L1:17 **Say it like this** Hören Sie und sprechen Sie nach.

2 Word focus Family members

a Werden diese Wörter für eine männliche oder eine weibliche Person oder für weibliche und männliche Personen verwendet? Haken Sie ab.

aunt			
brother			
child			
cousin			
daughter			
father			
grandchildren			
husband			

mother			
nephew			
niece			
parent			
sister			
son			
uncle			
wife			

b Schreiben Sie die Wörter in das Kreuzworträtsel.

1 Your male *(männlich)* child is your ~.
2 Your female *(weiblich)* child is your ~.
3 Your mother and father are your ~.
4 A married man has got a ~.
5 Your uncle is married to your ~.
6 Your female parent is your ~.
7 Your aunt and uncle's son is your ~.
8 Your aunt's husband is your ~.
9 Your brother's daughter is your ~.
10 Your sister's son is your ~.
11 A married woman has got a ~.

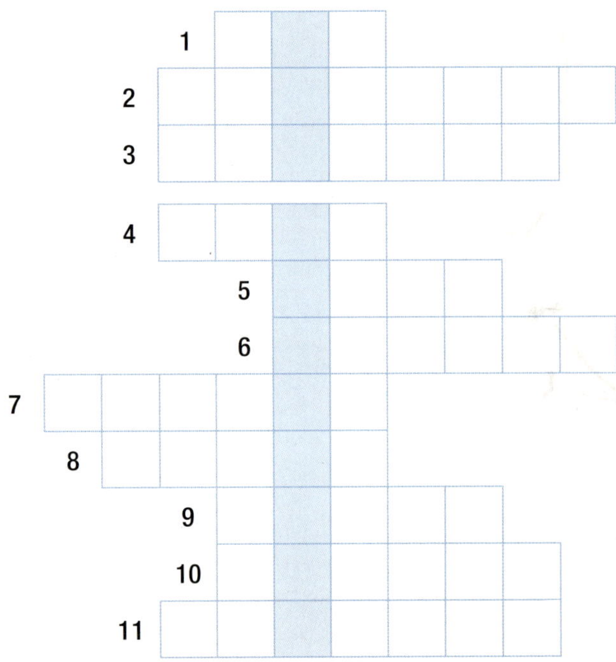

3 Grammar focus

3.1 *Have got*

→ G7 (S. 172)

Have you got a sister?	Yes, **I have**.
Have you got a brother?	No, **I haven't**.
I've got two sisters.	
I haven't got a brother.	
Has he got any children?	Yes, **he has**.
Has she got any children?	No, **she hasn't**.
He's got three sons.	
She hasn't got any children.	
Have you got a big family car?	No, **we haven't**.
We haven't got a big car.	
We've got a small car.	
Have John and Sue got a house?	Yes, **they have**.
They've got a house in London.	

a Sehen Sie sich die Sätze in der obigen Tabelle an. Beantworten Sie diese Fragen:

1 Has the woman got a daughter?

______, ______ ______.

2 Has the man got any sons?

______, ______ ______.

3 Have John and Sue got a house in London?

______, ______ ______.

b John und Sue sind verheiratet. Lesen Sie die Informationen über sie und schreiben Sie *'ve got, haven't got, 's got* oder *hasn't got* in die folgenden Sätze.

– two daughters, Anita and Jessica
– small house in London, no garden

– big, German car

– small, Italian car

1 She ______ a German car.

2 He ______ a big car.

3 They ______ two daughters.

4 They ______ a garden.

3.2 Possessive *'s*

→ G8 (S. 172)

a Lesen Sie diese Sätze laut.

He's my **brother's** best friend.
She's **John's** wife.

b Beantworten Sie diese Fragen zu John und Sue in Übung 3a und verwenden Sie dabei den Namen in Klammern.

1 Who is Sue? (John) – She 's John's wife.

2 Who is John? (Sue) – He ______.

3 Who is Anita? (Jessica) – She ______.

4 Who is Jessica? (Sue) – She ______.

4 Round up

Um spezifische Informationen herauszuhören, vergewissern Sie sich zuvor, dass Sie genau wissen, worauf Sie achten sollen. Lesen Sie zunächst die Aussagen weiter unten.

a L1:18 Zwei Mädchen aus England haben Informationen über ihre Familien und ihr Zuhause für eine Englischschule in Südamerika aufgenommen. Hören Sie und entscheiden Sie, ob diese Aussagen richtig (T) oder falsch (F) sind.

1 Danielle is an only child. ___

2 Danielle has got four sisters. ___

3 Danielle has got two grandmothers. ___

4 Becky has got a lot of friends, but she hasn't got any brothers or sisters. ___

5 Becky's father is in Ipswich. ___

6 Becky's mum's parents are in the next house. ___

S. 181

Jetzt kann ich …

andere nach ihrer Familie fragen.	○○○	www: U3A1 CD-R 1: 27
anderen von meiner Familie erzählen.	○○○	www: U3A2 CD-R 1: 29
über Dinge sprechen, die ich und andere haben und nicht haben.	○○○	www: U3A3 CD-R 1: 28

Part B Describing people

Describing someone's appearance and personality | Colours | Clothes | *can*

What sort of person are you?
Was für ein Mensch sind Sie?

a career person
a computer expert
a supermum
a feminist
a sports fan
A MACHO MAN
THE CLASS CLOWN
a pessimist
a party person
a superdad
an optimist

What can you do?

1 Ask a partner the questions in this personality quiz.
Stellen Sie einem Partner / einer Partnerin die Fragen aus diesem Persönlichkeitstest.

Can you play tennis?
☐ Yes, I can. ☐ No, I can't.

Can you swim 1km?
☐ Yes, I can. ☐ No, I can't.

Can you walk 8km?
☐ Yes, I can. ☐ No, I can't.

Can you run 5km?
☐ Yes, I can. ☐ No, I can't.

Can you use a computer?
☐ Yes, I can. ☐ No, I can't.

Can you repair a car?
☐ Yes, I can. ☐ No, I can't.

Can you cook spaghetti?
☐ Yes, I can. ☐ No, I can't.

Can you use a washing machine?
☐ Yes, I can. ☐ No, I can't.

Can you sing?
☐ Yes, I can. ☐ No, I can't.

Can you dance?
☐ Yes, I can. ☐ No, I can't.

Can you decorate a cake?
☐ Yes, I can. ☐ No, I can't.

Can you take good photos?
☐ Yes, I can. ☐ No, I can't.

Now add up your partner's score and tell him/her the result.
Ermitteln Sie nun die Punktezahl Ihres Partners / Ihrer Partnerin und teilen Sie ihm/ihr das Ergebnis mit.

Number of Yes answers
4 = You're very fit and sporty.
3 = You're fit.
2 = You aren't very fit.
1 or 0 = Go to a leisure centre.

Number of Yes answers
4 = You're very practical.
3 = You're practical.
2 = You aren't very practical.
1 or 0 = Do some courses.

Number of Yes answers
4 = You're very creative.
3 = You're creative.
2 = You aren't very creative.
1 or 0 = Find a creative hobby.

Tell the class some information you found out about your partner.
Erzählen Sie Ihrer Kursgruppe ein paar Dinge, die Sie über Ihren Partner / Ihre Partnerin herausgefunden haben.
Anke isn't very practical. She can't cook spaghetti and she can't repair a car.

2 Grammar focus

can

I can speak English.
I can't cook.

Can you dance? **Yes, I can. / No, I can't.**

can is the same for all persons – *I, you, he, she, it, we* and *they.*

2a T1:22 Listen and tick (✓) the word you hear.
Hören Sie und haken Sie das Wort ab, das Sie hören.

	can	can't		can	can't		can	can't
1	☐	☐	3	☐	☐	5	☐	☐
2	☐	☐	4	☐	☐	6	☐	☐

T1:23 **Say it like this** Listen and repeat.
Hören Sie und wiederholen Sie.

Colours

3 Word focus Colours

3a Write the names of the colours.
Schreiben Sie die Namen der Farben.
black | blue | brown | green | orange | red | white | yellow | grey | pink

3b Now try the *Stroop test* with a partner. In turns, read this list of colours. Don't read the *words*, say the *colour* the word is printed in.
Machen Sie nun zu zweit den *Stroop-Test*. Sagen Sie abwechselnd diese Farben. Lesen Sie nicht die *Wörter*, sagen Sie die *Farbe*, in der das Wort gedruckt ist.

green yellow red white blue pink green blue orange black

Clothes

4 Word focus Clothes

4a Match the words to the photos. Write the word under the photo.
Ordnen Sie die Wörter den Bildern zu. Schreiben Sie das Wort unter das Foto.
blouse | dress | jacket | jeans | pullover | shirt | shoes | skirt | trousers

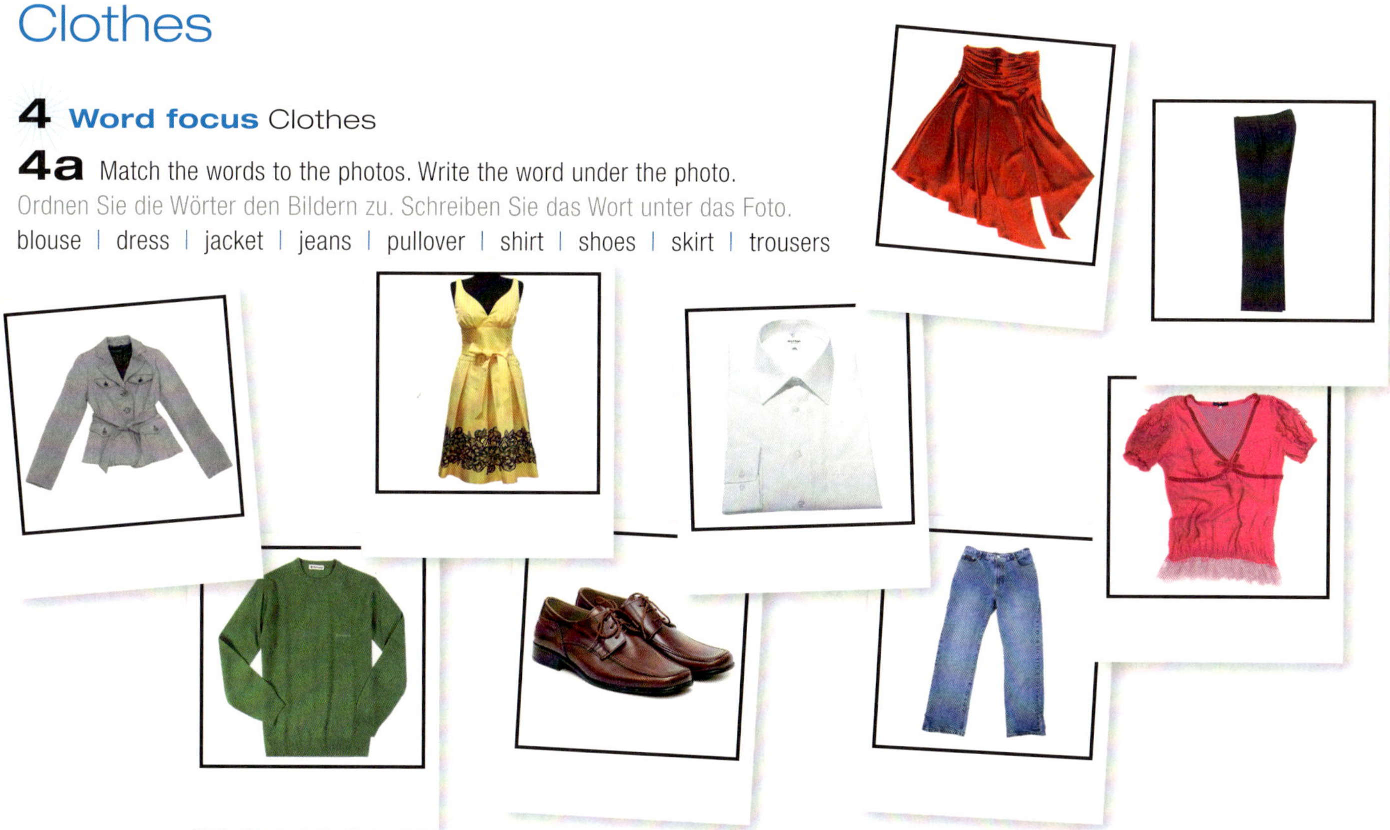

4b What colour are the clothes?
Welche Farben haben die Kleidungsstücke?
The shirt's white.
The trousers are black.

All types of trousers are plural.
My trousers ***are*** *black.*
My jeans ***are*** *blue.*
His shorts ***are*** *green.*

5 Describe another student's clothes. Your partner can guess who it is.
Beschreiben Sie die Kleidung von jemandem aus Ihrem Kurs. Ihr Partner / Ihre Partnerin kann raten, wer es ist.

He's got black trousers and a brown jacket.

Is it Ralf?

Appearance

a

Which man is the Russian visitor?
Welcher Mann ist der russische Besucher?

b

c

6a T1:24 David is at work with his personal assistant, Jill. Listen and choose the right answer.
David ist mit seiner Assistentin Jill auf der Arbeit. Hören Sie und wählen Sie die richtige Antwort.

- [ ] Jill must go to the airport and buy a ticket to Moscow.
- [ ] Jill must go to the airport and meet a Russian man.

6b T1:25 Listen again and fill in the information in Jill's notebook.
Hören Sie noch einmal und ergänzen Sie die Angaben in Jills Notizbuch.

Name: ______________________

Flight number: ______________________

Extra information: ______________________

____

7 How to describe someone's appearance

Wie Sie das Aussehen einer Person beschreiben.

Can you describe him/her?
She's black / white / Asian.
He's tall / short.
She's got black / brown / blonde / red / grey / white / short / long hair.
She's got blue / brown / green / big / small / nice eyes.
He's got glasses / a beard / a moustache.
She's beautiful. / He's/She's good-looking.

7a T1:26 Listen to descriptions of two people. Draw the faces in frames 1 and 2.
Hören Sie die Beschreibungen von zwei Personen. Zeichnen Sie die Gesichter in den Rahmen 1 und 2.

1

2

3

4

7b Draw a person in frame 3. Describe this person to a partner. Ask him/her to draw your person in his/her frame 4. Then you draw your partner's person in your frame 4.
Zeichnen Sie eine Person in Rahmen 3. Beschreiben Sie diese Person Ihrem Partner / Ihrer Partnerin. Bitten Sie ihn/sie ihre Person in seinem/ihrem Rahmen 4 zu zeichnen. Danach zeichnen Sie die Person Ihres Partners / Ihrer Partnerin in Ihrem Rahmen 4.

Flexizone

Task Adopt a Grandparent

Work in small groups. You work for the Adopt a Grandparent scheme. You get this letter.
Arbeiten Sie in Kleingruppen. Sie arbeiten für das Programm Adopt a Grandparent. Sie bekommen den folgenden Brief.

Dear Adopt a Grandparent
Hi! My name's Sam.
I'm 9. Can you find a grandparent for our family please?
From
Sam

What can you say about Sam's family?
Was können Sie über Sams Familie sagen?

Read the information about these 4 candidates.
Lesen Sie die Informationen über diese 4 Kandidaten.

Hattie (67)
What can you give a family?
I can cook, make cakes, make clothes and tell stories.
Is there anything you can't do?
Run, sports.
Favourite place:
On the sofa.

Tony (71)
What can you give a family?
Help with homework.
Is there anything you can't do?
Drive.
Favourite place:
Church.

Jimmy (68)
What can you give a family?
Fun. A lot of energy.
Is there anything you can't do?
No!
Favourite place:
Leisure centre.

Brenda (72)
What can you give a family?
Time, help with housework, songs, love.
Is there anything you can't do?
Use a computer.
Favourite place:
Clothes shops.

Who is the best candidate?
Wer ist der beste Kandidat?

I think (name) is interesting because … .

I think (name) is good for (Sam / Sam's big sister / Sam's baby sister/ Sam's dad) because … .

What do you think?

I think (name) is better because … .

Your turn Describing people (→ www)

1 How to …

Schreiben Sie die Wörter in die Lücken.

a Wie Sie nach dem Aussehen einer Person fragen.

Can | Can | describe | got | Has | Is | you

1 ________ you describe him?

2 ________ ________ ____________ him for me, please?

3 ________ she tall or short?

4 ________ he ________ long hair or short hair?

b Wie Sie jemanden beschreiben.

She is | He's got | He is | She's got

1 ________ ________ a long beard.

2 ________ ________ beautiful.

3 ________ ________ beautiful red hair.

4 ________ ________ a very tall man.

L1:19 Hören Sie und überprüfen Sie Ihre Antworten.

L1:20 **Say it like this** Hören Sie und sprechen Sie nach.

2 Word focus

a Colours

Vervollständigen Sie die Namen der Farben.

1 b _ _ _ k →

2 b _ _ e →

3 b _ _ _ n →

4 g _ _ _ n →

5 g _ _ y →

6 o _ _ _ _ e →

7 p _ _ k →

8 r _ d →

9 w _ _ _ e →

10 y _ _ _ _ w →

b Clothes

Vervollständigen Sie diese Sätze mit *His* oder *Her* und dem Namen des Kleidungsstücks.

1 ________ ____________ are black.

2 ________ ____________ is green.

3 ________ ____________ is yellow.

4 ________ ____________ is grey.

5 ________ ____________ are white.

6 ________ ____________ is blue.

7 ________ ____________ is green and yellow.

c A person's appearance

Wozu passen die folgenden Wörter? Tragen Sie sie ein bei *on the face*, *eyes* oder *hair*. Drei Wörter können sich sowohl auf die Augen als auch auf die Haare beziehen. Schreiben Sie diese in das gelbe Feld.

beard | beautiful | big | black | blonde | blue | brown | glasses | green | grey | long | moustache | red | short | small | white

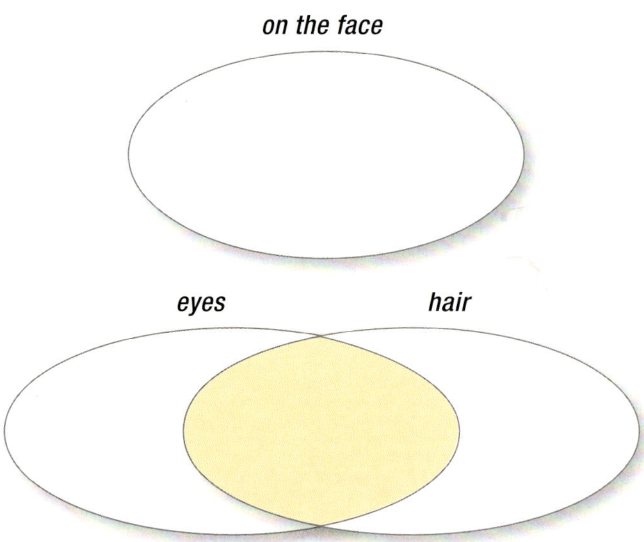

3 Grammar focus

can → G9 (S. 173)

Can you swim?	No, **I can't**.	**I can't** swim.
Can he cook? **Can she** sing?	Yes, **he can**. No, **she can't**.	**He can** cook fish. **She can't** sing.
Can you speak German?	Yes, **we can**.	**We can** speak German.
Can they dance?	Yes, **they can**.	**They can** dance.

Can und *can't* sind unveränderlich in allen Fällen.
Auf Englisch können Sie nicht *I can German* sagen. Sie müssen immer ein Verb verwenden: *I can* ***speak*** *German*.

a Schreiben Sie die (wahren!) Antworten in die Lücken.

1 Can you play tennis?

______, ______ ______.

2 Can your best friend speak English?

______, ______ ______.

3 Can your English teacher speak German?

______, ______ ______.

4 Can you and your best friend dance?

______, ______ ______.

5 Can very small babies walk?

______, ______ ______.

b Schreiben Sie die Wörter in der richtigen Reihefolge.

1 use | I | a | can | computer

______.

2 take | can | photos | She | good

______.

3 Spanish | can't | speak | They

______.

4 do | We | exercise | can | this

______.

c Was können sie tun?

	Mann	Frau
1 They ______ cook.	✓	✓
2 She ______ swim but he ______.	✗	✓
3 They ______ dance.	✗	✗
4 He ______ sing but she ______.	✓	✗

4 Round up

Manchmal müssen Sie anhand eines kurzen Gesprächsausschnitts raten, worüber jemand spricht. Achten Sie auf die Schlüsselwörter.

a L1:21 Hören Sie Ausschnitte aus einem Gespräch. Sprechen die Personen über das äußere Erscheinungsbild, die Kleidung oder darüber, was die Person tun kann? Schreiben Sie die Zahlen in die Kästchen.

a person's appearance ☐ ☐
what a person can do ☐ ☐

b Notieren Sie einige persönliche Informationen zu Ihrer Person.

All about me!

Name:

My appearance:

I can speak:

Things I can do:

S. 181

Jetzt kann ich …

fragen, wie jemand aussieht. — www: U3B1

beschreiben, wie jemand aussieht. — www: U3B2, CD-R 1: 35

sagen, was jemand kann und nicht kann. — www: U3B3, CD-R 1: 30+31

Reading A family story

The Chang family and the Foong family are from the same small town in China. The families are good friends. Mrs Chang and Mrs Foong have both got young sons and they're good friends, too.

The sons are now both married and their wives are pregnant. Mrs Chang is very happy – at 9 o'clock in the morning on February 25th, her son and his wife have a baby son, Yon Pok. Mrs Foong is happy, too when her granddaughter, Cheng Tai, is born – at 9 o'clock in the morning on February 25th! The grandmothers joke, "Now they're babies – but in twenty years, maybe they can be married!"

And today Chang Yon Pok and Foong Cheng Tai are husband and wife! And they've got 13 children – 10 daughters and 3 sons, 63 grandchildren, 54 great-grandchildren and a baby great-great-grandson. There are now more than 150 members of this five-generation family and every year on February 25th, they have a big family party.

Glossary

same der-/die-/dasselbe | pregnant schwanger | joke scherzen | great-great-grandson Ururenkel

Out and About

The doctor's son

A man telephones the hospital, "There's a car crash on the corner of West Street and Bridge Road. We need a doctor!"
The doctor is there in ten minutes. The car driver is a young man.
"Oh no," says the doctor, "that's my son!"
But the doctor isn't the young man's father. Can you explain this?

Find the solution in *Out and About*, page 14.
Die Lösung finden Sie in *Out and About*, S. 14.

Diese Testübungen orientieren sich an den Aufgabenformaten der Prüfung *telc English A1*. Bitte markieren Sie Ihre Antworten mit einem Querbalken (–) in den Antwortabschnitten rechts neben den Aufgaben.

1 Language elements

Markieren Sie (–) die richtige Antwort **a)** oder **b)** im Antwortabschnitt.

My best friend Jack ___1___ married. ___2___ wife's name is Sabine – ___3___ from Germany. She ___4___ speak German, French and English. They ___5___ two daughters, Amy and Kylie, and a son called Ted but they haven't got ___6___ grandchildren. ___7___ house is in ___8___ very small town near London. ___9___ some small shops in the town. Jack and Sabine ___10___ very happy there.

1 **a)** are **b)** is	3 **a)** it's **b)** she's	5 **a)** 's got **b)** 've got	7 **a)** His **b)** Their	9 **a)** There are **b)** There's
2 **a)** Her **b)** His	4 **a)** can **b)** can't	6 **a)** any **b)** some	8 **a)** a **b)** an	10 **a)** are **b)** is

Nun noch ein paar Informationen zu Jack und Sabine. Markieren Sie (–) die richtige Antwort **a)** oder **b)** im Antwortabschnitt.

Sabine ___11___ speak Spanish.	11	**a)** can	**b)** can't
Sabine ___12___ a grandmother.	12	**a)** is	**b)** isn't
Their son ___13___ a daughter.	13	**a)** 's got	**b)** hasn't got
Their daughters haven't got ___14___ children.	14	**a)** any	**b)** some
There ___15___ any big shops in their town.	15	**a)** are	**b)** aren't

1 Language elements

	a)	b)
1		
2		
3		
4		
5		
6		
7		
8		
9		
10		
11		
12		
13		
14		
15		

= ______ / 15

2 L1:22 Listening comprehension

Lesen Sie zunächst die Fragen. Hören Sie dann, was Jack über seinen Wohnort erzählt. Markieren Sie (–) die richtige Antwort **a)** oder **b)** im Antwortabschnitt.

16 What's the name of their road?
a) Windam Road
b) Wyndham Road

17 What number is Jack and Sabine's house?
a) 18
b) 80

18 What is there opposite their house?
a) a café in a park
b) a restaurant

19 Is there a big supermarket in his town?
a) Yes, there is.
b) There's a small supermarket.

20 What's Jack's phone number?
a) 01923 739886
b) 01923 739868

2 Listening comprehension

	a)	b)
16		
17		
18		
19		
20		

= ______ / 5

3 Situational responses

Part A L1:23

Sehen Sie sich zunächst die Erwiderungen **a)** – **d)** an.
Hören Sie dann, was drei Personen auf einer Büroparty sagen.
Markieren Sie (—) die richtige Antwort **a)**, **b)**, **c)** oder **d)** im Antwortabschnitt.

21 ______
22 ______
23 ______

a) No, I'm from Berlin.
b) Fine thanks, and you?
c) Hello, nice to meet you.
d) I'm from Germany.

Part B L1:24

Sehen Sie sich zunächst die Erwiderungen **e)** – **h)** an.
Hören Sie dann, was drei Personen auf der Straße sagen.
Markieren Sie (—) die richtige Antwort **e)**, **f)**, **g)** oder **h)** im Antwortabschnitt.

24 ______
25 ______
26 ______

e) Yes, there is. It's opposite the station.
f) You're welcome.
g) Thank you.
h) Yes, can I help you?

3 Situational responses

Part A				
21	a)	b)	c)	d)
22	a)	b)	c)	d)
23	a)	b)	c)	d)
Part B				
24	e)	f)	g)	h)
25	e)	f)	g)	h)
26	e)	f)	g)	h)

= ______ / 6

4 Reading comprehension

Lesen Sie die Informationen über die Stadt Middletown und beantworten Sie die folgenden Fragen.
Markieren Sie (—) die richtige Antwort **a)** oder **b)** im Antwortabschnitt.

Information

What can you find in our small town – Middletown?

➤ **In Station Road:**
Post Office
The Blue Café
The Red Lion Hotel (with The Otis snack bar)
The Readwell Bookshop

➤ **In Main Street:**
Tick-Tock Swiss Clocks and Watches
The Astra Cine-complex
Catholic Church
The Middletown Theatre

➤ **In London Road:**
Number One Supermarket
The Dubliner Irish Pub
The Victoria – our department store
Venezia Italian Restaurant
The 2000 Art Gallery
Church of England

27 It's 10.30 in the morning. You have got a cup of coffee and an ice cream. Where are you?
a) in Station Road
b) in Main Street

28 How many places are there in Middletown where you can have lunch with a friend?
a) two
b) four

29 Where can you go to see a film in Middletown?
a) to London Road
b) to Main Street

30 Where can you buy a book, a watch, spaghetti and a shirt?
a) in Main Street
b) in London Road

4 Reading comprehension

	a)	b)
27		
28		
29		
30		

= ______ / 4

total

= ______ / 30

S. 181

Daily life

Part A Routines

Telling the time | Days of the week | Present simple (1), *I / you* | Prepositions of time

How many clocks are there in your house? How many students in the class have got a watch on today? Are you a punctual person?

What's the time?

1a Look at these clocks.

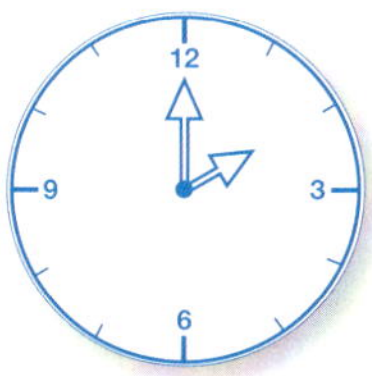

It's two o'clock.

It's five to two.

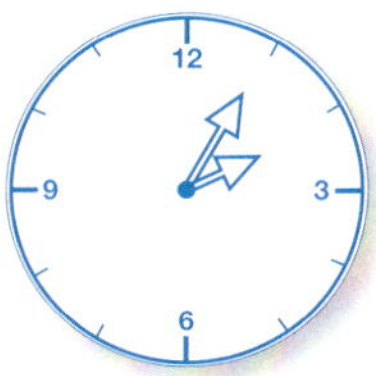

It's five past two.

9.30 = half past **nine**

1b Match the times to the clocks. Write the numbers in the boxes.

1

2

3

4

5

6

☐ It's twenty-five to eight.
☐ It's quarter to eight.
☐ It's quarter past seven.
☐ It's seven o'clock.
☐ It's half past seven.
☐ It's ten past seven.

2 How to tell the time

What's the time?
It's (one) o'clock.
It's five / ten / quarter / twenty / twenty-five / half past (one).
It's twenty-five / twenty / quarter / ten / five to (two).

In English, we don't use the 24 hour clock in everyday speech.
13.30 – *It's half past one.*

2a What's the time? Work with a partner

1 12:10 2 13:40 3 08:45 4 11:30 5 17:25 6 16:35

Daily routines

3 Look at Jill's daily routine.

3a Match the pictures to the phrases. Write the letters in the boxes.

- ☐ have breakfast
- ☐ do the housework
- ☐ finish work
- ☐ start work
- ☐ have lunch
- ☐ go to bed
- ☐ get up
- ☐ stay at home and relax
- ☐ have dinner

T1:27 Jill tells Richard about a typical day in her life. Listen to the order she does things every day and check your answers.

3b T1:28 Listen again. For each part of Jill's routine, write down the times she says on the clocks.

When you can't understand, say:
Sorry, I don't understand.

4 Grammar focus

Present simple *I / you*

What time **do you finish** work? — I **finish** work at 5.30.
Do you have lunch in the office? — **Yes, I do. / No, I don't.**
I don't go out for lunch.

4a Put the words in the correct order to make questions.

1 get up? | What time | do you
2 do you | in the morning? | do | What
3 lunch? | do you | have | Where
4 do | in the afternoon? | What | do you
5 do you | What time | dinner? | have
6 do you | in the evening? | What | do
7 to bed? | What time | go | do you

4b Ask a partner your questions.

5 Look at the title of this magazine questionnaire.

With a partner, do the questionnaire and find out how many students in the class are 'larks' and how many are 'owls'. Student A: Look at page 168. Student B: Look at page 167.

6 Word focus Days of the week

6a T1:29 Listen to the days of the week. Now put the days in the correct order.

Tuesday | Thursday | Saturday | Monday | Sunday | Friday | Wednesday

1 M ______ 5 ______
2 ______ 6 ______
3 ______ 7 ______
4 Th ______

T1:29 Listen again and check your answers.

T1:30 **Say it like this** Listen again and repeat the days of the week.

6b Tell your partner something you do (or don't do) on each day of the week.
On Mondays I go to work. On Tuesdays I don't go home after work – I come to my English course.

When's it open?

7 In this part of Unit 4, there are a lot of time phrases.

at six o'clock
from six o'clock **to** half past ten.
in the morning / afternoon / evening
at night
at lunchtime / dinnertime
after / **before** breakfast / lunch / dinner / work
on Monday(s)

Look at these signs. Work with a partner and say when each place is open.

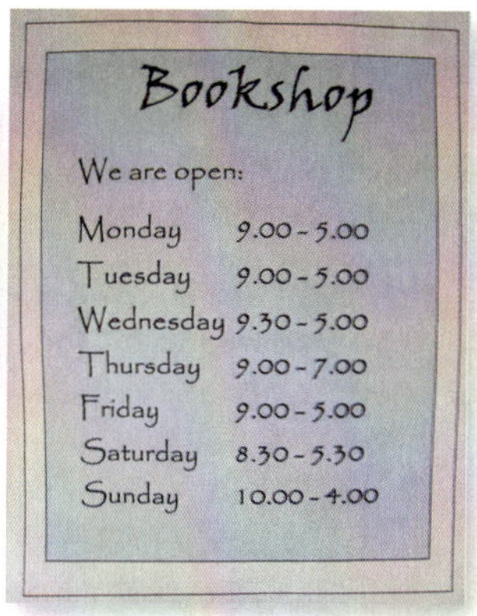

It's open from … to … .
It's open in the evening.
On Mondays it's open …

am is from midnight to midday (0–12).
pm is from midday to midnight (12–24).

Flexizone

A Ask your teacher some questions about his/her daily routine, e.g. *When do you …? What time do you …?.*

B What's your favourite day of the week? What do you do on that day?

Your turn Routines (→ www)

1 How to …

Schreiben Sie die Wörter in die Lücken.

a Wie Sie jemanden nach der Uhrzeit fragen.

Excuse me | please | the time | the time | what's

1 What's ______ ______?

2 ______ ______, what's the time?

3 Excuse me, ______ ______

______, ______?

b Wie Sie jemanden sagen, wie spät es ist.

half | past | past | o'clock | to

What's the time?

1 07:00 It's seven ______.

2 07:15 It's quarter ______ seven.

3 07:30 It's ______ ______ seven.

4 07:45 It's quarter ______ eight.

c Wie Sie über routinemäßige Handlungen sprechen.

after | at | at | before | from | in | on | to

1 I do that ______ 7 o'clock.

2 ______ 7 ______ 9.

3 ______ the mornings.

4 ______ or ______ lunch.

5 ______ lunchtime.

6 ______ Saturdays.

L1:25 Hören Sie und überprüfen Sie Ihre Antworten.

L1:26 **Say it like this** Hören Sie und sprechen Sie nach.

2 Word focus

a Days of the week

Schreiben Sie mithilfe der Buchstaben die Wochentage von Montag bis Sonntag.

Fr	i	~~M~~	nes	on	S	Sat
T	Th	ues	un	ur	urs	Wed

1 M______day 5 ______day

2 ______day 6 ______day

3 ______day 7 ______day

4 ______day

b In a day

Nummerieren Sie die Tageszeiten von 1–4 in der richtigen Reihenfolge.

☐ afternoon ☐ evening ☐ morning ☐ night

Nummerieren Sie die Mahlzeiten in der Reihenfolge, in der wir sie essen.

☐ breakfast ☐ dinner ☐ lunch

c The time

Welche Uhr passt zu welchem Ausdruck? Nummerieren Sie die Uhren von 1–6.

1 half past
2 o'clock
3 quarter past
4 quarter to
5 twenty-five past
6 twenty-five to

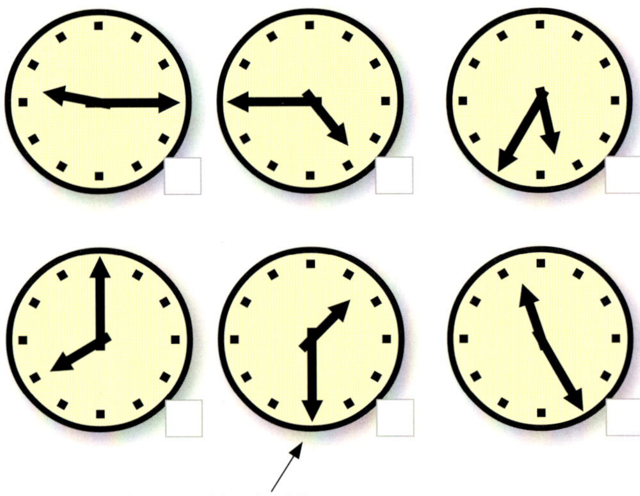

What's the time on this clock?

It's ______.

3 Grammar focus

Present simple *I / you*

→ G10 (S. 173)

Do you live near an airport?	No, **I don't**.
Do you live near a station?	Yes, **I do**.
Where **do you live**?	**I live** in a big town. **I don't live** in a small town.

a Verbinden Sie die Wörter, die zusammenpassen, mit einer Linie.

1 live	breakfast in the morning
2 get	champagne
3 go	in an office
4 have	near a cinema
5 like	to bed before midnight
6 work	up at 5.30 am

b Schreiben Sie Fragen. Verwenden Sie die Wörter aus 3a sowie das Wort *you*.

1 Do you live near a cinema?
2 ______ you ______
3 ______
4 ______
5 ______
6 ______

c Beantworten Sie jetzt die Fragen in 3b mit *Yes, I do.* oder *No, I don't.*

1 ______ 4 ______
2 ______ 5 ______
3 ______ 6 ______

d Schreiben Sie jetzt mit den Wörtern aus 3a zwei positive und zwei negative Sätze über sich.

1 ______
2 ______
3 ______
4 ______

4 Round up

a Lesen Sie, was Jill (J) in diesem Interview geantwortet hat. Schreiben Sie dann die Fragen des Interviewers (I). Benutzen Sie die Wörter in Klammern

I: *(live) Where* ______
J: I live in Wantage.

I: *(work) Do* ______
J: Yes, I do. I'm a PA.

I: *(like) Do* ______
J: My boss? Oh, yes – David is very nice.

I: *(get up) What* ______
J: At about 7 o'clock in the morning.

I: *(have) Do* ______
J: In a café? Oh, no. I have breakfast at home.

I: *(go out) Do* ______
J: Out for lunch? No, I don't, I have lunch in my office.

I: *(do) What* ______
J: After work I go home, or I go to the pub or to my yoga class.

I: *(go) When* ______
J: The class is on Mondays. At 6.30.

b L1:27 Hören Sie und überprüfen Sie Ihre Antworten. Der Interviewer stellt noch zwei weitere Fragen. Schreiben Sie sie und Jills Antworten auf.

I: ______
J: ______
I: ______
J: ______

S. 181

Jetzt kann ich ...

nach der Uhrzeit fragen.	www: U4A1
jemandem die Uhrzeit sagen.	www: U4A2 CD-R 1: 38
über routinemäßige Handlungen sprechen.	www: U4A3 CD-R 1: 37+39
über Tageszeiten und Wochentage sprechen.	www: U4A4 CD-R 1: 40+41

Part B Work

Jobs | Expressing opinions, agreeing and disagreeing | Present simple (2), *he/she*

What are children's typical dream jobs? Choose jobs from this list and write one in each gap. Then compare your answers.

housewife/househusband | pop star | train driver | teacher | police officer | model | formula one driver | footballer | astronaut | film star | TV presenter | shop assistant | pilot

2 dream jobs for girls	2 dream jobs for boys
______ and ______	______ and ______

What's his/her job?

1 Word focus Jobs

1a Write the names of the jobs under the photos.

sales manager | police officer | IT technician | nurse | PA (personal assistant) | lorry driver | shop assistant | doctor | builder

1 ______

2 ______

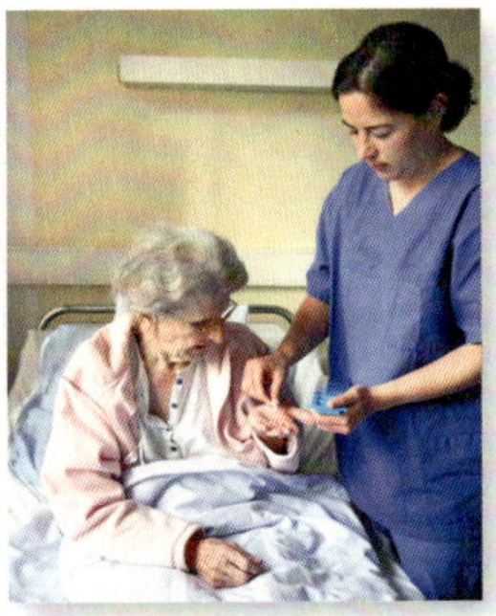

3 ______

4 ______

5 ______

6 ______

7 ______

8 ______

9 ______

1b Check your answers with a partner. Make sentences, e.g. *She's a PA.*

With jobs, use ***a*** / ***an***.
*She's **a** teacher.*
*He's **an** English teacher.*

What does he/she do at work?

2a Read these sentences about the people in the photos in exercise 1. Work with a partner and find two jobs for each sentence. Write the numbers in the boxes.

a	He/She wears a uniform.	☐	and	☐
b	He/She works in an office.	☐	and	☐
c	He/She sorts out problems.	☐	and	☐
d	He/She drives a lot.	☐	and	☐
e	He/She looks after people.	☐	and	☐
f	He/She earns a lot of money.	☐	and	☐
g	He/She works outside.	☐	and	☐
h	He/She goes to meetings.	☐	and	☐

2b Who is it?

1 She looks after people. She doesn't earn a lot of money. Who is it?
2 He drives a lot. He doesn't wear a uniform. Who is it?
3 She goes to meetings. She doesn't wear a uniform. Who is it?
4 He sorts out problems. He doesn't work outside. Who is it?
5 He works outside. He doesn't drive a lot. Who is it?

3 Grammar focus

Present simple *he / she*

He works outside.
He doesn't earn a lot of money.
Does he wear a uniform? **Yes, he does. / No, he doesn't.**

3a Work with a partner. Look again at the job photos in exercise 1. For each job, try to remember one sentence.

3b For each job, say two things that he/she **doesn't** do.
The PA doesn't wear a uniform and she doesn't work outside.

3c Student A: Choose one of the photos. Student B: Ask questions to guess who it is.
B: Does he wear a uniform? A: Yes, he does. / No, he doesn't.

If you don't know the English word for someone's job, you can say:
He works for (Siemens).
She works in an office / a bank / a hotel / a school.
I don't know the English word for her job,
but she helps people with their money.

A job at a hotel

4a Look at this photo. Say four things about the man in the photo.

4b Read this interview with the man. Match the questions and answers and write the numbers in the boxes.

1 What's your job?	☐ No, I don't. At the end of the day I go home to my wife.
2 What do you do at work?	☐ I'm a doorman at a five star hotel.
3 What do you wear at work?	☐ The tips. I often get a tip if I give good service.
4 Do you live in the hotel?	☐ I love it. On a warm summer morning, it's the perfect job.
5 What's the best thing about your job?	☐ The English winter. I'm out here in the rain and the snow.
6 What's the worst thing about your job?	☐ A traditional doorman's coat and hat. I think it's a very smart uniform.
7 Do you like your job?	☐ I stand outside the hotel and I welcome our guests when they arrive. I open the door for them. And I find a taxi for them when they leave.

T1:31 Listen and check your answers.

4c Talk with a partner and complete these sentences about the doorman:
He likes ….
He doesn't like …

4d Write three questions about the doorman:
What does he …? Does he …? What's …?
Now close your book. Take turns round the class to ask and answer questions.

I think it's a useful job

5 How to express opinions, agree and disagree

What about …?
What do you think?
I think …
I think it's …
Yes, I think so, too.
I don't think so.

When you don't understand a word, ask:
What does … mean?

a

interesting | boring
stressful | dangerous | useful
overpaid | underpaid

5a Work with a partner. Use the words in **a** to talk about the jobs in **b**. You can agree or disagree with your partner, e.g.

What about a nurse? What do you think?
I think it's a stressful job.
Yes, I think so, too. And I think it's boring.
Oh, I don't think so. I think it's interesting.

b

film star | hotel doorman | nurse
opera singer | police officer | formula one driver
shop assistant | taxi driver | teacher
television presenter | pilot

Flexizone

Task Present your Volunteer of the Year

Here are four volunteers. Each one works in his/her spare time for no money. Your teacher will make four groups and give each group a different volunteer. In your group, prepare a short presentation about your volunteer and his/her typical week.
Unten finden Sie Beschreibungen von vier Menschen, die ehrenamtlich tätig sind. Alle vier arbeiten in ihrer Freizeit ohne Bezahlung. Ihr Lehrer / Ihre Lehrerin wird Sie in vier Gruppen einteilen und jeder Gruppe einen Freiwilligen zuweisen. Bereiten Sie in Ihrer Gruppe eine kurze Präsentation über Ihren ehrenamtlich Tätigen / Ihre ehrenamtlich Tätige vor.

From Monday to Friday … but on Saturday …
He/She works / helps / goes …
I think his/her voluntary work is helpful / useful / dangerous …
I think he/she is a good candidate for Volunteer of the Year because …

Name: Maria Grigson
Job / Family: retired, married with three grandchildren
Voluntary work: hospital café volunteer
Voluntary organisation: League of Friends, Churchill Hospital, Oxford.

Key words: afternoon | café | tea and coffee | patients | families | talks | listens to

Name: Vanessa Clark
Job / Family: writer, three children
Voluntary work: minibus driver
Voluntary organisation: Oxfordshire District Society for the Blind
Key words: Friday | drives a minibus | takes | blind people | shops | friends | hospital

Name: Leesa Espley
Job: teacher
Voluntary work: lifeboatwoman
Voluntary organisation: The Royal National Lifeboat Institution
Key words: when someone is in danger | goes out to sea | boat | rescues | saves lives

Name: Graham Durrant
Job: salesperson
Voluntary work: Special Constable (volunteer policeman)
Voluntary organisation: Suffolk Police
Key words: Saturday | walks in the town | drives a police car | helps people | stops criminals

Now form new groups with one person from each old group. Present your volunteer to your new group.
Take a group vote: Who is your Volunteer of the Year?
Bilden Sie neue Gruppen mit jeweils einer Person der ursprünglichen Gruppen. Präsentieren Sie Ihren ehrenamtlich Tätigen / Ihre ehrenamtlich Tätige Ihrer neuen Gruppe. Stimmen Sie ab: Wer wird Ehrenamtlicher des Jahres?

Your turn Work (→ www)

1 How to …

Schreiben Sie die Wörter in die Lücken.

a Wie Sie über Berufe sprechen.

a | at | do | for | in | work | you

1 Where ______ ______ work?

2 I ______ ______ a shop.

3 I work ______ Lufthansa.

4 What do you do ______ work?

5 I'm ______ pilot.

b Wie Sie sagen, was Menschen mögen und nicht mögen.

I like | I don't like | likes | she doesn't like

1 Susan? She ______ her job but ______ ______ ______ her boss.

2 Me? ______ ______ my boss but ______ ______ ______ my office.

c Wie Sie Meinungen ausdrücken und auf die Meinungen anderer reagieren.

don't | boring | so | so | think | too

1 What do you ______?

2 I think it's a very ______ job.

3 Yes, I think ______, ______.

4 Oh, I ______ think ______.

L1:28 Hören Sie und überprüfen Sie Ihre Antworten.

L1:29 **Say it like this** Hören Sie und sprechen Sie nach.

2 Word focus Jobs

a Für welche Berufe stehen folgende Bilder?

1 t ______

2 t ______ d ______

3 p ______ o ______

4 o ______ s ______

5 h ______ d ______

6 s ______ a ______

7 n ______

8 t ______ d ______

9 t ______ p ______

☺ Which do you think is the best job? ______

☹ Which do you think is the worst job? ______

b Folgende Wörter können Berufe beschreiben. Ergänzen Sie die Vokale (a, e, i, o, u).

1 b_r_ng

2 d_ng_r_ _s

3 _nt_r_st_ng

4 _v_rp_ _d

5 str_ssf_l

6 _nd_rp_ _d

7 _s_f_l

3 Grammar focus

Present simple *he/she*

→ G10 (S. 173)

Zunächst ein Blick auf die Grammatik in Unit 4 Part A:

Do you live here? – Yes, I do. / No, I don't.
Where do you live? – I live in … / I don't live in …

Und nun:

Does he work in a bank?	No, **he doesn't**.
Does she work in a hotel?	Yes, **she does**.
Where does **he/she work**?	**He/She works** for the BBC. **He/She doesn't work** in a shop.

Beachten Sie: Mit *I/you* verwenden Sie *do* und *don't*, mit *he/she* verwenden Sie *does/doesn't*. Am Ende des Verbs in positiven Sätzen steht ein **s** *(he/she work**s**)*.

a Ergänzen Sie *do* oder *does* in den folgenden Fragen.

1 ________ you like your job?
2 ________ Patricia live in London?
3 ________ you drive a lot?
4 ________ your nephew go to school?

b Wo wohnt sie? Wo arbeitet er?
1 Anna: Scotland | 2 George: school

1 She ________
2 He ________

Und Sie? Wo wohnen oder wo arbeiten Sie?

____

c Schreiben Sie die Kurzantworten.

1 Does Anna live in London? ________
2 Does George work in a school? ________
3 Do you live in Berlin? ________

d Schauen Sie sich die Informationen über Anna und George an. Schreiben Sie über Anna, George und sich selbst.

1 Anna / London ________
2 George / school ________
3 I / school ________
4 I / near an airport ________

4 Round up

Die Übersicht unten zeigt Ihnen, was Jills Freundin Susie am Abend nach der Arbeit macht.

a L1:30 Hören Sie ein Gespräch zwischen Jill und Susie. Notieren Sie, was Susie zu bestimmten Zeiten macht.

	7	8	9	10	11
Monday	Italian Course				bed
Tuesday	stays at home all evening				
Wednesday					
Thursday					
Friday					

What does Susie do at these times?

1 She goes to an Italian course on Mondays 7.15 to 8.45.
2 She ________
3 She ________
4 She ________

b L1:31 Hören Sie nun Fragen zu Susie. Schreiben Sie die Antwort auf.

1 ________
2 ________
3 ________
4 ________
5 ________

S. 182

Jetzt kann ich …

über Berufe sprechen.	○○○	www: U4B1 CD-R 1: 44+45+48
sagen, was ich mag und was ich nicht mag.	○○○	www: U4B2 CD-R 1: 46
Meinungen ausdrücken und auf Meinungen reagieren.	○○○	www: U4B3 CD-R 1: 43

Reading The history of clocks

The word *clock* comes from the Latin word for bell: *clocca.*

The oldest clock, from around **3,500 BC**, is the sundial. But you can only use sundials in daylight.

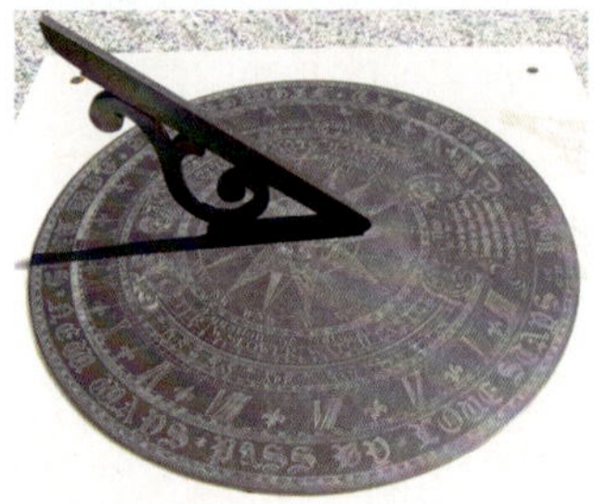

1400 BC The Egyptians invent the first water clock. They are popular in Greece, too. Water clocks are more accurate than sundials and you can use them day *and* night.

1510 Peter Henlein of Nuremberg invents the first 'modern' clock.

1656 Christian Huygens from Holland invents the first pendulum clock. Pendulum clocks are still popular today.

1920s Quartz clocks are relatively cheap to mass produce and they're accurate.

Today we've got radio controlled digital clocks – on our computers, for example. They're accurate to one second in one million years!

Glossary bell Glocke | around ungefähr | BC = Before Christ vor Christi Geburt | daylight Tageslicht | to invent erfinden | still noch | cheap billig

Out and About
How punctual?

You've got an invitation to an English birthday party. It starts at 8 o'clock.
Should you arrive at a) ten to eight, b) eight o'clock, or c) ten past eight?
Sie sind zu einem englischen Geburtstagsfest eingeladen, das um acht Uhr beginnt.
Wann sollen Sie erscheinen: a) um zehn vor acht, b) um acht oder c) um zehn nach acht.

Find the solution in *Out and About*, page 20.
Die Lösung finden Sie in *Out and About*, S. 20.

Active and healthy

Part A Keeping active

Free time activities | Saying how often you do things (1) | Expressing likes and dislikes | Present simple (3), *we / they*

Which of these sports do you watch on television? boxing | football | formula one | skiing | tennis
Which is the most popular sport on television in your class?

Free time activities

1 Word focus Free time activities

1a Fill in the missing vowels.

1 b___sk___tb___ll
2 ch___ss
3 sk______ng
4 sw___mm___ng
5 t___ble t___nn___s
6 w___lk___ng

1b Now write the words in the correct column.

I play …	I go …
__________	__________
__________	__________
__________	__________

Make sentences about you: *I don't go … / play …*

2a What activities can you see in these pictures?

T1:32 Now listen to a person from each photo talking about his/her group and check your answers.

2b T1:33 Read the sentences below. Which group is it? Listen again and write W (walkers), S (swimmers), B (basketball players) or C (chess players) in the boxes.

1 ☐ They meet once a week.
2 ☐ They meet twice a week.
3 ☐ They meet twice a month.
4 ☐ They have breakfast together once a week.
5 ☐ They go to the pub after a match.
6 ☐ They meet in the church hall.
7 ☐ They meet at about 6.30am.
8 ☐ They walk and talk.

2c T1:33 Listen again. Now make one question about each group.

How often do
What time do
What day do
Where do
What do

the walkers
the swimmers
the basketball players
the chess players

meet?
go walking?
play?
go swimmming?
do after a match?
do after their swim?

2d Memory test: Ask a partner your questions.

3 Grammar focus

Present simple *we / they*

We/They play tennis.
Do you/they play at the leisure centre?
Yes, we/they do. / No, we/they don't.
We/They don't play in the park.

3a Complete the questions about sports clothes. Use a word from the box.

1 Do swimmers wear …?
2 Do footballers wear …?
3 Do runners wear …?
4 Do boxers wear …?
5 Do basketball players wear …?

shoes
dresses
T-shirts
shorts
pullovers

3b Now ask a partner your questions. He/She will give a short answer: *Yes, they do. / No, they don't.*

4 How to say how often you do things

How often do you do sport?

I play football / tennis	*once* *twice* *three / four / five times*	*a week.* *a month.* *a year.*
I go skiing / swimming	*every*	*day / weekend / Tuesday.*

4a With a partner, ask and answer these questions about your free time activities.
How often do you …

1 walk in the countryside?
2 go swimming?
3 meet friends?
4 go on holiday?
5 talk to your neighbours?
6 run?
7 play cards?
8 go to the pub?
9 buy a newspaper?
10 phone your best friend?

5 Some people do unusual things in their free time.
Take a word from each box to make the names of these unusual activities.

wife | underwater | cheese

hockey | rolling | carrying

1 ______________________

2 ______________________

3 ______________________

What do you think about each activity?
I think it's fun / a good idea / silly / dangerous.

Likes and dislikes

6 How to express likes and dislikes

I love	*tennis.*
I like	*football.*
I don't like	*swimming.*
	playing tennis.
	watching tennis.

6a Complete these sentences about your likes and dislikes with *love, like,* or *don't like.*

1 I ______________ classical music.

2 I ______________ Scrabble.

3 I ______________ learning English.

4 I ______________ skiing.

5 I ______________ swimming in an outdoor swimming pool.

6 I ______________ meeting new people.

6b Show your answer… partner and tell the clas… for both of you. …le.

Katrín Elísdóttir's a swimmer from Iceland. She lives in Reykjavik with her husband and her two dogs.

+ + + My favourite things:
my husband and my dogs (in that order!)
súrmjólk (Icelandic sour milk)
chocolate (sportspeople need extra calories!)
winning medals
parties (with dancing and good music)

– – – Things I don't like:
training early in the morning
housework
negative people

…our book and see if every student in the class can remember one fact about Katrín.

She loves / likes … *She doesn't like …*

Flexizone

A Make two teams. In your team, make a list of places famous for a sport e.g. St Andrews. Ask the other team what sport people do there.
What do they do at (St Andrews)? ➔ *They (play golf).*

B On a piece of paper, draw a 🚹 or 🚺 to show if you are a man or woman. Write one thing you like and one thing you don't like.
I like … | *I don't like …*
Your teacher will collect the papers and give them out to different people. Read the new list to the class and the other students must guess who it is.
She likes beer gardens. She doesn't like big cities. ➔ *Is it Anke?*

Your turn Keeping active (→ www)

1 How to …

Schreiben Sie die Wörter in die Lücken.

a Wie Sie sagen, wie oft Sie etwas machen.

every day | How often | four times | twice a week | every weekend

______ ______ do you see your best friend?

– I see her ______ ______ – Monday to Friday – at work.

– I see him ______ ______ ______, on Tuesdays and Thursdays.

– I see him ______ ______, every Sunday.

– I see her about ______ ______ a year.

b Wie Sie sagen, wann Sie etwas machen.

at | on | What day | What time

■ ______ ______ do you go to your English lesson?

◆ ______ Wednesdays.

■ ______ ______ does the lesson start?

◆ ______ 7.30.

c Wie Sie über Vorlieben und Abneigungen sprechen.

don't like | enjoy | playing | watching

Do you like tennis?

Yes, I do. I ______ ______ tennis but I ______ ______ ______ it on television.

L1:32 Hören Sie und überprüfen Sie Ihre Antworten.

L1:33 **Say it like this** Hören Sie und sprechen Sie nach.

2 Word focus

a Free time activities

Auf welche Freizeitaktivitäten verweisen die Bilder? Brauchen Sie *play* oder *go*, um über sie zu sprechen? Schreiben Sie sie unter das richtige Verb.

I play …	I go …
… ______	… ______
… ______	… ______
… ______	… ______

b Word pairs

Was gehört zusammen? Schreiben Sie die Wörter zu den Verben, mit denen sie verwendet werden.

a lesson | breakfast | chess | golf | on holiday | new people | to a friend | swimming | about sport | my friends

1 go ______ ______
2 have ______ ______
3 meet ______ ______
4 play ______ ______
5 talk ______ ______

c Time

How long? When? Schreiben Sie die Wörter auf die Linien.

60 minutes = an h______

midnight → midnight = a d______

Saturday + Sunday = the w______

Monday → Sunday = a w______

January → December = a y______

3 Grammar focus

Present simple *we / they* → G10 (S. 173)

Zunächst ein Blick auf die Grammatik in Unit 4:

Do you live in …? – Yes, I do. / No, I don't.
Where do you live? – I live in … / I don't live in …
Does he/she live in …? – Yes, he/she does. –
No, he/she doesn't. – Where does he/she live? –
He/She lives in … – He/She doesn't live in …

Und nun:

Do you play table tennis?	No, **we don't**. / Yes, **we do**.
Where **do you play**?	**We play** at the leisure centre.
Do they like football?	No, **they don't**. / Yes, **they do**.
Which team **do they watch**?	**They watch** Chelsea.

Jetzt sehen Sie, dass es **nur** *he* und *she* (und *it*) sind, die *does* und *doesn't* brauchen.

a Ergänzen Sie die Fragen mit *Do* oder *Does* und beantworten Sie sie mit Kurzantworten.

1 ________ Jill play chess? – Yes, ________
2 ________ Jill and David work in Wantage? – Yes, ________
3 ________ David watch Chelsea? – No, ________
4 ________ you play basketball? – ________
5 ________ you and your friends speak English together? – ________

b L1:34 Hören Sie David und Jill. David erzählt Jill von seinem Freund Paul. Sind die folgenden Aussagen richtig (true = T) oder falsch (false = F).

1 Paul lives in Wantage, too. ☐
2 He works in a hospital. ☐
3 He and his wife go walking every weekend. ☐
4 They play chess in a chess club. ☐
5 Paul wins every time. ☐

Zwei der Sätze sind nicht richtig. Verneinen Sie diese Sätze.

____
____
____

4 Round up

Lesen Sie folgenden Text über Pauls Frau.

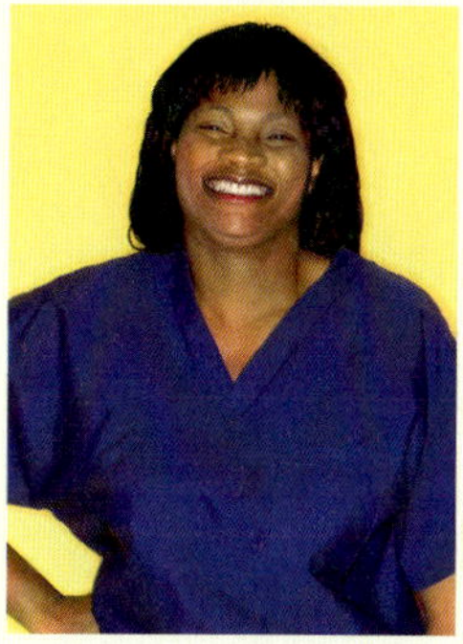

Paul's wife works in a hospital. She's a nurse. She starts work at 8 o'clock and she goes home at 6 o'clock. She likes her job but she doesn't like working on Sundays. In her free time she plays chess and she likes watching films on television. She's got a sister called Rita in Scotland. She sees her once or twice a year.

Schreiben Sie jetzt einen Paralleltext über Pauls Tochter und ihren Partner. Verwenden Sie die vorgegebenen Wörter.

9 o'clock 5 o'clock every weekend	read a lot listen to music ☺	school teachers jobs ☺ boss ☹ friend called Tom in Oxford

Paul's daughter and her partner work in ________. They are ________. They start work ________ and they ________

S. 182

Jetzt kann ich …

sagen, was ich mache und wie oft ich etwas mache. — www: U5A1, CD-R 1: 51

sagen, wann ich etwas mache. — www: U5A2

über meine Vorlieben und Abneigungen sprechen. — www: U5A3, CD-R 1: 50

Part B Keeping healthy

Talking about healthy and unhealthy lifestyles | Saying how often you do things (2) | Making suggestions

What do you think are the most important factors in good health? Put these in order.

a good doctor | healthy food | good genes | an active life | family and friends | money | an interesting job | sport

Healthy or unhealthy?

1a Work with a partner. Read these sentences and decide if they are about a healthy (✓) or an unhealthy (✗) lifestyle.

- ☐ I do sport twice a week.
- ☐ I sit at a computer all day.
- ☐ I've got a stressful job.
- ☐ I don't smoke.
- ☐ I drink a lot of coffee.
- ☐ I like walking.
- ☐ I drive a lot.
- ☐ I eat a lot of salad and other fresh food.

1b Now tell a partner some healthy and unhealthy things about your lifestyle.

T1:34 **Say it like this** Listen to these words with *th* in them. Then listen and repeat the sentences.

2a T1:35 Jill's talking to a friend about her new partner, Richard. Listen and tick (✓) the true sentence.

- ☐ Jill thinks that Richard's lifestyle is unhealthy.
- ☐ Richard thinks that Jill's lifestyle is unhealthy.

2b T1:36 Listen again to Jill and underline the words she uses.

1 We *sometimes* / *always* go out.
2 I *often* / *never* say 'I could cook something healthy for us at home.'
3 We *sometimes* / *never* walk to a restaurant.
4 He *usually* / *always* sits next to the buffet.
5 He *sometimes* / *usually* dances with me but he *sometimes* / *usually* sits and drinks.

2c Put the words in order of frequency from *always* to *never*.

always | sometimes | usually | often | never

always → ______ → ______ → ______ → never

3 Grammar focus

Adverbs of frequency

I	**always**	dance at parties.
	usually	
	often	
	sometimes	
	never	

Word order with *to be*:
I'm usually active. / She's always tired. / Parties are often loud.

3a What do you usually do at parties? Fill in the gaps with *always, usually, often, sometimes* or *never*.

1 I ________________ dance at parties.
2 I ________________ eat a lot of party food.
3 I ________________ drink cocktails at parties.
4 I'm ________________ loud at parties.
5 I ________________ smoke at parties.
6 I'm ________________ ill the next morning.

Read your answers to your partner.

4a Match the pairs of opposite sentences. Write the numbers in the boxes.

1 I eat healthy food.	☐ I go to bed late.
2 I'm active in the evenings.	☐ I eat unhealthy food.
3 I say 'No thank you' to alcohol.	☐ I sit and watch television in the evenings.
4 I walk (or run) upstairs.	☐ I say 'Yes, please' to alcohol.
5 I go to bed early.	☐ I take the lift or escalator.

4b Talk to a partner. Use the pairs to make sentences about yourself with *always, usually, often, sometimes* or *never*, e.g.
I always eat healthy food and I never eat unhealthy food. or
I usually eat healthy food, but I sometimes eat unhealthy food.

Making suggestions

5a Do you remember Jill's problem (from exercise 2)? Jill's friend has got some ideas to help. Put the words in the correct order to make suggestions.

1 Why don't you | with healthy salads? | to a good restaurant | take him
2 You could | dance course | do a | together.
3 finish | with him. | You could
4 about the problem? | talk to him | Why don't you

T1:37 Listen and check your answers.

5b T1:38 Listen again. Which suggestion does Jill like best?

6 How to make suggestions and respond to them

Why don't you ... ? *You could ... .*	*That's a good idea.* *I don't think that's a very good idea.* *Maybe.*

6a Work with a partner. Student A: You have one of these problems. Explain your problem and react to your partner's questions and suggestions. Student B: Listen to your partner's problem. Ask some questions to get more information and make some suggestions to help your partner. Then change roles.
Arbeiten Sie zu zweit. Student A: Sie haben eines dieser Probleme. Erläutern Sie Ihr Problem und reagieren Sie auf die Fragen und Vorschläge Ihres Partners / Ihrer Partnerin. Student B: Hören Sie sich das Problem Ihres Partners / Ihrer Partnerin an. Stellen Sie Fragen, um weitere Informationen zu erhalten, und machen Sie ein paar hilfreiche Vorschläge. Tauschen Sie dann die Rollen.

I can't sleep.

I want to meet new people.

I'm always tired.

I do too much sport.

I want to get fit but I don't like sports.

I want to stop smoking.

6b Choose your partner's best suggestion. Tell this suggestion to the class. The other students guess what your problem is.

Flexizone

Task Activity week

You're on holiday and the town has a week of free activities for local people and visitors. Work in small groups and choose three things to do together.
Sie sind im Urlaub und die Stadt bietet in dieser Woche kostenlose Aktivitäten für Einheimische und Besucher an. Arbeiten Sie in kleinen Gruppen und wählen Sie drei Dinge, die Sie gemeinsam machen können.

You can:
Say what you find interesting: *Look at this. / What about this? / This is interesting.*
Work together to understand: *What's this? / What does this mean?*
Make suggestions: *Why don't we … ? / We could … . / What do you think?*
React to suggestions: *That's a good idea. / Maybe. / I don' t think that's a very good idea.*
Say what you like and don't like: *I (don't) like (creative activities).*
Ask and answer questions: *When … ? / What time …? / Where … ?*

Activity week

Why don't you try something new this week?
All activities are FREE!

PAPERMAKING Make new paper from old. Use traditional methods and Japanese techniques to make beautiful paper.
Arts centre, Tues & Thurs, 1pm

COMPOSTING FOR BEGINNERS Compost – it's free, it's fun, it's fantastic for the garden.
Sat & Sun 10am – 2.30pm at Bonnington Garden Centre, Standlake Rd.

ALEXANDER TECHNIQUE FOR BEGINNERS Learn how to sit, stand and walk with minimum stress on your body.
St Paul's church hall, Saturday 10 – 3

APPLE DAY Learn about traditional local apples and meet the people who grow them.
Market place, Tues 9.30 – 2.30pm.
'Cooking with apples' demonstration, 11am

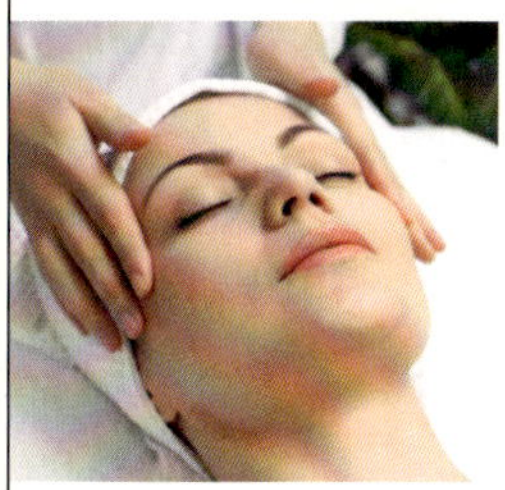

MASSAGE Learn the basic techniques of Indian head massage. Bring a partner. Relax and enjoy!
Leisure centre, Sun 2pm & Wed 10am

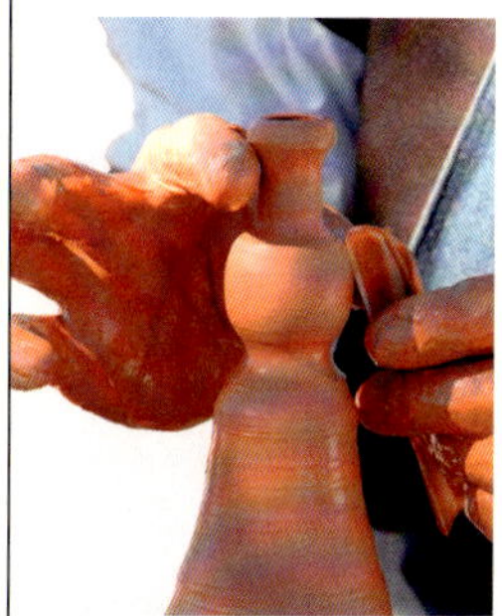

CERAMICS Come and make a pot or a vase with our ceramics group.
Arts centre, Tues 8pm. Phone Hilary on 303897 for more information

CREATIVE WRITING Have you got a book in you? Come and find out at this relaxed and practical seminar with a local author and teacher.
Freelands School, Mon 4pm

KICKBOXING Kick your stress away as you try this fun sport. Great for general fitness.
Leisure centre, Wed 7pm & Thurs 8pm

LINGUA-SHOCK! Try a new language every evening. Which languages? Come and find out! Dynamic and different.
Freelands School, Mon – Fri 7.30 – 9.00pm

AQUAROBICS Arthritis or knee problems? Or just bored with normal aerobics? Try this low-impact alternative. Ideal for all ages.
Leisure centre, Wed 11.45am

Your turn Keeping healthy (→ www)

1 How to …

Schreiben Sie die Wörter in die Lücken.

a Wie Sie Vorschläge machen.

could | don't | Why | You | you

I've got a problem and I don't know what to do.

1 ______ ______ ______ ask a friend?

2 ______ ______ ask a friend.

b Wie Sie auf Vorschläge reagieren.

don't think | excellent | good idea | maybe | that's

■ Why don't you start boxing in your free time?

◆ I ______ ______ that's a very ______ ______!

■ Well … you could go running.

◆ Hmm – ______.

■ Or, I know, you could buy a fitness DVD.

◆ Now ______ an ______ idea!

c Wie Sie sagen, wie oft Sie etwas machen.

always | never | often | sometimes | usually

1 **** I ______ walk to work – every day.

2 *** I ______ walk up the stairs – but not when I'm very tired.

3 ** I ______ go running – two or three times a week.

4 * I ______ go swimming – about once a month.

5 I ______ smoke.

L1:35 Hören Sie und überprüfen Sie Ihre Antworten.

L1:36 **Say it like this** Hören Sie und sprechen Sie nach.

2 Word focus Lifestyles

1 He never buys ~ food from the market.
2 He smokes a lot and doesn't want to stop ~.
3 His job is very ~ but he works 12 hours every day.
4 He sits at a computer ~ day.
5 He ~ to work *every* day in his car.
6 He always takes the ~, he never walks up the stairs.
7 He goes to bed late, so he's always ~.
8 His job is very ~, it's a job for two people.
9 He always drinks ~ at parties (and at home).
10 He doesn't have a ~ lifestyle.
11 He drinks too much ~.
12 He ~ goes swimming, he doesn't like water!

1 f ______
2 s ______
3 i ______
4 a ______
5 d ______
6 l ______
7 t ______
8 s ______
9 c ______
10 h ______
11 a ______
12 n ______

______ ______ is very ______.

3 Grammar focus

Adverbs of frequency

→ G11 (S. 174)

Zunächst ein Blick auf die Grammatik in Unit 4 und 5 Part A:

I/You/We/They go to a leisure centre once a week.
He/She goes walking every weekend.

Und nun:

I **always / usually / often / sometimes / never** eat unhealthy food.

I am **always / usually / often / sometimes / never** tired.

He **always / usually / often / sometimes / never** goes running after work.

He is **always / usually / often / sometimes / never** at home in the evenings.

Häufigkeitsadverbien stehen vor dem Verb. Eine Ausnahme: Die Häufigkeitsadverbien stehen hinter dem Verb *to be*.

a Schreiben Sie die Wörter in der richtigen Reihenfolge.

1 often | to | She | walks | work

2 Saturdays | never | He | works | on

3 job | Her | stressful | is | sometimes

4 go | They | at 6 | always | home

5 I | early | bed | usually | to | go

b Was können Sie über diese Menschen sagen?

- get up early | usually
- go to work at 8 | always
- eat Chinese food | often
- come to the lesson late | never
- be tired on Fridays | sometimes

1 He usually gets up early.
2
3
4
5

4 Round up

a L1:37 Hören Sie eine Fitness-Expertin im Radio. Machen Sie bei den Dingen, die sie nennt, ein Häkchen.

- [ ] active lifestyle
- [ ] healthy food
- [ ] smoking
- [ ] alcohol
- [ ] stressful job
- [ ] walking
- [ ] sleep
- [ ] good friends
- [ ] sport
- [ ] free time

b L1:38 Hören Sie noch einmal und vervollständigen Sie die Vorschläge, die sie macht. Halten Sie die Aufnahme an, damit Sie die Vorschläge aufschreiben können.

1 Why don't you ______ ?
2 You could ______
3 Why don't you ______ ?
4 You could ______
5 Why don't you ______ ?

c ☺ Which is the best suggestion for you?

Suggestion number __ .

☹ Which is the worst suggestion for you?

Suggestion number __ .

S. 182

Jetzt kann ich ...

über meinen Lebensstil reden.	www: U5B1 / CD-R 1: 54+57
Vorschläge machen.	www: U5B2 / CD-R 1: 56
auf Vorschläge reagieren.	www: U5B3
sagen, wie häufig ich etwas mache.	www: U5B4 / CD-R 1: 55

Reading Chess boxing

The first European Chess Boxing Champion is from Bulgaria. In October, Tihomir 'Tiger' Titschko won the title at the Chess Boxing Championships in Berlin, Germany.

The WCBO (World Chess Boxing Organisation) organises these big chess boxing events. Chess boxers play a four-minute round of chess and then a two-minute round of boxing. They play a maximum of eleven rounds. A knockout or checkmate can stop the game before that.

Twenty-six-year-old Titschko beat the German champion Andreas 'D' Schneider with a checkmate in the ninth round.

A spokesperson for the World Chess Boxing Organisation said, "The basic idea in chess boxing is to combine the number one thinking sport and the number one fighting sport. Chess boxers must be fit both mentally and physically." ■

Glossary

won hat gewonnen | beat hat geschlagen | spokesperson Sprecher/-in | thinking sport Denksport | fighting sport Kampfsport | physically physisch

Out and About

Logic puzzle

Five friends, **Peter**, **Tom**, **Diana**, **Wendy** and **Sophie**, have got five different hobbies: **swimming**, **golf**, **tennis**, **skiing** and **jogging**. Read this information and find out their hobbies.

- Sophie and Peter don't use a ball for their sport.
- Tom always plays with a partner.
- The swimmer is a woman.
- Peter thinks skiing is dangerous.
- Wendy doesn't wear shoes for her sport.
- Tom always wears traditional white clothes for his game.

Find the solution in *Out and About*, page 23.
Die Lösung finden Sie in *Out and About*, S. 23.

Food and drink

Part A Eating out

Food and drink | Ordering in a café or restaurant | Places to eat | *would like (to do)*

What's your favourite restaurant, café or bar in your town? Where is it? Why do you like it? You can use the words below to talk about it.

atmosphere | food | service | prices

Food and drink

1 Word focus Food and drink

Match the pictures to the words. Write the numbers in the boxes.

☐ bread	☐ chicken	☐ ham	☐ pasta
☐ cake	☐ eggs	☐ milk	☐ vegetables
☐ cheese	☐ fish	☐ orange juice	☐ wine

T1:39 Listen and check your answers. Now tell a partner how often you eat (or drink) three of these things.

2a Here are some different sorts of food and drink from around the world. Work in small groups. Ask and answer questions, e. g.
What's brie? ➔ *It's a sort of cheese. I think it's from France.*

brie | Sachertorte | feta | baguette | pitta | súrmjólk | tortellini | baklava | Verlängerter | Bürli | Bordeaux | Darjeeling

If you don't know a word in English, the phrase *sort of* can help.
Cheddar? ➔ *I think it's a sort of cheese.*

2b Think of more sorts of cheese, cake, bread, wine or beer from round the world. Ask the other students:
What's (champagne)? Where's it from?

In a café

3a Look at this menu with a partner and find …
1 something made with eggs.
2 two fruit juices.
3 a typical British meal.
4 a sort of fish.

3b T1:40 Listen to some customers in the Corner Café. Fill in the gaps in the waiter's notebook.

Customer 1
coffee
______ cake

Customer 2
______ salad
______ juice

Customer 3
omelette with ______
mineral water

Corner Café – Menu

Soups
Tomato soup, chicken soup, vegetable soup (all with bread)

Salads
Ham salad, Greek salad, tuna salad

Sandwiches or baguettes
Ham, cheese, tuna or chicken

Hot meals
Fish and chips
Omelette (with chips or salad)

Cakes
Apple cake, chocolate cake

Hot drinks
Coffee, tea

Cold drinks
Orange juice, apple juice, mineral water

3c T1:41 Read these phrases. Then listen again and tick (✓) the phrases you hear.

- ☐ What can I get you?
- ☐ I'd like …
- ☐ I want …
- ☐ Can I have …?
- ☐ Could I have …?
- ☐ Bring me …
- ☐ We've got …
- ☐ Would you like …?

In English, it isn't polite to say *Bring me …* or *I want …* when you order things in a restaurant.

4 How to order in a café or restaurant

I'd like (a cheese sandwich), please.
Can I have (a tuna salad), please?
Could I have (a mineral water), please?
Would you like (chips)? > Yes, please. / No, thank you.

4a With a partner, use these phrases and the menu in exercise 3a to do a role play in a café. Student A: You're the waiter. Student B: You're the customer. Then change roles.

5 Grammar focus

would like (to do)

Would you like to eat out tonight?
Yes, I would.
Where **would you like to go**?
I'd like to go to a Turkish restaurant.

would like is the same for all persons – *I, you, he, she, it, we* and *they*.

'd = would

5a Which restaurant would you like to go to – Chinese, Greek, Italian or Spanish? Walk round the class and ask:
Which restaurant would you like to go to tonight?
Make a group with other students who would like to go to the same restaurant as you.
Then tell the class which restaurant your group would like to go to.

5b Which of these sentences is more polite?
A I'd like to see the menu. B I want to see the menu.

Change these sentences, to make them more polite. Take turns with your partner.
1 I want to speak to the manager.
2 Do you want to order drinks?
3 My wife wants to see the dessert menu.
4 Do you want coffee?
5 We want a table in the corner.
6 I want the bill, please.

Unusual places to eat

6 This is an unusual place to eat – they're in a swimming pool! It's the world's first underwater dinner.

I asked for a steak and a water, not a steak under water!

Now read about some more unusual places to eat. Make groups of three or four students.
Student A: Look at page 161.
Student B: Look at page 162.
Student C: Look at page 163.
Student D: Look at page 164.

Flexizone

A Play a game round the class. The first student says *I'd like (a cappuccino)*. The next student says *He'd/She'd like a cappuccino and I'd like (a Greek salad)*. Continue round the class, until you come back to the first student. He/She must try to remember the full list.

B Every second student in the class stands up. You are the waiters / waitresses. The other students are the customers. The waiters have three minutes to take orders from as many customers as they can. The customers can say who is the best waiter / waitress. Then change roles.

Your turn Eating out (→ www)

1 How to …

a Wie Sie über Ihre Vorlieben sprechen. Schreiben Sie die Wörter in die Lücken.

What is | Where is | Who is

1 ________ ________ your favourite dessert? – Ice cream.

2 ________ ________ your favourite café? – Opposite the station.

3 ________ ________ your favourite singer? – Frank Sinatra.

b Wie Sie etwas in einem Restaurant bestellen. Schreiben Sie Ihren Teil des Dialogs.

Mineral water, please. | Yes, I'd like the chicken, please. | No, thank you – I don't drink wine. | Yes, could I have the menu, please? | Can I have chips and salad? | Thank you.

(A = waiter, B = you)

A: Good evening, can I help you?

B: ________________________________.

A: Yes, of course. Here it is.

B: ________________________________.

A: Would you like to order now?

B: ________________________________.

A: With chips or with salad?

B: ________________________________.

A: Yes, of course. And would you like to see the wine menu?

B: ________________________________.

A: What would you like to drink then?

B: ________________________________.

A: Thank you.

L1:39 Hören Sie und überprüfen Sie Ihre Antworten.

L1:40 **Say it like this** Hören Sie und sprechen Sie nach.

2 Word focus Food and drink

a Was sehen Sie hier?

1 t ________	9 f ________
2 a ________	10 h ________
3 e ________	11 c ________
4 c ________	12 b ________
5 c ________	13 v ________
6 o ________	14 p ________
7 t ________	15 m ________
8 w ________	16 s ________

b Ergänzen Sie jeden Satz mit zwei Nahrungsmitteln.

1 I can make soup with ________________ and ________________.

2 I can put ________________ and ________________ in a salad.

3 I can drink ________________ and ________________.

4 I can make a sandwich with ________________ and ________________.

3 Grammar focus

Would like a … / Would like to …

➔ G12 (S. 174)

What **would you like**?	A salad, please. **I'd like** a salad, please.
Would you like a ham salad? **Would you like** bread with it?	Yes, please. No, thank you.
What **would you like** to drink?	Coffee, please. **I'd like** a coffee, please.
Where **would you like to go** this evening?	**I'd like to go** to an Indian restaurant.
Would you like to go to the Taj Mahal restaurant?	Yes, **I would**.

Would like bleibt bei allen Personen gleich – es ändert sich nie. Wenn Ihnen etwas angeboten wird, sollten Sie mit *Yes, please.* oder *No, thank you.* antworten.

a Schreiben Sie die Wörter in der richtigen Reihenfolge.

1 a | cup | like | of | tea | Would | you | ?

2 like | now | order | to | Would | you | ?

3 your | chips | like | omelette | with | Would | you | ?

4 like | What | would | you | ?

5 like | order | to | What | would | you | ?

b Nummerieren Sie folgende Sätze mit 1, wenn es sich um eine Vorliebe/Abneigung, mit 2, wenn es sich um eine Bestellung in einem Restaurant, und mit 3, wenn es sich um einen Wunsch handelt.

☐ I'd like to eat at home this evening.
☐ I don't like red wine.
☐ I'd like chips with it, please.
☐ I like Chinese food.
☐ I'd like chicken soup to start, please.
☐ I'd like to have a Chinese meal this evening.

4 Round up

Wenn Sie bei gesprochenen Texten auf bestimmte Informationen warten, sollten Sie sich dessen bewusst sein, dass die Informationen nicht unbedingt in der von Ihnen erwarteten Reihenfolge kommen. Seien Sie offen für jede Art von Information.

a L1:41 Eine lokale Radiostation hat drei Reporter zum Essen in drei verschiedene Restaurants geschickt. Sie sollten über Atmosphäre, Essen, Service und Preise berichten. Hören Sie den Beitrag und ergänzen Sie die Resultate.

The points system:
5 points = fantastic
4 points = very good +
3 points = good / OK
2 points = not really good
1 point = not good

	The Chinese Garden	The Taj Mahal	The Pizza Palace
atmosphere			
food			
service			
prices			
TOTAL			

b Beantworten Sie jetzt Fragen zu den Restaurants:

1 Which restaurant has the best atmosphere?

2 Which restaurant has the best food?

3 Which restaurant has the best total?

4 Which restaurant would you like to go to?

S. 183

Jetzt kann ich …

über meine Vorlieben sprechen. ○○○ www: U6A1 / CD-R 1: 59

eine Bestellung in einem Restaurant machen. ○○○ www: U6A2 / CD-R 1: 60+61+62

jemandem etwas zu essen und zu trinken anbieten. ○○○ www: U6A3

einen einfachen Radiobericht verstehen. ○○○ www: U6A4

Part B A party

Months and dates | Organising an event | Invitations | *How much? / How many?*

What do you usually do on your birthday?

Dates

1 Word focus Months of the year

1a Find the months of the year in this puzzle. Then write the names of the months in the correct order.

J	S	E	P	T	E	M	B	E	R	A
A	A	F	E	B	R	U	A	R	Y	U
N	P	D	E	C	E	M	B	E	R	G
U	R	N	O	V	E	M	B	E	R	U
A	I	M	A	R	C	H	M	A	Y	S
R	L	J	U	L	Y	J	U	N	E	T
Y	O	C	T	O	B	E	R			

1 ______________ 7 ______________

2 ______________ 8 ______________

3 ______________ 9 ______________

4 ______________ 10 ______________

5 ______________ 11 ______________

6 ______________ 12 ______________

1b T1:42 Listen and check your answers. Underline any months that you find a bit difficult to say.

T1:43 **Say it like this** Listen again and repeat the months.

2 When you hear the names of some months, you think of a special food or drink. Complete these sentences with the name of a month.

1 People often drink Glühwein at Advent parties in ______________.

2 The Munich Oktoberfest starts in ______________.

3 Some people give chocolates on St Valentine's Day in ______________.

4 Children like eating chocolate Easter eggs in ______________ or ______________.

3 Word focus Ordinal numbers

3a T1:44 Listen to these ordinal numbers.

1st | 2nd | 3rd | 4th | 5th | 6th | 7th | 8th | 9th | 10th | 12th | 20th | 21st | 22nd | 30th

T1:45 **Say it like this:** Now listen and repeat the numbers.

3b Now match the numbers to the words and write them on the lines.

second ______	seventh ______	first ______
thirtieth ______	fourth ______	ninth ______
twenty-first ______	twentieth ______	twelfth ______
third ______	tenth ______	fifth ______
eighth ______	sixth ______	twenty-second ______

4 T1:46 Listen to three dialogues and circle the dates you hear.

July						
Sun	Mon	Tue	Wed	Thu	Fri	Sat
				1	2	3
4	5	6	7	8	9	10
11	12	13	14	15	16	17
18	19	20	21	22	23	24
25	26	27	28	29	30	31

Check your answers with a partner.

We write *1st September.*
We say ***the** first **of** September.*

5 With a partner, take turns to choose a square in the grid below and say the date. Write your name in your square. The first person to have a line of four down (↓), across (→) or diagonally (↗) is the winner.
Arbeiten Sie zu zweit. Wählen Sie abwechselnd ein Quadrat aus dem Raster aus und nennen Sie das Datum. Schreiben Sie Ihren Namen in das Quadrat. Der Spieler / Die Spielerin, der / die zuerst eine Zeile (→) eine Spalte (↓) oder eine Diagonale (↗) hat, hat gewonnen.

21st Sept	19th Jan	1st Sept	27th Nov	31st July
30th Aug	1st June	20th Feb	5th May	12th Dec
24th July	21st Oct	my birthday	2nd Mar	6th Nov
3rd Aug	3rd Apr	2nd Feb	25th Jan	30th Apr
4th Mar	13th May	11th June	15th Oct	29th Dec

Organising an event

6a T1:47 David and his PA, Jill, are at work. They want to organise a party because the company is ten years old. Jill wants to buy the food for the party. Before she goes to the supermarket, she asks David some questions. Listen and tick (✓) the correct information.

They want to have ☐ an informal buffet.
☐ a formal dinner.

6b T1:48 Look at Jill's notes. Listen again and write in the numbers on Jill's list.

Food and drink for ____ guests

Ham sandwiches – ____
Cheese sandwiches – ____
White wine – ____ bottles
Red wine – ____ bottles
Juice – ____ bottles

Budget: £____

6c T1:48 Listen again. Cross out the wrong word in each question.

1 How *much* / *many* guests …?
2 How *much* / *many* sandwiches …?
3 How *much* / *many* wine …?
4 How *much* / *many* juice …?
5 How *much* / *many* money …?

7 Grammar focus

How much? / How many?

Things you can count	Things you can't count
How many sandwiches ...?	**How much** wine ...?
Not many. / A lot.	**Not much. / A lot.**

7a Work with a partner and sort these food items into two groups.

apples | cola | eggs | orange juice | tomatoes | tomato soup | apple juice | milk | oranges | coffee | sandwiches | hamburgers | wine

How many ...?	How much ...?

7b Student A: Choose the right word and ask your partner these questions. Student B: Answer with *A lot / Not much / Not many* or a number, e.g. *Two or three cups.* Then change roles.

1 How *much / many* coffee do you drink every day?
2 How *much / many* sandwiches do you eat every week?
3 How *much / many* tea do you drink every day?
4 How *much / many* eggs do you eat every week?

Invitations

8 Jill writes an invitation to send to the party guests. Read her email and fill in the missing words.

wine | see | party | come | Friday

Dear Jeanette

Would you like to ____________ to a party next month?

It's for our company's tenth anniversary. It's at our office in

Wantage on ____________ 30th September at 3pm.

Come and have a glass of ____________ with us. We'd

love to ____________ you.

Best wishes
Jill

Check your answers with a partner.

9 **How to** invite someone and respond to invitations

Would you like to come to dinner / lunch / my party on Saturday?
Yes, I'd love to. / Yes, that would be very nice.
I'm sorry, I can't come. But thanks for the invitation.

9a Choose one of these events.

lunch | dinner | your birthday party | a cocktail party | a jazz evening | a gallery opening | a film

Walk round the class. Invite the other students to your event. You can say *yes* or *no* to the other students' invitations, but you must be polite! You can ask extra questions, e.g. *When is it? Where is it?*

Flexizone

Task Find someone who ...

Look at the pictures and the questions. Walk round the class and ask the questions to the other students. For each picture, you must find the name of someone in the class and write it on the line.
Sehen Sie sich die Bilder und Fragen an. Gehen Sie in der Klasse herum und stellen Sie anderen Kursteilnehmern die Fragen. Für jedes Bild sollen Sie einen Namen eines Kursteilnehmers / einer Kursteilnehmerin finden. Schreiben Sie ihn auf die Zeile.

Do you like sushi?

_______________ *likes sushi.*

Would you like to work in a restaurant?

_______________ *would like to work in a restaurant.*

How often do you eat in a restaurant?

_______________ *eats out more than once a week.*

How often do you cook?

_______________ *cooks every day.*

Can you make bread?

_______________ *can make bread.*

How much cheese do you eat?

_______________ *eats a lot of cheese.*

Report one fact to the class.
Berichten Sie dem Kurs, was Sie zu einem Bild herausgefunden haben.

Your turn A party (→ www)

1 How to …

Schreiben Sie die Wörter in die Lücken.

a Wie Sie jemanden einladen.

Can | come | invite | like | Would | you

1 ________ ________ ________ to come to dinner on Friday?

2 I'd like to ________ you to my party on Saturday.

________ you ________?

b Wie Sie auf Einladungen reagieren.

can't | love | sorry | Thank | thanks

Would you like to come to dinner on Friday?

I'm ________, I ________ come on Friday. But ________ for the invitation.

Well, can you come on Saturday?

Oh yes, I'd ________ to. ________ you.

L1:42 Hören Sie und überprüfen Sie Ihre Antworten.

L1:43 **Say it like this** Hören Sie und sprechen Sie nach.

c L1:44 Wie Sie das Datum sagen. Sprechen Sie nach den Zahlen 1, 2, 3 usw. Danach hören Sie das Datum und können Ihre Antworten überprüfen.

1 13th Apr	5 21st Dec	9 30th Nov
2 1st Aug	6 3rd Sept	10 2nd Mar
3 22nd Oct	7 18th Feb	11 11th July
4 5th Jan	8 7th June	12 29th May

2 Word focus

a Dates

Schreiben Sie die Daten aus, wie im Beispiel.

14th Aug	the fourteenth of August
3rd Feb	
15th June	
1st Nov	
10th Sep	
31st Jan	
22nd Mar	
12th Apr	
4th July	
5th Oct	
20th Dec	
19th May	

b From 24 hours to a year

Ergänzen Sie die fehlenden Wörter.

24 hours = 1 ________

7 ________ = 1 ________

4 ________ = 1 ________

12 ________ = 1 year

c Events

1

2

3

4

Um welche Ereignisse handelt es sich?

1 a c________ party

2 a b________ party

3 a j________ evening

4 a g________ opening

5 an a________ party

6 a d________ party

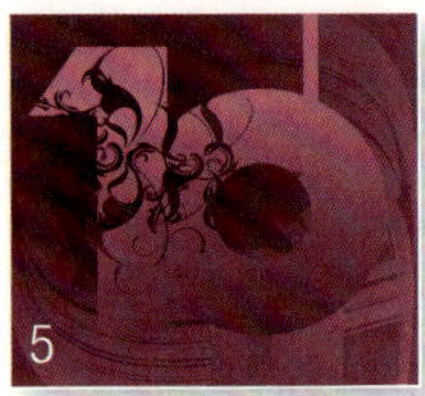
5

6

3 Grammar focus

How much …? / How many …?

→ G5 (S. 171)

Things you can count e. g. books, bottles, children	**How many** bottles of wine have you got at home? **Not many.** / I hav**en't** got **many** bottles. **A lot.** I've got **a lot of** bottles of wine.
Things you can't count e. g. water, time, money	**How much** money have you got? **Not much.** / I hav**en't** got **much** money. **A lot.** I've got **a lot of** money.

Beachten Sie bitte: Sie können *euros* und *pounds* zählen, aber nicht *money*; Sie können *hours* zählen, aber nicht *time*.

a Schreiben Sie *How much* oder *How many* an den Anfang der Fragen.

1 ______ books have you got at home?
2 ______ chocolate do you eat?
3 ______ friends have you got?
4 ______ free time do you have?
5 ______ pullovers have you got?
6 ______ water do you drink?

b Schreiben Sie Kurzantworten zu Fragen in 3a: *Not much.*, *Not many.* oder *A lot.*

1 ______ 4 ______
2 ______ 5 ______
3 ______ 6 ______

c Ergänzen Sie die fehlenden Wörter: *many*, *much* oder *lot*.

1 ☐ I haven't got ______ books.
☐ I've got a ______ of books.
2 ☐ I eat a ______ of chocolate.
☐ I don't eat ______ chocolate.
3 ☐ I haven't got ______ friends.
☐ I've got a ______ of friends.
4 ☐ I don't have ______ free time.
☐ I have a ______ of free time.

Die Sätze sind mögliche Antworten auf einge der Fragen in 3a. Welche Antworten treffen auf Sie zu? Machen Sie ein Häkchen.

4 Round up

a L1:45 Hören Sie das Telefongespräch. Pete lädt Hilary zu seiner Party ein. Sind folgende Aussagen richtig (true = T) oder falsch (false = F)?

1 It's an anniversary party. ☐
2 Hilary lives very near Pete. ☐
3 Hilary can go to the party. ☐

b Hilary stellt während des Gesprächs mehrere Fragen. Schreiben Sie die Fragen auf.

1 party | Where | the | is | ?
______
2 party | time | does | the | What | start | ?
______
3 something | Can | bring | I | ?
______
4 the | near | Is | hotel | there | a | small | club | ?
______
5 is | station | from | the | How | taxi | a | much | ?
______

c L1:46 Hören Sie das Gespräch noch einmal. Überprüfen Sie dabei die Fragen, die Sie aufgeschrieben haben.

d Was antwortet Peter auf Hilarys Fragen?

1 ______
2 ______
3 ______
______
4 ______
5 ______

S. 183

Jetzt kann ich …

jemanden einladen.	www: U6B1 CD-R 1: 67
auf Einladungen reagieren.	www: U6B2
das Datum sagen.	www: U6B3 CD-R 1: 64+65
über Mengen sprechen.	www: U6B4 CD-R 1: 66

Reading Waiter jokes

Glossary

spider Spinne | he's afraid of er hat Angst vor | frogs' legs Froschschenkel | I walk like this ich gehe so | thumb Daumen | cream Sahne

Out and About

In the restaurant

1 What do you say? When you call the waiter, you say: *Excuse me! / Hello!*
2 What do you do? When the waiter gives you the menu, you *eat / read* it.
3 Who is it? In a restaurant, the chef is the *cook / boss*.

Find the solution in *Out and About*, page 26.
Die Lösung finden Sie in *Out and About*, S. 26.

Diese Testübungen orientieren sich an den Aufgabenformaten der Prüfung *telc English A1*. Bitte markieren Sie Ihre Antworten mit einem Querbalken (–) in den Antwortabschnitten rechts neben den Aufgaben.

1 Language elements

Markieren Sie (–) die richtige Antwort **a)** oder **b)** im Antwortabschnitt.

Jack: ___1___ you like your new boss, Sabine?
Sabine: No, I ___2___. He ___3___ very friendly to me.
Jack: ___4___ he speak to you when he ___5___ you?
Sabine: Yes, he ___6___ but he ___7___ smiles.
Jack: How ___8___ time do you work together with him each day?
Sabine: We ___9___ together from 9 o'clock to 10 o'clock. ___10___ like to have a new boss!

1 a) do b) does
3 a) does b) isn't
5 a) sees b) see
7 a) always b) never
9 a) works b) work

2 a) do b) don't
4 a) do b) does
6 a) does b) do
8 a) much b) many
10 a) I b) I'd

Nun noch ein paar Informationen zu den Personen, mit denen Sabine zusammenarbeitet. Markieren Sie (–) die richtige Antwort **a)** oder **b)** im Antwortabschnitt.

Three people ___11___ with Sabine. — 11 a) work b) works
She ___12___ them very much. — 12 a) like b) likes
They ___13___ all like to have a friendly boss. — 13 a) do b) would
Their boss is ___14___ in meetings, but not all the time. — 14 a) always b) often
Sabine and her colleagues ___15___ know what to do do. — 15 a) doesn't b) don't

1 Language elements

	a)	b)
1		
2		
3		
4		
5		
6		
7		
8		
9		
10		
11		
12		
13		
14		
15		

= ______ / 15

2 L1:47 Listening comprehension

Lesen Sie zunächst die Situationen und die Aussagen, die ihnen folgen. Hören Sie dann die Aufnahme. Markieren Sie (–) die richtige Antwort **True (T)** oder **False (F)** im Antwortabschnitt.

16 *Situation:*
You'd like a table for six in the Bodega Spanish restaurant on Friday. You phone the restaurant.
There isn't a table for you on Friday.

17 *Situation:*
Your friend, Alan, phones you.
He wants to invite you for dinner tomorrow.

18 *Situation:*
You are in a restaurant.
You can have what you want to eat.

19 *Situation:*
You are at home. Your television is on.
The film that you want to watch starts in 15 minutes.

20 *Situation:*
You are at the leisure centre.
You can stay all evening.

2 Listening comprehension

	T	F
16		
17		
18		
19		
20		

= ______ / 5

3 Situational responses

Part A L1:48

Sehen Sie sich zunächst die Erwiderungen **a)** – **d)** an.
Hören Sie dann die Aufnahme.
Markieren Sie (–) die richtige Erwiderung **a)**, **b)**, **c)** oder **d)** im Antwortabschnitt.

21 ______
22 ______
23 ______

a) A coffee, please.
b) Yes, I'd love to.
c) No, I wouldn't.
d) Yes, please.

Part B L1:49

Sehen Sie sich zunächst die Erwiderungen **e)** – **h)** an.
Hören Sie dann die Aufnahme.
Markieren Sie (–) die richtige Erwiderung **e)**, **f)**, **g)** oder **h)** im Antwortabschnitt.

24 ______
25 ______
26 ______

e) At the cinema.
f) At the weekends, usually.
g) About once a month.
h) At half past seven, I think.

3 Situational responses

Part A				
21	a)	b)	c)	d)
22	a)	b)	c)	d)
23	a)	b)	c)	d)
Part B				
24	e)	f)	g)	h)
25	e)	f)	g)	h)
26	e)	f)	g)	h)

= ______ / 6

4 Reading comprehension

Lesen Sie die Speisekarte und beantworten Sie die folgenden Fragen.
Markieren Sie (–) die richtige Antwort **a)** oder **b)** im Antwortabschnitt.

The ABC Café and Restaurant

23 Main Street
Middletown
01743-629345

Opening hours:
Tues – Sat 10.30 – 23.00
Sunday 11.00 – 15.00

New in Middletown
Opening next week!

➤ **Lunch menu (Tuesday to Saturday)**

1 **Start with ...**
Tomato soup *or* Vegetable soup *or* Mixed salad

2 **Then choose from ...**
The ABC Big Salad — Lasagne
Pizza (Napoli *or* Quattro stagioni) — Fish and chips

3 **Finish with ...**
Fruit salad *or* Apple strudel *or* Ice cream

➤ Choose from '2' only: **£6.25**
➤ Choose from '1+2' or '2+3': **£7.25**
➤ Choose from '1+2+3': Best buy **£8.00**

➤ House red, House white, Beer **£3**
➤ Other drinks **£2**

See our Sunday lunch and evening menu on
www.ABCmiddletown.co.uk

27 When can you go to the ABC for the first time?
a) today
b) next week

28 When can customers have lunch at the ABC?
a) every day
b) Tuesday to Sunday

29 How much does this lunch cost?
a soup + a big salad + 1 glass of red wine + 1 mineral water
a) £12.25
b) £13.00

30 Where can you look at the evening menu today?
a) in the restaurant
b) on the Internet

4 Reading comprehension

	a)	b)
27		
28		
29		
30		

= ______ / 4

total

= ______ / 30

S. 183

On holiday

Part A Summer holidays

Talking about holidays | Holiday shopping | Prices | Past of *to be* | *There was / There were*

Do you send postcards when you're on holiday? Who to? And do you buy presents for people at home, too?

Holiday shopping

1 Word focus Holiday items

Write the words under the photos.

bag | camera | guidebook | postcards | suitcases | suncream | sunglasses | towels

The word *glasses* is always plural. *How much* **are** *the sunglasses? Where* **are** *my glasses?*

2 How to ask for and say prices

How much is the …?
How much are the …?

£10 – ten pounds
£10.50 – ten (pounds) fifty
£0.50 / 50p – fifty pence / fifty p

That's cheap / OK / a good price / a bit expensive.

2a T2:2 Look again at the holiday items in exercise 1. Listen to some customers and write the missing prices.

2b Work with a partner. Student A: Look at page 163. Student B: Look at page 164.

A holiday postcard

3 Word focus Adjective pairs

Write the opposites.

awful | bad | cold | dirty | expensive | unfriendly

good / ____________

fantastic / ____________

clean / ____________

friendly / ____________

cheap / ____________

warm (or hot) / ____________

4

David is on holiday with his wife, Mel. Read this postcard from David to Jill, his PA. Write in the missing words.

next | sunny | people | beach

Dear Jill,
Hello from Spain! We're on the ____________.
It's warm and ____________. Everything's great.
There are a lot of ____________ on the streets
today because there's a festival this evening.
Mel says 'hello', too.
See you ____________ week.
Best wishes,
David

Read the postcard to a partner and check your answers.

5a

T2:3 David comes back to work and tells Jill about his holiday. Listen and tick the present he gives her.

5b

T2:4 Read these sentences. Listen again and say if they are true (T) or false (F).

1 The hotel was good. ☐
2 The sea was a bit cold. ☐
3 The beaches were dirty. ☐
4 The wine was expensive. ☐
5 The people were friendly. ☐
6 They were in a big town. ☐
7 There were some small shops and a market. ☐
8 There was a fish restaurant opposite the hotel. ☐
9 The present for Jill was David's idea. ☐

5c

Check your answers in class. Look again at the sentences you think are false. Take turns to correct the sentences, e.g. 3 *The beaches were clean.*

6 Grammar focus

Past of *to be*: *was / were*

I was happy because **the beer was** cheap.
We were in a small town and **the people were** friendly.

It wasn't expensive because **we weren't** in a five star hotel.

Was the hotel nice? **Yes, it was. / No, it wasn't.**
Were the restaurants good? **Yes, they were. / No, they weren't.**

6a

With a partner, take turns to ask and answer questions about David and Mel's holiday.

1 weather | nice? *Was the weather nice? → Yes, it was.*

2 hotel | good?
3 the sea | warm?
4 people | friendly?
5 food | good?
6 beaches | clean?
7 wine | expensive?

6b

Now ask and answer questions about a summer holiday you each remember. Here are some words to help you.

weather, hotel, people, beaches, sea, beer, food, wine

good, friendly, cheap, nice, warm, clean, expensive

Two festivals

7a T2:5 When David was on holiday last week, there was a festival in the town. Listen to David. Tick the things and the people he talks about.

- ☐ children and babies
- ☐ live music
- ☐ men and women
- ☐ beer
- ☐ tourists
- ☐ food and wine
- ☐ dancers
- ☐ fireworks

7b Most plural words end in *-s*, e.g. *tourists, beaches, families.* But some plurals are irregular, e.g. *person / people, child / children.* Find the plurals of these words in exercise 7a.

1 man ________ 2 woman ________

7c T2:6 Listen again. What does David say?

1 ________ live music.

2 ________ Spanish dancers.

3 ________ a lot of Spanish food and wine.

4 ________ fireworks in the evening.

There's a big festival every summer.
There was a big festival last week.

There are a lot of tourists every summer.
There were a lot of tourists last week.

8 David gets an email from some friends on holiday in Sicily. Read the mail. Then talk to a partner and compare the Spanish and Sicilian festivals. What was the same, what was different?

Dear David and Mel

We were in Palermo last week for the festival of Santa Rosalia. They call it the 'little festival' *(festino)* but it really wasn't small! There were five days of fun and on the last day there was a big show and an evening of music and fireworks. There was a live orchestra. It was fantastic. The best thing was the atmosphere. There were a lot of tourists on the streets and a lot of the Sicilian people were in traditional costumes. There was music, food and Sicilian wine – what more can you want?

See you soon
Fran and Charlie

9 Now think of a street festival, market, carnival, flower festival or sports event that you remember from a holiday or from your town. Tell a partner four or five things about it.

I was in …
We were in …
There was …
There were …
It was …
The best thing was …

Flexizone

A Where were you last weekend? Think of a place and tell the class three or four things about it. The other students must guess where you were, e.g. *It was Sunday afternoon. There were a lot of old things. There were some things from Greece and Rome. It was very interesting. It was quiet. Where was I?* → *Were you in a museum?*

B One student chooses an item in the classroom. He/She writes a realistic price for this item on a piece of paper and hides it. The next student must guess the price, e.g. *Is it ten euros?* The first student can say *more* or *less*. Then the next person can guess and the game continues round the class until someone guesses the right price. Then this person chooses another item.

Your turn Summer holidays (→ www)

1 How to …

Schreiben Sie die Wörter in die Lücken.

a Wie Sie nach Preisen fragen.

How much are | How much are | How much is | How much is

1 ___ ___ ___ the guidebook?

2 ___ ___ ___ these postcards?

3 ___ ___ ___ the sunglasses?

4 ___ ___ ___ the suitcase?

b Wie Sie Preise sagen.

Beantworten Sie die Fragen aus 1a. Schreiben Sie die Preise in Worten.

1 The guidebook ___ ___ ___ ___.

2 The postcards ___ ___ ___.

3 The sunglasses ___ ___ ___.

4 The suitcase ___ ___ ___ ___ ___.

c Wie Sie Gründe nennen.

Verwenden Sie die Verben und bilden Sie zwei Sätze.

drinks | is | like | speak

He can … French	because	he doesn't … it.
He never … wine		his mother … French.

___

___

___

___

L2:2 Hören Sie und überprüfen Sie Ihre Antworten.

L2:3 **Say it like this** Hören Sie und sprechen Sie nach.

2 Word focus

a Holiday items

Was geht mit auf die Reise?

1 ___ 4 ___

2 ___ 5 ___

3 ___ 6 ___

b Holiday activities

Was können Sie in Ihrem Urlaub machen?

I can stay in a h___ and eat in the r___ there. I can swim in the s___ and then sit on the b___ and write some p___ to my friends or read my b___. I can go to a m___ and buy some p___ for people at home. I can eat good f___ and drink good w___.

c People

Welche Menschen sehen Sie?

There are nine ___: two ___, three ___ and four ___.

d Adjectives

Schreiben Sie die fehlenden Vokale und verbinden Sie Wörter mit gegenteiliger Bedeutung mit Linien.

c _ ld ○	○ _ nfr _ _ ndly
b _ d ○	○ cl _ _ n
d _ rty ○	○ f _ nt _ st _ c
fr _ _ ndly ○	○ g _ _ d
_ wf _ l ○	○ _ xp _ ns _ v _
ch _ _ p ○	○ h _ t

3 Grammar focus

Past of *to be*: *was / were* → G13 (S. 174)

Zunächst ein Blick auf die Grammatik in Unit 1 und 2:

I am …, I'm not … You are …, You aren't … He/She/It is …, He/She/It isn't …	We are …, We aren't … You are …, You aren't … They are …, They aren't …
There is …, There isn't …	There are …, There aren't …

Und nun:

Were you on holiday in June?	No, **I wasn't** on holiday. **I was** at work.
Was he/she at the last lesson?	No, **he/she wasn't** at the lesson. **He/She was** on holiday.
Was it a good holiday?	Yes, **it was**. / No, **it wasn't**.
Were you happy with your hotel?	**We were** happy with the room. **We weren't** happy with the restaurant.
Were they at home on Sunday?	Yes, **they were** at home all weekend.
Was there a swimming pool? **Were there** any nice bars?	No, **there wasn't**. Yes, **there were**.

a Streichen Sie die falschen Verben.

1 John and Sue *was / were* in Crete last July.
2 The hotel *was / were* a bit expensive.
3 The food *wasn't / weren't* very good.
4 The people there *was / were* very friendly.
5 The beach *was / were* clean.
6 The rooms *wasn't / weren't* very big.

b Schreiben Sie *was, wasn't, were* oder *weren't* in die Lücken.

1 ________ there a swimming pool in the hotel?
Yes, there ________ but it ________ very big.

2 ________ there any good restaurants near the hotel?
No, there ________ but there ________ a good pizzeria in the town.

3 ________ John and Sue happy there?
Yes, they ________. It ________ a very holiday.

c L2:4 Hören Sie die Fragen und schreiben Sie Kurzantworten.

Example: Was it cold last Saturday?

Yes, it was. or *No, it wasn't.*

1 ________.
2 ________.
3 ________.

4 Round up

David hat Jill eine Urlaubskarte geschrieben. Hier finden Sie Teile eines ähnlichen Grußes. Setzen Sie sie zusammen und schreiben Sie sie auf die Postkarte.

See you next week. Hi from Barcelona. Dear Sue,
We're in a restaurant near the sea for lunch. Karin
I've got a big salad and Tom's got some fish. Best wishes,
The red wine is great (and not very expensive).
There are some flamenco dancers at the hotel this evening!

S. 183

Jetzt kann ich …

nach Preisen fragen und Preise sagen.	www: U7A1 CD-R 2: 1
über Ferien sprechen.	www: U7A2 CD-R 2: 2+3+4+5
eine Urlaubskarte schreiben.	www: U7A3
Gründe nennen.	www: U7A4

Part B Around the world

More about holidays | Past simple (1), positive sentences

Which of these holidays would you like best? Take a class vote.

A week on a sunny beach | A weekend in a European capital city | Two months in India with a rucksack | A safari in Africa | A month in Australia

Famous tourist attractions

1a Match the tourist attractions with their names and countries. Write the numbers of the photos in the boxes.

☐ Australia ☐ Canada ☐ China ☐ England ☐ the USA

☐ Ayers Rock ☐ the Rocky Mountains ☐ the Grand Canyon ☐ Stonehenge ☐ the Great Wall

T2:7 Now listen to some tourists and check your answers.

1b Fill in the missing words.

saw | Last | went

__________ year they __________ to the USA and __________ the Grand Canyon.

1c Now speak to a partner and make sentences about the other tourist attractions.

They went to __________ and they saw __________.

A fly drive holiday

2a T2:8 Listen to Jill talking about a holiday she had with her ex-husband, Mike, ten years ago. Mark their route on the map.

2b T2:9 Listen again. Which place is Jill talking about: New York (NY), Boston (B), Portland (P) or the Adirondack Park (AP)?

1 ☐ We flew there.
2 ☐ We stayed in a very nice hotel.
3 ☐ I took photos of all the famous buildings.
4 ☐ We did the Freedom Trail.
5 ☐ I found a wonderful market.
6 ☐ Mike visited an old lighthouse.
7 ☐ We saw mountains, waterfalls and bears.
8 ☐ I bought a teddy bear.

3a Write these past forms in the gaps.

went | saw | flew | stayed | hired | took | wanted | did | loved | found | visited | bought | had | came | drove

1 buy ______	5 find ______	9 hire ______	13 take ______
2 come ______	6 fly ______	10 love ______	14 visit ______
3 do ______	7 go ______	11 see ______	15 want ______
4 drive ______	8 have ______	12 stay ______	

T2:10 Listen and check your answers.

T2:11 **Say it like this** Now listen and repeat the past forms of the verbs.

3b Look again at the list of verbs in exercise 3a. Which ones have *-ed* in the past? These are called *regular verbs* (regelmäßige Verben). The others are called *irregular verbs* (unregelmäßige Verben).

4 Grammar focus

Past simple (positive sentences)

Regular verbs	Irregular verbs
stay → stay**ed**	go → **went**
hire → hir**ed**	see → **saw**
love → lov**ed**	fly → **flew**
visit → visit**ed**	have → **had**
want → want**ed**	come → **came**

The past simple is the same for all persons – *I, you, he, she, it, we, they*.

4a Think about the last time you flew – on holiday or for your work. Tick sentences that are true for you.

1 ☐ I flew alone.
2 ☐ I had a lot of bags.
3 ☐ I bought a newspaper or magazine at the airport.
4 ☐ I had lunch on the plane.
5 ☐ I watched a film on the plane.
6 ☐ I worked on the plane.
7 ☐ I talked to the person next to me on the plane.
8 ☐ I hired a car at the airport.

4b Compare the answers with a partner and try to find something that was the same for you. Tell the class:
Ben and I both had a lot of bags.

5 You have seen some phrases we use to talk about the past, e.g. last year, ten years ago. Which of these words go with *last …* and which go with *… ago*?

year | two years | month | three months | six weeks | week

last …	… ago

6 How to talk about past holidays

Work in small groups. Tell your group four or five things about your best holiday.

Last … / … ago
We went to / …
We flew / drove / …
We saw / bought / visited / …
The weather / hotel / town / food was …
The people / beaches / mountains were …
There was a market / festival / museum / …
There were a lot of tourists / restaurants / shops / …

Flexizone

Task Detective work

a You are a private detective. Read this email.

This man is Mr M. Follow him on his 'holiday' to Munich. Take photos and report back to me.
Be careful!
H

You follow Mr M. You take some photos and find some other information.

1 Person
Dick Tracy
Reihe F
Platz 12
20:30
Preis Euro 8,50

Suitehotel
RECHNUNG-NR. 61 133754/1

Gast-Nr.	: 9257733
Zimmer-Nr.	: 142 / Einzelzi.
Dauer	: 2 Nächte

pizzabella
Ristorante – Pizzeria

#008
RECHNUNG
Tischnummer 4

2 Mittagsmenue	9,00	*18,00
1 kl.Salat	3,50	*3,50
Zwischensumme		*21,50
netto		*17,41
MwSt 19%		*4,09

Es bediente Sie Kellner 3

Car hire reservation
Pick-Up/Return Location:
Munich Airport, Franz-Josef-Strauß Airport, Munich, DE
Pick-Up: Fri, 28 Mar, 2008 at 15:00
Return: Sun, 30 Mar, 2008 at 16:00
Car Type Mercedes A-Class, 2-4 Door Automatic, air con, sat nav

Flight number: BA0952
From: Heathrow (London) Terminal 5
To: Munich
Depart: 28 Mar 12:30
Arrive: 28 Mar 15:15

Flight number: BA0955
From: Munich Terminal 1
To: Heathrow (London)
Depart: 30 Mar 2008 17:30
Arrive: 30 Mar 2008 18:30

b Where did Mr M go? What did he do? Who did he meet? Talk in small groups. Use these verbs.

bought | flew | had | hired | met | saw | stayed | talked | visited | was/were | walked | went

c Write a short report to H.

Dear H
We followed Mr M.

____

____

____

____

____

Best wishes

Your turn Around the world (→ www)

1 How to ...

a Wie Sie über die Vergangenheit sprechen.
Schreiben Sie die Wörter in rückwärts gerichteter Reihenfolge, ausgehend von der Gegenwart.
last year | ten days ago | last month | two years ago

I saw him last night.
________ ________.
________ ________ ________.
________ ________.
________ ________ ________.

b Wie Sie sagen, wann etwas in der Vergangenheit stattgefunden hat.

1 Write today's date here: __ __ / __ __ / __ __ __ __
2 And the date a week ago? __ __ / __ __ / __ __ __ __
3 Last month was ________________,
4 Last year was __ __ __ __.
5 When was your birthday? – It was ________ ________ ago.
6 When was your last holiday? – It was ________ ________ ago.
7 When was your last English lesson? – It was ________ ________ ago.

c Wie Sie über einen vergangenen Urlaub sprechen.
Schreiben Sie die Wörter in die Lücken.
bought | saw | stayed | went | were

1 We ________ to Paris.
2 We ________ in a small hotel.
3 We ________ some presents and postcards.
4 We ________ very happy there.
5 We ________ the Eiffel Tower.

L2:5 Hören Sie und überprüfen Sie Ihre Antworten.

L2:6 **Say it like this** Hören Sie und sprechen Sie nach.

2 Word focus

a Words that often go together
Schreiben Sie die blauen Wörter auf die blauen Linien neben das richtige Verb.
in a hotel – a film – a car – photos – lunch – a friend

have		
hire		
stay		
take		
talk to		
watch		

Wo passen folgende roten Wörter dazu? Schreiben Sie sie auf die roten Linien.
breakfast – my teacher – at home – a football match

b A holiday in Canada
Ordnen Sie die Wörter richtig zu.

art gallery	buy presents	mountains	take photos
bears	lighthouse	museum	visit buildings
book	magazine	newspaper	waterfall

Three things you can see in a national park in Canada:
____
____
____

Three things you can read on holiday:
________ ________
____

Three buildings you can visit on holiday:
____
____
____

Three things you can do on holiday:
________ ________
____

3 Grammar focus

Past simple (positive sentences)

➔ G15 (S. 175)

regular	irregular	
hire – hir**ed**	Ergänzen Sie die Vokale in den Vergangenheitsformen:	
like – lik**ed**	buy – b __ __ ght	fly – fl __ w
live – liv**ed**	come – c __ m __	go – w __ nt
love – lov**ed**	do – d __ d	have – h __ d
park – park**ed**	drive – dr __ v __	see – s __ w
stay – stay**ed**	find – f __ __ nd	take – t __ __ k
talk – talk**ed**		
visit – visit**ed**		
want – want**ed**		
watch – watch**ed**		
work – work**ed**		

Denken Sie auch an das unregelmäßige Verb *to be*: *was* oder *were*

a Schreiben Sie die Verben in die Lücken (Sie finden die Verben im Kasten oben).

Last year John and Sue (1) ________ to Crete for their summer holiday. They (2) ________ from Heathrow Airport. John (3) ________ to the airport and (4) ________ his car there. In London it (5) ________ cold and grey but in Crete it (6) ________ warm and sunny. They (7) ________ a driver to drive them to their hotel. He (8) ________ near the hotel, so he (9) ________ to John and Sue all the time about his town. On the way they (10) ________ the sea and a lot of people on the beaches. The hotel (11) ________ very nice and the people there (12) ________ very friendly but their room (13) ________ a bit small. John and Sue (14) ________ Crete. At home they (15) ________ very hard every day before their holiday – but there in Crete, they (16) ________ breakfast very late and then they (17) ________ to the markets and (18) ________ some presents or they (19) ________ some old buildings … and they (20) ________ to the beach every day. John (21) ________ a lot of photos with his digital camera. They (22) ________ in Crete for two weeks.

b L2:7 Hören Sie zehn Sätze. Handeln sie von der Vergangenheit oder der Gegenwart? Machen Sie ein Häkchen in der richtigen Box.

	1	2	3	4	5	6	7	8	9	10
past										
present										

4 Round up

Wenn Sie zuhören, ist es sinnvoll, dass Sie das, was Sie hören, mit dem vergleichen, was Sie schon wissen. Um das zu tun, müssen Sie auf Unerwartetes achten.

a Bevor Sie hören, lesen Sie den Text über Johns und Sues Urlaub im *Grammar focus*. Überprüfen Sie Ihre Antworten mithilfe des Schlüssels. Lesen Sie den Text noch einmal und prägen Sie sich die Details ein.

b L2:8 Hören Sie nun einen Radiobericht über den Urlaub einer anderen Person. Notieren Sie Unterschiede zum Urlaub von John und Sue.

1 ~~Crete in summer~~ She went ________ .
2 ~~flew to Crete~~ She ________ .
3 ~~warm and sunny~~ It ________ .
4 ~~saw the sea~~ She ________ .
5 ~~small room~~ She ________ .
6 ~~breakfast late~~ She ________ .
7 ~~two weeks~~ She ________ .

S. 184

Jetzt kann ich …

sagen, vor welcher Zeit/wann etwas geschah.	○○○	www: U7B1 CD-R 2: 8+9
über Details eines Urlaubs sprechen.	○○○	www: U7B2 CD-R 2: 6+7+10
etwas, das ich höre, mit dem vergleichen, das ich schon kenne.	○○○	www: U7B3

Reading Weekend breaks

Most people go on holiday in the summer or in the school holidays, and the hotels are usually full and expensive at that time. But the months from January to March and from October to November are not very popular for holidays so a lot of hotels offer weekend breaks. You can stay at a good hotel from Friday to Sunday and it's not too expensive. To make it more attractive, some hotels have theme weekends.

Chocoholic weekend

Chocolate from morning to night – a chocoholic's paradise! Visit a chocolate shop in town and watch them make their speciality, chilli chocolate.
In the afternoon, learn how to make and decorate a fantastic chocolate cake. And at bedtime? A cup of hot chocolate, of course.

Antiques weekend

Interested in antiques? Come to the Antiques weekend at Holstead Castle. On Saturday, you can have a tour of the castle, and you can enjoy a medieval dinner in the evening. There's an antiques fair on Sunday afternoon in the castle gardens.

Romantic weekend

February 14th is Valentine's Day. Enjoy a romantic weekend with your partner at the Glenderry Hotel. A weekend with soft lights and soft music and a candlelit dinner on Saturday evening.

Glossary

offer anbieten | enjoy genießen | soft lights sanftes Licht | castle Schloss | medieval mittelalterlich

Out and About
How much was it?

You bought a guidebook and a map. Together they cost £25.50.
The book was £20.00 more than the map.
How much was the guidebook?
And how much was the map?

Find the solution in *Out and About*, page 31.
Die Lösung finden Sie in *Out and About*, S. 31.

Entertainment
Part A Culture

Dance, films, music and literature | Biographies | Years | Past simple (2), negative sentences

Fill in the missing letters to make different sorts of dance.

_ lam _ n _ o   j _ v _   p _ _ ka   t _ ng _   sa _ s _   tw _ s _   b _ _ let

Where are these dances from? How many sorts of dance can the students in your class do?

A famous entertainer

1a Here are some kids in Havana, Cuba. What do you think they do every day?

1b Now read the first paragraph of a magazine article about a boy from Cuba and fill in the fact file.

Carlos Acosta was born in Havana. He was the eleventh (and youngest) child of a poor Cuban truck driver. Young Carlos loved break-dancing and playing football on the streets. Carlos and his friends had a lot of free time because they didn't go to school. His father wanted more for Carlos and sent him away to a ballet school. But Carlos didn't want to be a ballet dancer. He wanted to be a footballer. "I didn't like ballet and I ran away from school twice. But my father always sent me back."

Fact file

Name: ____________

Home town: ____________

Nationality: ____________

Father's job: ____________

Brothers and sisters: ____________

Favourite free time activities: ____________

School: ____________

Dream job: ____________

1c What do you think happened to Carlos? Talk to a partner.

1 He became a professional *footballer / dancer.*
2 He started to work hard at his dancing *when his father died / because he saw a very good ballet.*
3 He *won a lot of prizes / didn't win any prizes.*
4 People *loved / didn't like* his style.
5 He *forgot / didn't forget* his family.

1d Did you guess correctly what happened to Carlos? Read and check.

When he was 13, Carlos saw the Cuban National Ballet and from that moment he wanted to make a career in ballet. He practised a lot and won a lot of prizes. Carlos stayed at school for four more years. When he left school he became a professional dancer.
Carlos had talent, power, style and charisma. He danced classical ballet with Cuban flair. Audiences loved his style and they loved him. He danced with all the famous ballet companies in the world and was soon the most popular dancer of his generation. He didn't forget his family or his home town and he gave a lot of money to projects for kids in Havana. And what's next for Carlos? He wants to be a father.

2 Grammar focus

Past simple (negative sentences)

They didn't go to school.
He didn't want to be a ballet dancer.
I didn't like ballet.

Remember: The past simple is the same for all persons – *I, you, he, she, it, we* and *they*.

2a Look again at both parts of the article about Carlos Acosta and find three more examples of verbs with *didn't*.

2b Make these sentences true about you, when you were ten years old.

1 I *went / didn't go* to ballet classes.
2 I *went / didn't go* to school from Monday to Friday.
3 I *won / didn't win* a prize for my schoolwork.
4 We *sang / didn't sing* at school.
5 We *had / didn't have* a lot of homework.
6 We *played / didn't play* football on the streets.
7 I *wanted / didn't want* to be a footballer.
8 I *left / didn't leave* primary school when I was ten.

Compare answers with a partner and try to find one thing that was the same for both of you. Tell the class:
Anke and I both went to ballet classes.

Say it like this These words all have the sound [æ] in them.

ballet | classical | family | had | happy | practise | ran | talent

T2:12 Listen and repeat the words.

Work with a partner. Take turns to make sentences about Carlos with some of these words. Read a sentence to the class.

Music, films and literature

3 Work in small groups. Cross out the wrong information.

1 Lennon and McCartney wrote *Jumpin' Jack Flash, All you need is love* and *Yesterday*.
2 The film *Titanic* won eleven Oscars, a Nobel Prize and four Golden Globes.
3 Shakespeare wrote *Romeo and Juliet, Faust* and *Hamlet*.
4 Arnold Schwarzenegger starred in *The Terminator, Conan the Barbarian* and *Pretty Woman*.
5 Abba sang *Rivers of Babylon, Waterloo* and *Money, Money, Money*.

Report to the class.

We think that Lennon and McCartney wrote *All you need is love* and *Yesterday*, but they didn't write *Jumpin' Jack Flash*.

If you can't agree, look at page 187 for the answers.

4 How to say years

Before 2000	After 2000
1800 – *eighteen hundred*	2000 – *two thousand*
1900 – *nineteen hundred*	2001 – *two thousand and one*
	2009 – *two thousand and nine*
1901 – *nineteen oh one*	
1907 – *nineteen oh seven*	2010 – *twenty ten*
	2015 – *twenty fifteen*
1921 – *nineteen twenty-one*	2021 – *twenty twenty-one*
1982 – *nineteen eighty-two*	

4a In class, take turns to say these years.

1900 | 1908 | 1978 | 1982 | 1997 |
2000 | 2005 | 2008 | 2013 | 2025

Carlos Acosta **was born** in Havana in 1973.
Where **were you born**?
I **was born** in Bremen in 1968.

5 T2:13 Listen to a radio quiz called *Who is it?* about a famous person from the world of entertainment – an actor, a singer, a dancer or a writer. Listen to the clues and fill in the missing information below.

Job: ____________

Born: (country) ____________, (year) ________

Died: (year) ________

Married: _____ times.

Most famous film: ____________

Initials: _____

In class, work out the name of the person. You can check your answer on page 187.

6 How to give biographical information

I was born in …
I went to school / university in …
I left school / university in …
I started my first job in …
I worked there from (1990) to (1995).
I worked there for (five) years.
I met my (first) husband / wife in …
I got married / divorced in …
My first child was born in …
Then I worked / went to / met / …

6a Work in small groups. Tell the other students about the important years and places in your life.

Flexizone

A Tell the class something you did last weekend e.g. *I had breakfast in bed.* The other students must say if they did that too, e.g. *I had breakfast in bed, too.* or *I didn't have breakfast in bed.* Try to find something that no other students did.

B Write three clues about a famous person from the world of films, music or books, e.g. *She wrote / sang / starred in / made / won / was born in …* . Read your sentences to the class. The other students guess who the person is.

Your turn Culture (→ www)

1 How to ...

a Wie Sie biografische Informationen angeben.
Schreiben Sie die Wörter in die Lücken.

got divorced | got married | met | started | was | was born | was married | went | worked

1 I ______ born in 1968 in Hamburg.
2 I ______ to school in Hamburg.
3 After that I ______ work.
4 I ______ in my first job for 6 years.
5 I ______ ______ in 1994.
6 Our first child ______ ______ in 1997.
7 I ______ ______ from 1994 to 2003.
8 Then we ______ ______.
9 I ______ my new partner about six months ago.

b Wie Sie über Jahre und Orte sprechen.
Schreiben Sie die Wörter in die Lücken.

for | from | in | in | in | in | to | to

1 My cousin was born ______ 1971.
2 Her family lived ______ London.
3 She started school ______ 1976.
4 She went ______ school there ______ 13 years.
5 She worked ______ a hotel ______ 1999 ______ 2002.

L2:9 Hören Sie und überprüfen Sie Ihre Antworten.

L2:10 **Say it like this** Hören Sie und sprechen Sie nach.

c Wie Sie Jahreszahlen sagen.
Sehen Sie sich die Jahreszahlen an. Überlegen Sie für sich, wie man sie sagt.

1 1800	3 1746	5 1997	7 2004	9 2012
2 1702	4 1860	6 2000	8 2006	10 2020

L2:11 Starten Sie nun die Aufnahme und sagen Sie eine Jahreszahl nach der anderen. Überprüfen Sie mit der CD, ob Sie sie richtig gesagt haben.

2 Word focus

a Dances
Suchen Sie die sieben Wörter in dem Gitterrätsel und schreiben Sie sie auf die Zeilen.

m	o	l	e	i	j	a	p
j	b	a	l	l	e	t	o
i	v	e	f	w	j	e	l
v	m	s	t	w	i	s	t
t	w	a	p	o	v	d	a
p	o	l	k	a	e	a	n
i	n	s	a	l	s	n	g
f	l	a	m	e	n	c	o

______ ______
______ ______
______ ______
______ ______

b Jobs in entertainment
Welche Berufe üben diese Menschen aus? Wo üben sie sie aus?

1 
2 
3 

Kombinieren Sie die Wörter und bilden Sie Sätze über die Menschen.

who	what	where
~~dancer~~ singer writer	writes ~~dances~~ sings	in opera houses at home ~~in theatres~~

1 She's a dancer. She dances in theatres.
2 ______
3 ______

3 Grammar focus

3.1 Past simple (negative sentences)

→ G15 (S. 175)

positive sentences	negative sentences
I worked yesterday.	I **didn't work** yesterday.
You did your homework.	You **didn't do** your homework.
He had lunch at home.	He **didn't have** lunch at home.
She came to the lesson.	She **didn't come** to the lesson.
We went to the pub.	We **didn't go** to the pub.
They drove to London.	They **didn't drive** to London.

Went ist die Vergangenheitsform von *go*. Der verneinte Satz ist *We* ***didn't go*** *to the cinema. Didn't* ist für alle Personen gleich.

Ergänzen Sie die verneinten Sätze.

1 Carlos Acosta danced in Havana last weekend.
He didn't __________ in London.

2 David and Mel went to Spain on holiday.
They __________ __________ to Austria.

3 John had lunch at home yesterday.
He __________ __________ lunch in a restaurant.

4 Sue bought a DVD yesterday.
She __________ __________ a book.

3.2 Was / Were born

→ G14 (S. 175)

Where **were you** born? – **I was born** in Munich.

When **was he/she** born? – **He/She was** born in 1984.

Were **you/they born** in Germany?
– Yes, **we/they were**.
– No, **we/they weren't**.

Beantworten Sie folgende Fragen.

1 Were you born in Germany? __________
__________.

2 Was your father born in Paris? __________
__________.

3 Were the Beatles born in Germany? __________
__________.

4 Where was Carlos Acosta born? __________
__________.

4 Round up

a L2:12 Hören Sie ein Interview mit dem Schauspieler Jason Bell. Kreuzen Sie die richtige biografische Information an.

1 He was born in:
☐ London ☐ Manchester ☐ Dublin

2 He went to school for:
☐ 11 years ☐ 12 years ☐ 13 years

3 He finished school when he was:
☐ 16 ☐ 17 ☐ 18

4 After school he went to:
☐ acting school ☐ university ☐ work

5 Two years after that he went to:
☐ acting school ☐ university ☐ work

6 His first job was:
☐ on TV ☐ in a theatre ☐ in Hollywood

7 Now he is:
☐ a TV actor ☐ a film actor ☐ a TV presenter

8 He met her:
☐ last year ☐ two years ago ☐ ten years ago

9 He's got:
☐ one child ☐ two children
☐ He hasn't got any children.

b Lesen Sie die Antworten oben sowie die Sätze in Übung 1b + 1c. Schreiben Sie dann mindestens fünf Sätze mit biografischen Informationen über sich.

____
____
____
____
____
____

S. 184

Jetzt kann ich ...

Jahreszahlen sagen.	○○○	www: U8A1 CD-R 2: 12
biografische Informationen geben.	○○○	www: U8A2 CD-R 2: 13+15
über einige Aspekte von Unterhaltung sprechen.	○○○	www: U8A3
über Dinge, die in der Vergangenheit passiert sind, sprechen.	○○○	www: U8A4 CD-R 2: 14

Part B Staying in and going out

Television and other entertainment | Past simple (3), questions

You can do all of these things at home or in town. Which do you think is better?

have a coffee | see friends | have breakfast | do exercise | see a film | listen to music

I think it's better to …

Staying in

1a Read this article from a British magazine and, with a partner, choose the best headline for it.

British people don't like films

Staying in is 'in', going out is 'out'

My boring weekend

What did you do last weekend? Did you go to a museum? Did you go to a restaurant? Or an art gallery? Or did you stay at home? Did you sit on the sofa and watch TV? Did you spend a lot of time online?

Here in Britain, the average person watches television for 148 minutes every day and spends about 164 minutes online – that makes over five hours a day! We go to the cinema three times a year. And high culture … well, when did you last go to the ballet or the opera?

Our homes are warmer and more comfortable than in our grandparents' time. We've got fantastic home entertainment systems. Technology brings the world into our homes. We can find information, entertainment, culture, games, new friends and partners – all from the sofa. And we don't want to go out any more!

1b Underline all the questions in the article. Ask a partner the questions about his/her weekend:

What did you do last weekend? ➔ *I cleaned the flat on Saturday and I made dinner for some friends on Sunday.*
Did you go to a museum? ➔ *Yes, I did. / No, I didn't.*

2 Grammar focus

Past simple (questions)

What **did you do** last weekend? – I stayed at home.
Did you watch television? – **Yes, I did. / No, I didn't.**
When **did you** last **go** to the cinema? – Two weeks ago.

2a When did you last do these things? Work in small groups.

When did you last …
1 go on holiday?
2 start a new free time activity?
3 make a new friend?
4 buy a book?
5 send an email?
6 work in the garden?
7 give someone flowers?
8 make a cup of coffee for someone?

Last summer.
A long time ago.
Two years ago.
Yesterday.
In February.

2b One student tells the class something he/she did last weekend. The other students ask questions with *Did you…?* or *Was it …?*

I went to the cinema on Saturday afternoon.

Did you see an American film?

Was it good?

An evening in front of the television

3 Word focus Adjectives

Choose the best adjective to describe each type of film or television programme and write it on the line.

exciting | frightening | funny | romantic | sad | serious

1 a documentary __________
2 a comedy __________
3 a love story __________
4 an action film __________
5 a tragedy __________
6 a horror film __________

4 Do you like watching television? Make two groups. Group A: look at page 165. Group B: look at page 166.

5 How to talk about a film or television programme

I saw (title).
I saw it on television / at the cinema.
It was a documentary / a comedy / …
It was good / interesting / boring / exciting / …
It wasn't very good.
It was with (name of TV presenter or actor).

5a Write a few sentences about a film or a television programme you enjoyed, or didn't enjoy. Then work in small groups. Read out your paragraph to your group. They can ask you some questions.

Going out – a day in London

6a Jill's got two grandchildren, Amy and Jack. She thinks they stay in too much and watch too much television, so she likes taking them out to interesting places when she's got time. Yesterday they spent the day together and she took them to London. Look at this tourist information Jill has got.

Child-friendly London

- **V&A (Victoria and Albert Museum)**
World famous museum of art and design. Fashion, textiles, sculpture, ceramics, glass and much, much more. Great cafés. Family activities. Free.

- **V&A Museum of Childhood**
Find out about children's lives through the years at this child-centred museum in East London. Teddy bears, dolls and many other toys. Free.

- **Tate Modern**
Gallery of modern art next to the Thames. Family-friendly activities at weekends and in the school holidays. Free.

The V&A (Victoria and Albert Museum)

The V&A Museum of Childhood

The Tate Modern

6b T2:14 Now listen to Jill talking to David, her boss. Where did she take her grandchildren?

6c T2:15 Listen again and say if the information is true (T) or false (F).

1 Amy loved the dolls.
2 Jack loved the trains.
3 They learnt a lot about children's lives through the years.
4 They spent six hours in the museum.
5 The train to London was very cheap.
6 They had lunch in the museum café.
7 The children wanted to buy everything in the gift shop.
8 Jill gave them a bit of money to spend in the gift shop.
9 They bought a postcard and they sent it to their aunt and uncle.
10 The postcard was Jill's idea.

With a partner, correct the six false sentences together.

to spend time – Zeit verbringen
to spend money – Geld ausgeben

6d Write three questions about Jill's trip to London.

Where did …?
What did …?
Did …?
Was …?

Close your book. Take turns round the class to ask and answer questions.

Flexizone

Game Biography game

Play in pairs. To win a square, you must identify the person and say:
His/Her name was …
He/She was born in (year) and died in (year).

And give **one** new piece of information, e.g.
He was / had / lived / worked / danced / said / sang / played / had / wrote / was /…

When you win a square, write your initials in it. Then the other person can play.

At the end of the game, when you have won as many squares as you can, give points:

each line of two squares = 2 points
each line of three squares = 3 points
each line of four squares = 4 points
each line of five squares = 5 points

The winner is the player with the most points. If there were some people you didn't know, check the answers on page 187.

JL 1940–1980 His wife, Yoko, was Japanese.	**GG** 1905–1990 She said 'I want to be alone'.	**JP II** 1920–2005 He lived and worked in the Vatican for 26 years.	**CC** 1889–1977 He didn't speak in his films.	**AE** 1879–1955 He found that $E = mc^2$.
QV 1819–1901 Her husband, Albert, was German.	**WAM** 1756–1791 He wrote operas and other classical music.	**JFK** 1917–1963 His wife's name was Jackie.	**WS** 1564–1616 He was born in Stratford-upon-Avon.	**S** 1837–1898 Romy Schneider played her in three films.
MD 1901–1992 She sang Lili Marleen.	**D** 1961–1997 She divorced her husband, Charles.	**FA** 1899–1987 He danced with Ginger Rogers.	**MT** 1910–1997 She lived in Calcutta but she wasn't Indian.	**MM** 1926–1962 Her real name was Norma Jeane.
RM 1940–2005 He had a black moustache and a dog called Daisy.	**RB** 1943–1991 His real name was Gerd Höllerich.	**EP** 1935–1977 He lived at Graceland.	**FJS** 1915–1988 Munich airport has got his name.	**MLK** 1929–1968 He said 'I have a dream'.

Your turn Staying in and going out (→ www)

1 How to …

a Wie man sich nach einem Besuch im Restaurant erkundigt. Schreiben Sie die Wörter in die Lücken.

Did | Was | Were | What | Where | Which

1 ______ did you go?
2 ______ restaurant did you go to?
3 ______ did you eat?
4 ______ the food good?
5 ______ you have a good time?
6 ______ the waiters friendly?

b Wie Sie über Filme sprechen, die Sie gesehen haben. Schreiben Sie die Wörter in die Lücken.

actors | cinema | sad | story | TV

1 I saw it on ______.
2 I saw it at the ______.
3 The ______ was very exciting.
4 But the end of the film was a bit ______.
5 The ______ were fantastic.

c Wie Sie jemandem von einem Abend zu Hause erzählen. Nummerieren Sie die Sätze der Reihe nach. Die fettgedruckten Wörter helfen Ihnen.

☐ **After** my dinner, I watched a film on TV.
☐ 8 I went to bed at 11.30.
☐ **Then** I phoned and ordered some food.
☐ 1 I arrived home at about 7.30.
☐ **Before** the food arrived, I spent half an hour online.
☐ **The first thing I did** was to look at the Chinese restaurant menu.
☐ The food came at 8.30 – it was very good.
☐ **Before** I went to bed, I phoned two friends.

L2:13 Hören Sie und überprüfen Sie Ihre Antworten.

L2:14 **Say it like this** Hören Sie und sprechen Sie nach.

2 Word focus

a Staying in

Welche der blauen Verben passen zu den roten Wörtern? Schreiben Sie die Nummern in die Kästchen.

1 read	5 have	☐ dinner with friends	☐ to music
2 watch	6 spend	☐ emails	☐ television
3 listen	7 phone	☐ a book	☐ friends
4 play	8 write	☐ time online	☐ cards

b Adjectives

Sie alle waren gestern Abend im Kino. Was für einen Film haben sie gesehen? Schreiben Sie die Adjektive.

1

2

3

4

5

6

1 They saw a f______ film.
2 She saw a s______ film.
3 He saw a f______ film.
4 She saw a b______ film.
5 He saw an e______ film.
6 They saw a r______ film.

c A newspaper article

Was können Sie auf der Seite sehen? Schreiben Sie die Ziffer neben das Wort.

___ a picture
___ paragraph 1
___ the page number
___ the headline
___ paragraph 2

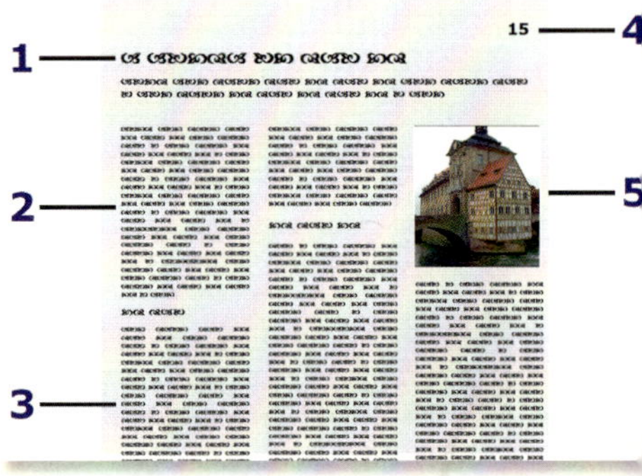

3 Grammar focus

Past simple (questions)

→ G15 (S. 175)

Zunächst ein Blick auf die Grammatik in Unit 7, Part B und Unit 8, Part A:

positive	negative
I met her yesterday.	I didn't meet her yesterday.
They worked yesterday.	They didn't work yesterday.

Und nun:

questions	answers
Did you see her yesterday?	Yes, **I did**. / No, **I didn't**.
Did he/she work yesterday?	Yes, **he/she did**. / No, **he/she didn't**.
Where did they go?	**They went** to the theatre.
When did you last go to the cinema?	Three weeks ago.

a Bilden Sie Fragen, indem Sie die Wörter in die richtige Reihenfolge bringen.

1 did | film | yesterday | Which | see | you | ?

2 the | start | What time | did | film | ?

3 film | Was | good | the | ?

4 see | did | Where | film | the | you | ?

b Schreiben Sie Fragen, auf die die fettgedruckten Wörter antworten.

1 They went **to London**.
Where ______

2 They had lunch **in a Chinese restaurant**.
Where ______

3 They sent **three** postcards.
How many ______

4 They saw **a ballet** in the evening.
What ______

4 Round up

In folgender Übung hören Sie drei verschiedene Arten von Information. Überlegen Sie vorher, was Sie wissen wollen und worauf Sie sich deshalb konzentrieren müssen. Lassen Sie sich nicht von unwichtigen Dingen ablenken.

a L2:15 Hören Sie eine Nachrichtensendung im Radio. Kreuzen Sie die drei Themen an, von denen der Nachrichtensprecher gesprochen hat.

- ☐ a football match
- ☐ the weather
- ☐ a film star
- ☐ an opera
- ☐ shop opening hours
- ☐ a museum
- ☐ something that happened in a restaurant

b Schreiben Sie das Thema des Gehörten in die gelben Felder.

L2:16 Hören Sie noch einmal und schreiben Sie die Zahl, die bei jedem Thema genannt wird, ins grüne Feld.

Topic 1

Topic 2

Topic 3

c L2:16 Hören Sie noch einmal. Achten Sie dieses Mal auf den Satz, in dem die Zahl genannt wird, die Sie notiert haben. Schreiben Sie ihn in das weiße Feld.

S. 184

Jetzt kann ich ...

danach fragen, wie jemand den Abend verbracht hat.	www: U8B1
übers Ausgehen sprechen.	www: U8B2 CD-R 2: 17
über einen Abend sprechen, den ich zu Hause verbracht habe.	www: U8B3

Reading Ballet debut

You're never too old ...

88-year-old John Lowe from Cambridge made his stage debut on Sunday in the Lantern Dance Theatre Company's performance of Prokofiev's The Stone Flower.

Mr Lowe, a retired teacher, had his first ballet lesson when he was 79! The idea for his new hobby came from his daughter, a professional dancer. And so he went to the dance school in his town and had ballet lessons.

He says, "I practise at home and I don't really have any problems with the routines because I exercise a lot and I'm very fit. Dancing is a wonderful thing to do and I can't understand why more men don't do it." ■

Glossary

stage debut Bühnendebüt | performance Vorstellung | retired pensioniert | understand verstehen

Out and About

Socks

A dance school has got twelve pairs of warm socks – six white pairs and six black pairs – for its students. The 24 socks are in a big bag. Of course, when a student wants to have a pair of socks, they must be the same colour – how many socks must the student take out of the bag to be sure he/she has got a pair?

Find the solution in *Out and About*, page 37.
Die Lösung finden Sie in *Out and About*, S. 37.

Doing things your way

Part A Doing things differently

People in the news | Adverbs of manner | Apologising and giving reasons | Question words

What makes you different from other people? Think about your clothes, your job, your free time activities and your lifestyle.

Fast or slow?

1a This is Sonya Thomas from Virginia, USA. She's a world champion speed eater. She can eat a lot of food, very fast.

Sonya with a snack!

Look at the information about her world records in this table. With a partner, make sentences about Sonya. e.g.
In 2004 she ate five kilos of cheesecake in nine minutes.

Year	Food	How much/many?	Minutes
2004	cheesecake	5 kg	9
2004	eggs	52	5
2004	tacos	48	11
2007	chicken wings	173	12

1b Read this interview with Sonya Thomas. Match the questions and answers and write the letters in the boxes.

1 ☐ When did you start speed eating?
2 ☐ How often do you do competitions?
3 ☐ What do you usually eat?
4 ☐ Do you enjoy cooking?
5 ☐ How often do you train?
6 ☐ What's your dream?

a I want to be the number one competitive eater in the world.
b Yes, I do, but I don't have much time for it.
c I eat a lot of healthy food – fruit, vegetables, rice, fish and chicken. I sometimes enjoy sweets, but not too many.
d I don't train very often because it isn't healthy to eat a lot of food very fast very often. I sometimes go to all-you-can-eat buffets in restaurants.
e I only do them once or twice a month.
f In 2002. I saw the world number one, Takeru Kobayashi, eat 50 hot dogs on television and I wanted to do the same thing. In June 2003 I won my first speed eating competition.

1c Check your answers with a partner. Then read the interview aloud together.

2a T2:16 Listen to a news report about this man, Greg Billingham. Tick (✓) the right sentence.

- [ ] Greg Billingham ran the London Marathon fast.
- [ ] Greg Billingham ran the London Marathon slowly.

2b T2:17 Listen again and cross out the wrong information.

1 Greg Billingham finished *two days / a week* after the other runners.
2 He made *£14,000 / £40,000* for children with leukaemia.
3 He *trained hard / didn't train much*.
4 He thanked *his wife / the public*.
5 An *African / American* runner won the race.
6 Mr Billingham *didn't want his photo in the newspaper / smiled happily for the cameras*.

3 Grammar focus

Adjectives and adverbs

Regular adverbs end in *ly*.
He's a **slow** runner. He ran the marathon **slowly**.
He was **happy**. He smiled **happily**.

Irregular adverbs.
He had a **good** race. It went **well**.
It was a **hard** race. He trained **hard**.
Sonya Thomas is a **fast** eater. She can eat really **fast**.

3a What do you find helpful in your English course? Choose an adverb for each sentence.

1 It helps me when my English teacher speaks *clearly / unclearly*.
2 It helps me when the people speak *slowly / fast* on the CD.
3 It helps me when the other students work *well / badly* in group work.
4 It helps me when everyone works *happily / unhappily* together.

4a Word focus Question words

Match the question words with the answers.

1 ☐ Why ...?	a	Slowly.
2 ☐ How ...?	b	Because ...
3 ☐ How much ...?	c	On Sunday.
4 ☐ When ...?	d	In London.
5 ☐ Where ...?	e	The London Marathon.
6 ☐ Which ...?	f	£40,000.

3b Read these sentences and tick (✓) the ones that are true for you.

1 ☐ I usually walk slowly.
2 ☐ I usually eat fast.
3 ☐ I often talk very fast.
4 ☐ I drive very well.
5 ☐ I work well in a team.
6 ☐ I worked hard yesterday.
7 ☐ I always work hard in my English class.
8 ☐ I can sing beautifully.

Compare your answers with a partner and find something that you both do / did. Tell the rest of the class:
Anke and I both work well in a team.

4b Test your memory. Use the question words from exercise 4a to write five questions about the slow runner in exercise 2. Then close your books and ask and answer the questions in small groups.

Early or late?

5 People often say that German and Swiss people are very punctual. Write *always, usually, often, sometimes* or *never* in each of these sentences about you.

When I go to the doctor's, I'm ________ ten minutes early.

When I visit friends, I'm ________ punctual.

When I come to my English lesson, I'm ________ late.

Listen to your teacher's sentences. Who is more punctual – you or your teacher?

6a T2:18 It's quarter past nine in the morning in David and Jill's office. Listen. Who's late for work this morning?

6b T2:19 Listen again and match these problems and reasons.

1 ☐ Jill's late for work.
2 ☐ Jill's daughter phoned.
3 ☐ David's tired.

a He/She didn't sleep well last night.
b His/Her daughter phoned.
c He/She had a problem with the children.

With a partner, take turns to read out your answers. Use *because* to join the two parts.
1 *Jill's late for work because …*

6c What does Jill say? Put these words in order.

I'm | late. | sorry | I'm

What does David say?

alright. | That's | problem. | No

7 How to apologise and give a reason, and how to react to apologies

I'm sorry.	*It was because …*	*That's alright.*
I'm sorry I'm late.	*I had a problem at work / at home / at the airport / …*	*No problem.*
	I had a problem with my car / my boss / the babysitter / …	*Don't worry.*
	My train / bus / tram / flight was late.	

7a Read this dialogue with a partner. Then read it again, changing the words in the coloured blocks. Swap roles and read it a third time with different changes.

A: Hello, (name).
B: Oh, hi (name). I'm sorry I'm late.
A: No problem. Is everything OK? — That's alright. Don't worry.
B: Yes, thanks. I had a small problem at work. — the office home
A: Was it serious?
B: No, it wasn't. My boss wanted to talk about his/her new idea at one minute to five. — colleague assistant / car grandchild
A: That sounds exciting. — interesting boring
B: And then when I arrived at the station I found I didn't have my ticket so I walked here. — tram stop bus stop / any money my handbag
A: How long did it take?
B: About fifteen minutes. So, I'm very sorry. — ten twenty
A: Don't worry! You're here now. What would you like to drink?

Flexizone

A Ask your teacher questions with *fast, slowly, well, badly, late* and *early*. Use *Can you …? Do you …?* and *Did you …?*

B You're late for a meeting. Think of a reason why you're late. Stand up and walk around the class. Say sorry to the other students and tell them why you're late. Who has the best reason?

Your turn Doing things differently (→ www)

1 How to …

Schreiben Sie die Wörter in die Lücken.

a Wie Sie sich entschuldigen.

I can't | I didn't | I'm | sorry | sorry | sorry

1 I'm ______________ ______________ late.

2 I'm ______________ ______________ ______________ phone you yesterday.

3 I'm ______________ ______________ ______________ meet you this afternoon.

b Wie Sie erklären, warum Sie sich entschuldigen.

busy | day | yesterday evening | had | this morning | was

1 I ______________ a problem with my daughter at breakfast ______________ ______________!

2 I'm ______________ all ______________ today.

3 I ______________ very tired ______________ ______________.

c Wie Sie auf Entschuldigungen reagieren.

alright | problem | worry

1 No ______________. Can you call me this evening?

2 Don't ______________, you're here now.

3 That's ______________, but I'd like to see you soon.

L2:17 Hören Sie und überprüfen Sie Ihre Antworten.

L2:18 **Say it like this** Hören Sie und sprechen Sie nach.

d Setzen Sie nun die Sätze aus a, b und c so zusammen, dass kurze Dialoge entstehen.

	from **a**	from **b**	from **c**
dialogue 1	1		
dialogue 2	2		
dialogue 3	3		

Überprüfen Sie Ihre Antworten im Lösungsschlüssel.

2 Word focus

a Opposites

Suchen Sie im Gitterrätsel fünf Wortpaare mit gegenteiliger Bedeutung. Davon ist jeweils ein Wort waagerecht und eines senkrecht. Beginnen Sie mit den Wörtern, die waagerecht stehen. Schreiben Sie die Paare auf die Zeilen unten.

a	b	s	l	o	w	l	y
b	a	l	c	o	m	e	e
e	d	w	e	l	l	n	s
a	l	w	a	y	s	e	m
r	y	v	r	f	u	v	t
n	o	b	l	a	t	e	l
n	g	i	y	s	r	r	o
p	o	m	i	t	v	a	n

no + *yes*

______________ + ______________

______________ + ______________

______________ + ______________

______________ + ______________

______________ + ______________

b Question words

Schreiben Sie die Fragewörter an den Anfang der Sätze.

How | What | When | Where | Which | Who | Why

☐ ______________ do you always walk to work?

☐ ______________ does your teacher speak?

☐ ______________ did you have dinner with yesterday?

☐ ______________ is your favourite food?

☐ ______________ do you live?

☐ ______________ sport do you like watching on TV?

☐ ______________ do you do sport?

c L2:19 Hören Sie nun die kurzen Antworten zu diesen Fragen. Schreiben Sie die Nummern der Antworten neben die Sätze.

3 Grammar focus

3.1 Adjectives

→ G16 (S. 176)

He's a **nice** man. The man is very **nice**. He's very **nice**.	They're **nice** children. The children are very **nice**. They're very **nice**.

Adjektive sagen etwas über Menschen, Orte oder Dinge. Sie können vor dem Nomen stehen oder nach *is / are / was / were*. Adjektive ändern ihre Form nie.

Schreiben Sie die Wörter in der richtigen Reihenfolge.

1 a | good | marathon | last | saw | We | year

____

2 African | very | The | ran | fast | runners

____

3 very | was | It | exciting

____

3.2 Adverbs

→ G16 (S. 176)

He's a slow runner. He runs **slowly**.
She's a beautiful dancer. She dances **beautifully**.

I'm a fast walker. I walk **fast**.
He's a good driver. He drives **well**.
They're hard workers. They work **hard**.

Regelmäßige Adverbien werden gebildet, indem man *-ly* an Adjektive anhängt. Wenn ein Adjektiv auf *-y* endet, wird es zu *i*: *happy* → *happily*.
Fast, *hard* und *well* sind unregelmäßige Adjektive.

a Schreiben die Sätze um und verwenden Sie Adjektive.

1 He's a slow writer. He writes ______________.

2 She's a good cook. She cooks ______________.

3 He's a fast driver. He drives ______________.

b Beantworten Sie Fragen. Verwenden Sie die Adverbien wie im Beispiel.

Is he a fast walker? No, he walks very slowly.

1 Are they bad dancers? No, ______________.

2 Is she a slow worker? No, ______________.

3 Is he a clear speaker? Yes, ______________.

4 Round up

Füllen Sie folgenden Fragebogen aus. Treffen die Aussagen auf Sie zu oder nicht?

AM I THE SAME AS OTHER PEOPLE OR AM I DIFFERENT?

		True	Not true
1	People say that I eat too fast.	☐	☐
2	I can sing beautifully.	☐	☐
3	I think speed eating world records are interesting.	☐	☐
4	I'd like to go to a speed eating competition.	☐	☐
5	I think sports world records are more interesting.	☐	☐
6	I like eating a lot of food.	☐	☐
7	People say I drive very well.	☐	☐
8	I like working in groups in the class.	☐	☐
9	I worked very hard yesterday.	☐	☐
10	I think I can run a half marathon.	☐	☐
11	I'm always punctual for everything.	☐	☐
12	I always apologise when I'm late.	☐	☐
13	I think it's good to give flowers when I say 'sorry'.	☐	☐
14	I usually sleep very well.	☐	☐

Vergleichen Sie Ihre Antworten mit den Antworten eines Partners / einer Partnerin – am Telefon oder vor Beginn der nächsten Unterrichtsstunde. Sind Sie sich ähnlich oder sind Sie eher verschieden? Wie viele Fragen haben Sie anders beantwortet?

S. 185

Jetzt kann ich ...

mich entschuldigen und eine Erklärung geben.	○○○	www: U9A1 CD-R 2: 20
auf Entschuldigungen reagieren.	○○○	www: U9A2
beschreiben, wie Menschen Dinge tun.	○○○	www: U9A3 CD-R 2: 22

Part B Doing the right thing

Talking about etiquette and rules | Saying the right thing | *must, mustn't*

What does your class know about Japan? What's the capital city? What's it like? Can you name two more Japanese cities? Do you know any Japanese words?

Life in Japan

1a Rearrange the letters to find the names of these things.

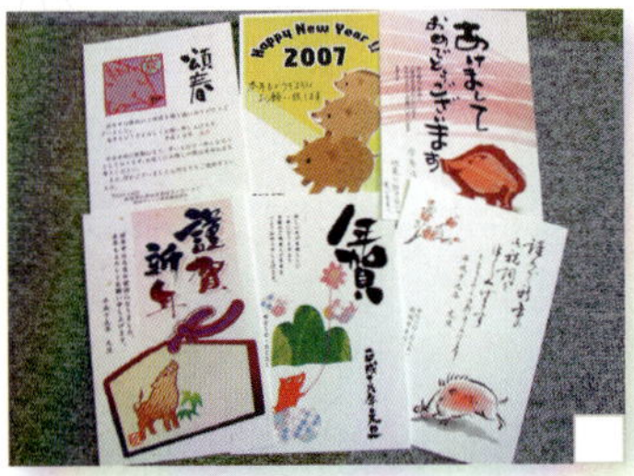

DRACS ____________

DRAGNE ____________

THAB ____________

RSEETNPS ____________

HOSES ____________

LOITET ____________

1b T2:20 Hiroko is Japanese and her new partner, Stephen, is English.

Hiroko tells Stephen about some of the things he must learn about Japanese life before he visits her family. Listen to Hiroko. What does she talk about? Tick three photos.

1c T2:21 Listen again and cross out the wrong word.

1 You *must / mustn't* wear your shoes in the house.
2 You *must / mustn't* leave your shoes at the door.
3 You *must / mustn't* wear your normal slippers in the toilet.
4 You *must / mustn't* wash in the bath.
5 You *must / mustn't* wash before your bath.
6 You *must / mustn't* leave the bathwater for the next person.

Check your answers in class.

2 What does it mean? Tick (✓) the right sentence.

You must leave your shoes at the door.

a ☐ Please leave your shoes at the door. This is very important.

b ☐ You can leave your shoes at the door, or not. No problem.

You mustn't wear your shoes in the house.

a ☐ Please don't wear your shoes in the house. This is very important.

b ☐ You can wear your shoes in the house, or not. No problem.

3 Grammar focus

must, mustn't

You must leave your shoes at the door.
You mustn't wear your shoes in the house.

Must and *mustn't* are the same for all persons – *I, you, he, she, it, we, they.*

3a Here are some more rules about Japanese etiquette. Talk to a partner and write the missing words in the spaces.

At dinner:

must | must | mustn't

You ________ be punctual.

You ________ take a small present for your host.

You ________ mix the rice with the other food.

Talking to people:

directly | loudly | politely

You mustn't speak ________.

You must speak ________ and respectfully.

You mustn't look ________ into someone's eyes for a long time.

At a business meeting:

give | put | wear

You must ________ conservative clothes.

You must ________ your business card with both hands.

You mustn't ________ the other person's business card in your pocket.

Presents:

open | small | white

When you give a present, you must say 'It's only a ________ thing, but ...'.

You mustn't give ________ flowers.

When you get a present, you mustn't ________ it immediately.

Check your answers in class.

3b In small groups, write four rules for Japanese visitors to your country. Read your rules to the class.

Saying the right thing

4 Word focus Special days in the year

4a Fill in the missing vowels *(a, e, i, o, u)* to make these special days and festivals.

1 Chr__stm__s D__y
2 b__rthd__y
3 M__th__rs' D__y
4 N__w Y____r's D__y
5 V__l__nt__n__'s D__y
6 F__th__rs' D__y
7 E__st__r S__nd__y
8 w__dd__ng __nn__v__rs__ry

4b Now work with a partner. Look at the list of special days above. When do you give (or get) presents?

5

Are these usually happy or unhappy events? Is it good news or bad news? Talk to a partner and tick (✓) the right box. You can agree or disagree.

	☺	☹	
1	☐	☐	A friend's got a good result in his/her English test.
2	☐	☐	A friend's got a bad result in his/her English test.
3	☐	☐	It's your friend's birthday.
4	☐	☐	You're late for work.
5	☐	☐	Your boss is on holiday next week.
6	☐	☐	Someone gives you some flowers.
7	☐	☐	A friend has got a job interview today.
8	☐	☐	You send a Christmas card to a friend.

6 How to say the right thing in social situations

a *Good luck. I hope it goes well.*
b *Have a nice holiday. Have a good trip.*
c *Happy birthday. Have a great day.*
d *Merry Christmas. Happy New Year.*
e *Thank you. Thanks very much.*
f *Well done. Congratulations.*
g *Oh dear. That's a pity.*
h *I'm sorry I'm late. The train was late.*

T2:22 **Say it like this** Listen and repeat the phrases.

6a Match the phrases in the box to the situations in exercise 5. Write the letters in the boxes.

1 f 2 ☐ 3 ☐ 4 ☐ 5 ☐ 6 ☐ 7 ☐ 8 ☐

7

Choose a situation.

1 You've got some English books as presents for the other students in the class.
2 You can't come to your English course next week because you're on holiday.
3 You're in a sports team and you've got an important match on Saturday.
4 You've got a job interview next Monday.
5 It's your birthday today.
6 You've got a new baby.
7 You've got a new job.

Walk around the class and talk to the other students.
Tell them your news and react to their news.

Flexizone

Game The Yokohama Landmark Tower

The Landmark Tower is a very tall building in Yokohama. There are shops, offices and a hotel in it. Visitors can go up the tower (in a super-fast lift) and enjoy a fantastic view of the city. From the top, you can see another famous Japanese tourist attraction – play the game and find out!

Play in groups of two or three. Take turns to play. Use a 2 euro coin (number side = go forward 2, picture side = go forward 3). When you land on a box, tell the other players what you did on your trip to Japan, e.g.

1 You had a good flight to Japan.

I had a good flight to Japan.

That's good.

The other players must react to what you say, e.g.

Positive reactions: That's good. / Well done. / You did the right thing. / That's polite in Japan. / I think that's normal in Japan.

Negative reactions: Oh dear. / That's not so good. / Oh no. / That's not very polite in Japan. / You mustn't do that in Japan.

The first player to arrive at the top of the tower is the winner. Winner: go to page 166 and tell the other players what you can see from the top of the Landmark Tower.

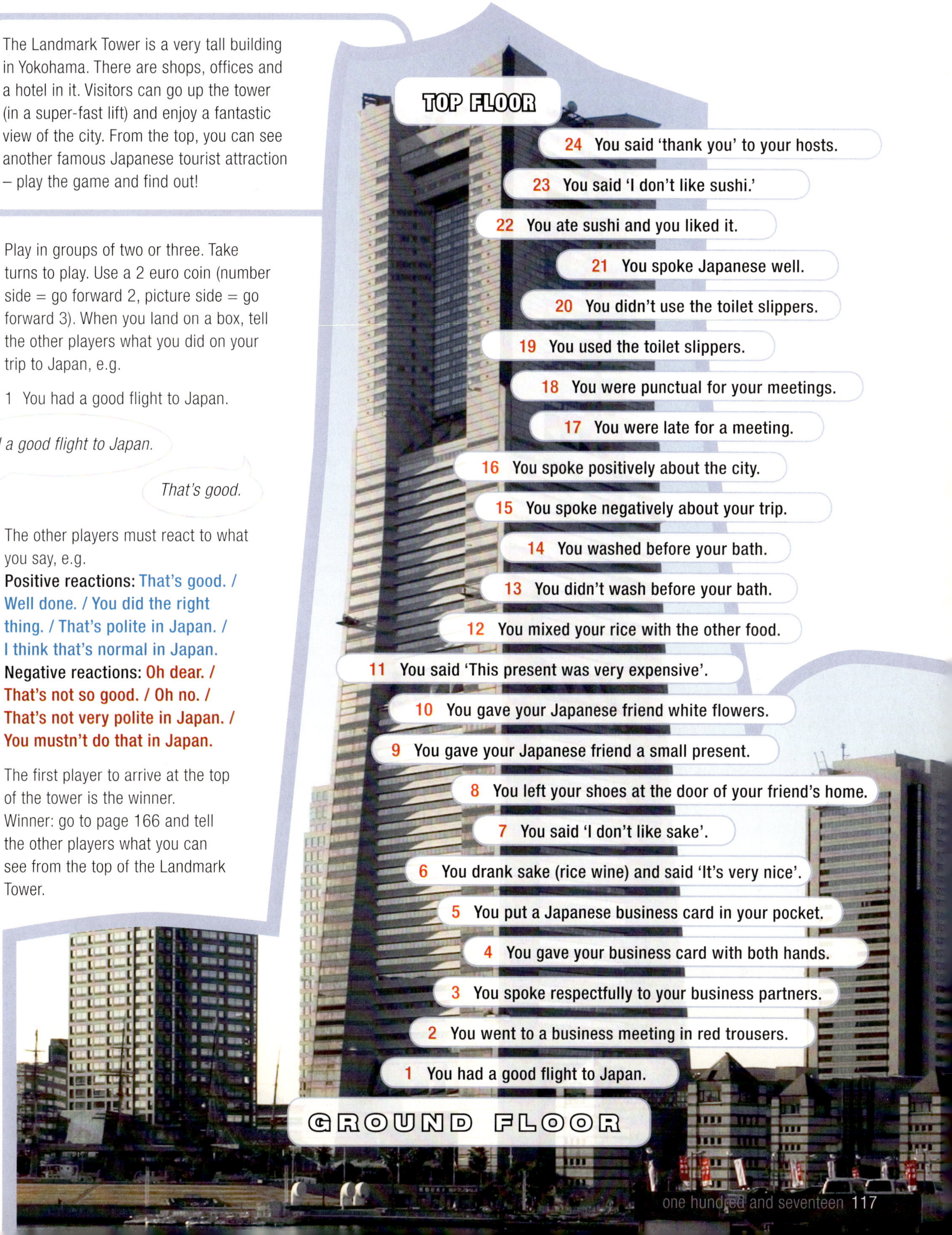

TOP FLOOR

24 You said 'thank you' to your hosts.

23 You said 'I don't like sushi.'

22 You ate sushi and you liked it.

21 You spoke Japanese well.

20 You didn't use the toilet slippers.

19 You used the toilet slippers.

18 You were punctual for your meetings.

17 You were late for a meeting.

16 You spoke positively about the city.

15 You spoke negatively about your trip.

14 You washed before your bath.

13 You didn't wash before your bath.

12 You mixed your rice with the other food.

11 You said 'This present was very expensive'.

10 You gave your Japanese friend white flowers.

9 You gave your Japanese friend a small present.

8 You left your shoes at the door of your friend's home.

7 You said 'I don't like sake'.

6 You drank sake (rice wine) and said 'It's very nice'.

5 You put a Japanese business card in your pocket.

4 You gave your business card with both hands.

3 You spoke respectfully to your business partners.

2 You went to a business meeting in red trousers.

1 You had a good flight to Japan.

GROUND FLOOR

Your turn Doing the right thing (→ www)

1 How to …

Wie Sie bei geselligen Anlässen reagieren.
Schreiben Sie die Wörter in die Lücken.

a pity | birthday | Christmas | good trip | luck | very much | New Year

1 Merry ________.
2 Good ________.
3 Thanks ________ ________.
4 Happy ________.
5 Have a ________ ________.
6 Oh, that's ________ ________.
7 Happy ________ ________.

Schreiben Sie nun die Nummern 1–7 neben die richtige Sprechblase.

A I'm 35 today! ☐
B I've got my driving test this afternoon. ☐
C I'm on a walking holiday for the next three weeks. ☐
D Hi, it's 25th December here in New Zealand. ☐
E I'm ill, so I can't come with you. ☐
F Here's an English magazine for you. ☐
G Hello Mum, it's midnight … and it's goodbye to the old year. ☐

L2:20 Hören Sie und überprüfen Sie Ihre Antworten.

L2:21 **Say it like this** Hören Sie und sprechen Sie nach.

2 Word focus

a Special days

Wie heißen folgende Festtage? Schreiben Sie auf.

1 
2 
3 
4 
5 
6 

1 ________
2 ________
3 ________
4 ________
5 ________
6 ________

b Find the words

Erinnern Sie sich an die Wörter, die in folgende Sätze passen? Wenn nicht, schauen Sie in Unit 9, Part B nach.

1 London is the c________ of England, it's a fantastic city.
2 Our house has got a nice g________ with beautiful flowers.
3 He gave me his business c________ after the meeting.
4 She always gives him a Christmas p________ – socks!
5 He's always p________ – never early and never late.
6 I've got some good n________ for you. Your test results are fantastic.
7 He's got an i________ for a job next Monday.
8 Japanese people always l________ their shoes at the door.

3 Grammar focus

Must / mustn't

→ G17 (S. 176)

In Japan
You **must** be punctual when you go to someone's house for dinner.
You **must** take a present when you go to someone's house for dinner.
You **mustn't** give white flowers when you go to someone's house for dinner.
You **mustn't** speak loudly at the dinner table.

Mustn't = *must not* = nicht dürfen
Die Wörter *must* und *mustn't* bleiben immer gleich.

a Schauen Sie sich die Schilder an. Welches Schild und welche Regel passen zusammen? Was dürfen Sie hier nicht tun?

1 
2 
3 
4 
5 
6 
7 
8 

- ☐ I mustn't drive fast.
- ☐ I mustn't smoke.
- ☐ I mustn't put my feet on the seat.
- ☐ I mustn't take photos.
- ☐ I mustn't eat ice cream.
- ☐ I mustn't park my car.
- ☐ I mustn't use my mobile phone.
- ☐ I mustn't drive into this street.

b Morgen früh um 8 Uhr haben Sie ein Bewerbungsgespräch für eine Stelle, die Sie unbedingt haben wollen. Vervollständigen Sie die Sätze mit *must* oder *mustn't*.

1 I ______ go to bed early this evening.
2 I ______ drink a lot of alcohol this evening.
3 I ______ be late for the interview.
4 I ______ speak clearly at the interview.
5 I ______ go to a nightclub this evening.
6 I ______ ask good questions at the interview.
7 I ______ be friendly but not *too* friendly.
8 I ______ relax for five minutes before the interview.

4 Round up

Wenn Sie Menschen zuhören, erschließt sich Ihnen einiges, wenn Sie auf deren Tonfall achten und Ihr Weltwissen zu Hilfe nehmen.

a L2:22 Hören Sie Menschen zu, die anderen etwas zu Regeln und Vorschriften sagen. Machen Sie ein Häkchen bei den Bildern, die die im Dialog angesprochene Situation zeigen.

1

☐

☐

2

☐

☐

b L2:23 Hören Sie noch einmal und vervollständigen Sie die Sätze für die Situationen 1 und 2.

The woman mustn't ______
She must ______
The man mustn't ______
He must ______

S. 185

Jetzt kann ich ...

in verschiedenen gesellschaftlichen Situationen reagieren.	www: U9B1 CD-R 2: 27
über Regeln und Umgangsformen reden.	www: U9B2 CD-R 2: 25+26
über Dinge reden, die nicht erlaubt sind.	www: U9B3

Reading An email from an au pair

Charlotte is an English au pair in Leipzig. Here's an email to her friend Claire.

Hi Claire
Or *Guten Tag* as they say here! I still go to my German course every morning when the kids are at school. German's really difficult – they've got a lot of words just for the word *the*! And some of the words are so long. Do you like this one? *Volkshochschulkursleiter* – that's the word for my teacher!

Hey, I told you about my new boyfriend, Tobi. Well, here's a photo of him. He's really nice.
I met his parents last week. They speak a bit of English, so that was OK. I liked them a lot – but I don't think they liked me! You see, they invited me for dinner and I made so many mistakes.

First, Tobi introduced me to his parents (I remembered to shake hands!) and I said, "Nice to meet you, Rosi" to his mother. She looked really shocked! I forgot that they don't use first names here – only with people they know very well, or members of the family. And the older person must 'offer' their first name to the younger person. Yes, I know all that – but I was a bit nervous about meeting them and so I just forgot!

The next problem was the flowers. I took some flowers for his mum but when I gave them to her, she looked a bit – well, strange. Tobi told me later that when you give flowers here, you mustn't give them with the paper on. I didn't know that. There are so many little things that are different here. It's good that Tobi studied in England for a year so he knows that we do some things differently.

You can meet Tobi in August. He wants to come back to England with me. Then he can meet my parents and do things the English way! I must go and make some lunch for the kids now. They come home from school at one o'clock.
Say hi to Emma from me. I miss you all.
Love
Charlotte

Glossary
still noch | told erzählte | look shocked schockiert ausschauen | forgot vergaß | strange merkwürdig

Out and About
Faux pas – What cultural mistakes did this man make?
I was in Korea on business last week. I went to a party and I took Dae, my hostess, four yellow roses. I made a nice card for her with: *Thank you, Dae* on it. But she didn't look happy – I don't know why. I made a business contact – he gave me his business card and I put it in my bag. I think the people at the party liked my shoes because they all looked at them and smiled.

Find the solution in *Out and About*, page 38.
Die Lösung finden Sie in *Out and About*, S. 38.

Diese Testübungen orientieren sich an den Aufgabenformaten der Prüfung *telc English A1*. Bitte markieren Sie Ihre Antworten mit einem Querbalken (—) in den Antwortabschnitten rechts neben den Aufgaben.

1 Language elements

Markieren Sie (—) die richtige Antwort **a)** oder **b)** im Antwortabschnitt.

Jack and Sabine ___1___ in Edinburgh ___2___ weekend. They ___3___ to see one of ___4___ daughters – it ___5___ her birthday on Sunday. They ___6___ her out for dinner. They ___7___ buy her a present but they ___8___ her ___9___ money. Jack and Sabine ___10___ in Edinburgh for very long – only two days.

1 **a)** was **b)** were
3 **a)** did **b)** went
5 **a)** was **b)** wasn't
7 **a)** didn't **b)** don't
9 **a)** any **b)** some

2 **a)** next **b)** last
4 **a)** there **b)** their
6 **a)** invite **b)** invited
8 **a)** gave **b)** give
10 **a)** wasn't **b)** weren't

Nun noch ein paar Informationen zu Jacks und Sabines Tochter.
Markieren Sie (—) die richtige Antwort **a)** oder **b)** im Antwortabschnitt.

She ___11___ born in London.	11 **a)** is	**b)** was
She went to Edinburgh two years ___12___.	12 **a)** ago	**b)** before
She ___13___ happy there at first, but she loves Edinburgh now.	13 **a)** was	**b)** wasn't
She ___14___ like the weather when she first arrived.	14 **a)** wasn't	**b)** didn't
And she didn't ___15___ any money!	15 **a)** have	**b)** had

1
Language elements

	a)	b)
1		
2		
3		
4		
5		
6		
7		
8		
9		
10		
11		
12		
13		
14		
15		

= _______ / 15

2 L2:24 Listening comprehension

Lesen Sie zunächst die Fragen. Hören Sie dann, was Jack erzählt.
Markieren Sie (—) die richtige Antwort **a)** oder **b)** im Antwortabschnitt.

16 Where do Jack and Sabine have breakfast?	**a)** in a café	**b)** at home
17 What time does Sabine leave the house?	**a)** 8 o'clock	**b)** 8.30
18 How often does Jack work on a Saturday morning?	**a)** once a month	**b)** three times a month
19 When does Sabine work all day?	**a)** on Tuesdays	**b)** on Saturdays
20 When does Jack cook for Sabine?	**a)** Saturday lunchtimes	**b)** Saturday evenings

2
Listening comprehension

	a)	b)
16		
17		
18		
19		
20		

= _______ / 5

3 Situational responses

Part A L2:25

Sehen Sie sich zunächst die Erwiderungen **a)** – **d)** an.
Hören Sie dann die Aufnahme.
Markieren Sie (—) die richtige Erwiderung **a)**, **b)**, **c)** oder **d)** im Antwortabschnitt.

21 ______
22 ______
23 ______

a) Yes, how much are they?
b) Can I help you?
c) Yes, I do – but it's a bit too expensive.
d) It's £3.50.

Part B L2:26

Sehen Sie sich zunächst die Erwiderungen **e)** – **h)** an.
Hören Sie dann die Aufnahme.
Markieren Sie (—) die richtige Erwiderung **e)**, **f)**, **g)** oder **h)** im Antwortabschnitt.

24 ______
25 ______
26 ______

e) You're welcome.
f) Good luck.
g) That's alright.
h) And tomorrow?

3 Situational responses

Part A				
21	a)	b)	c)	d)
22	a)	b)	c)	d)
23	a)	b)	c)	d)
Part B				
24	e)	f)	g)	h)
25	e)	f)	g)	h)
26	e)	f)	g)	h)
= ______ / 6				

4 Reading comprehension

Lesen Sie diese Texte 27 – 30 aus dem Informationsblatt eines Sommerhotels.
Wählen Sie die beste Überschrift für die Texte.
Markieren Sie (—) die richtige Antwort **a)**, **b)**, **c)**, **d)** oder **e)** im Antwortabschnitt.

a) Food and drink
b) Evening entertainment
c) Sport for all the family
d) In the restaurant
e) Play and learn

27

Beach volleyball, tennis and swimming – lessons for children aged 10 to 15. Every morning from 9 to 11.

Mum and dad can have a long (and quiet!) breakfast.

28

Every day – music and dancing for all the family 20.00 – 24.00
Saturday – Disco Augusta *and* swimming pool cinema 20.00 (begin)
Sunday – show with flamenco dancers and singers 20.30 – 23.00

29

We have tables for two and tables for four. We also have family tables and once a week we have 'children only' tables.
Please reserve before 11 a.m.

30

Come to our paella and Rioja evening. Children can come too – they can have our special 'paella junior' and cola.

4 Reading comprehension

	a)	b)	c)	d)	e)
27					
28					
29					
30					
= ______ / 4					

total

= ______ / 30

S. 185

Home and away

Part A Houses and flats

Talking about homes | Rooms and furniture | How to describe a house or flat | Comparatives

Talk in small groups. Do you live in a house or a flat? Do you live alone or with another person / other people? What's the name of your street? What is there in your street or near your home?

Houses

1a This is 10 Downing Street.
It's the British prime minister's house.

Whose house is it?
It's the prime minister**'s**.

Here are some more houses. For each picture, talk to a partner and ask: *Whose house is it?* There's a clue under each picture, to help you.

1

To be, or not to be?

2

a doll

3

A Little Night Music

4

a colour

5

a dog

1b Write a sentence about one of the houses.

I think (Mozart's) house is	quite very	big. small. old. new. beautiful. comfortable.

Read your sentence to the class.

1c In small groups, read these sentences and decide if you think they are true (T) or false (F). Do you all agree?

1 The White House is bigger than 10 Downing Street. ☐
2 Mozart's house is more beautiful than Shakespeare's house. ☐
3 Shakespeare's house is taller than Mozart's house. ☐
4 The White House is older than Shakespeare's house. ☐
5 Barbie's house is cleaner than Snoopy's house. ☐
6 10 Downing Street is more comfortable than Shakespeare's house. ☐

2 Grammar focus

Comparatives

Short adjectives	Shakespeare's house is	**older/bigger**	**than**	10 Downing Street.
Adjectives ending with *-y*	Snoopy's house is	**dirtier**	**than**	Barbie's house.
Long adjectives	The White House	**more beautiful**	**than**	10 Downing Street.

2a In class, compare these places.

1 a big house / a small flat (cheap): *A small flat is cheaper than a big house.*
2 a small flat / a big house (expensive)
3 a small town / the capital city (important)
4 a park / a garden (big)
5 New York / London (old)
6 Frankfurt airport / Graz airport (busy)
7 Munich's football stadium / Hamburg's football stadium (new)

T2:23 **Say it like this** In Unit 5 you practised the sound *th*, as in *think*, *three*, *Thursday*.
There is another *th* sound, as in *than*. Listen and repeat: than | they | this | other | mother | brother | father
My brother is taller than my father. My father is taller than my mother.

3 Word focus Rooms and other parts of the house

3a T2:24 Listen. Where are these people? Number the places 1–7.

☐ living room ☐ bedroom ☐ office ☐ bathroom ☐ garage ☐ balcony ☐ kitchen

3b Read these questions about life at home.

Where do you usually …			**What colour is …**		
eat breakfast?	listen to music?	watch television?	your bathroom?	your kitchen?	your bedroom?

Ask the questions to people in your class.

4 Word focus Things in the home

You can find all these things in a house or flat. Write them in the correct groups.

bath | bookcase | chair | cooker | dishwasher | fridge | shower | sofa | toilet

Three things in the living room	______________,	______________	and	______________
Three electrical things in the kitchen	______________,	______________	and	______________
Three important things in the bathroom	______________,	______________	and	______________

5 How to describe a house or flat.

It's old / modern / big / small.
For a flat: *It's on the ground floor / first floor / second floor.*
It's in / near / next to / opposite …
It's got … / There's a … / There are two …

5a Work in small groups. Tell the other students about your house or flat.

Flats

6a Read this information about two places to stay in Brighton – a holiday flat and a holiday house.

Modern holiday flat on the third floor (no lift) of an elegant building in the town centre.
Small garden.
Bedrooms: one double, one single.
Shops, restaurants, pubs, nightclubs: in the same street.
£800 per week. Extra costs: electricity, towels, cleaning.
No dogs, please. Nice children welcome.

Lovely large holiday house with big garden in quiet street.
Bedrooms: one double, one with three single beds.
Supermarket: 5 mins.
Pubs, restaurants: 10 mins.
£800 per week, no extra costs.
Dogs and children welcome.

Is it the flat (F) or the house (H)? Talk to a partner.

1 It's bigger. ☐
2 It's more expensive. ☐
3 It's more modern. ☐
4 It's nearer shops and restaurants. ☐
5 It's quieter. ☐
6 It's got more beds. ☐
7 It's got a bigger garden. ☐
8 It looks friendlier. ☐
9 It's nicer for families. ☐

6b Talk to a partner. You can agree or disagree.

I think …
Yes, I think so, too.
Oh, I don't think so.

Irregular comparative
good → better
bad → worse

Which place is better for …
1 a family with three children?
2 a young couple with a new baby?
3 a couple without a car?
4 an older couple with their grandchild?
5 a family with one child and a dog?
6 you?

7 Read this advert for a holiday home.
With a partner, work out what the advert means.

> ***Cornwall.*** Sea 2 mins. Quiet, v comf. Mod ktchn, bath. £100 / nt (£600 / wk). May – Oct. 03637 239017

Flexizone

A Compare your living-room and your classroom. Write three sentences. Here are some words to help you:
big | clean | cold | comfortable | interesting | old | warm
Now swap sentences with a partner and read your partner's sentences.

B Each student prepares one question to ask the teacher about his/her home, e.g *Where …? / What …? / Do you …? / Is there …? / Have you got …? / Is it …? / What colour's …?*

Your turn Houses and flats (→ www)

1 How to …

a Wie Sie sich nach der Wohnung von jemandem erkundigen. Schreiben Sie die Wörter in die Lücken.

a flat | building | live | modern | near | street | the name | Where is

1 Do you _____ in a house or _____ _____?

2 _____ _____ your flat?

3 How many floors are there in the _____?

4 Is your flat _____ the station?

5 Is it old or _____?

6 What's _____ _____ of your _____?

b Wie Sie Ihre Wohnung beschreiben. Schreiben Sie die Wörter in die Lücken.

bathroom | bedrooms | big house | ground floor | live | old

1 I _____ in a flat.

2 My friends live in a _____ _____.

3 My flat is very _____.

4 It's on the _____ _____.

5 There is one _____ in my flat.

6 There are two _____ in my flat.

Amerikaner nennen das Erdgeschoss *first floor*, Briten *ground floor*.

L2:27 Hören Sie und überprüfen Sie Ihre Antworten.

L2:28 **Say it like this** Hören Sie und sprechen Sie nach.

c Wie Sie Meinungen anderer Leute zustimmen oder sie ablehnen.

L2:29 Hören Sie zu und schreiben Sie auf, was John sagt.

Sue: I think this is a lovely house.

John: _____

Sue: But the garden is a bit small.

John: _____

2 Word focus

a Which floor?

Benennen Sie die Stockwerke.

the _____ _____

the _____ _____

the _____ _____

the second floor

the _____ _____

the _____ _____

b Which room?

Schreiben Sie unter die Bilder, wie die sechs Zimmer heißen.

1 _____

2 _____

3 _____

4 _____

5 _____

6 _____

c Which things?

Grenzen Sie mit vertikalen Linien die Wörter, die Dinge bei Ihnen zu Hause bezeichnen, voneinander ab.

c h a i r | t e l e v i s i o n b e
d s o f a b a t h f r i d g e c o o
k e r c o m p u t e r t a b l e t o
i l e t l a m p

3 Grammar focus

3.1 Comparatives

→ G18 (S. 177)

old: My father is **older than** my mother.
An kurze Adjektive hängen Sie *-er* an. Nach kurzem, betontem Vokal wird, wenn Sie *-er* anhängen, der Endkonsonant verdoppelt: *big* → *bigger than*.
dirty: My son's hands are always **dirtier than** his face!
Endet ein Adjektiv auf *-y*, wird vor dem *-er* das *y* zu einem *i*.
expensive: Houses are usually **more expensive than** flats.
Bei längeren Adjektiven verwenden Sie *more*.
The weather is **bad** today, it's **worse than** yesterday. Her new flat is really **good**, it's **better than** her last flat.
Die Steigerungsformen von *good* und *bad* sind unregelmäßig.

a Ergänzen Sie die Steigerungsformen in folgenden Sätzen.

1 *(big)* Germany is ______ Switzerland.
2 *(good)* My English is ______ my Italian.
3 *(healthy)* Fruit is ______ chocolate.
4 *(popular)* Coffee is ______ tea.
5 *(bad)* This café is ______ the old one!

b Vergleichen Sie die beiden Männer.

Mark	Paul
1.89 metres 80 kilos fitness – excellent	1.82 metres 88 kilos fitness – OK

1 *(short)* ______
2 *(fit)* ______
3 *(heavy)* ______
4 *(tall)* ______

3.2 Whose

→ G8 (S. 172)

Whose book is it?	It's Sue's book. / It's Sue's.

Lesen Sie die Informationen über John und Sue auf Seite 37. Beantworten Sie dann folgende Fragen.

1 Whose car is the Fiat? ______
2 Whose car is the Volkswagen? ______

4 Round up

Wenn Sie Bilder beschriften oder Post-its an Dinge hängen, hilft Ihnen das, sich Wörter besser einzuprägen.

a Beschriften Sie den Grundriss einer Wohnung.

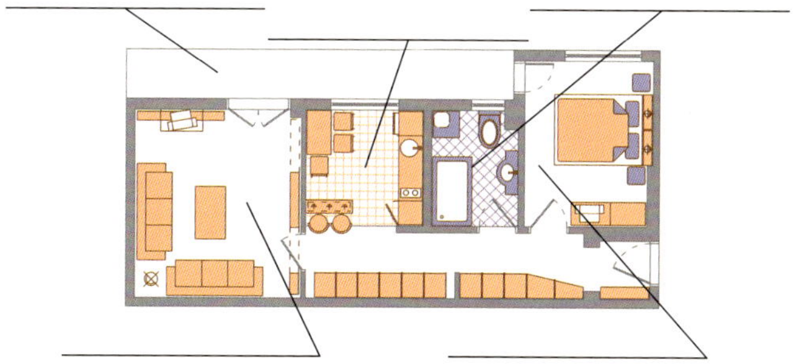

b L2:30 Gestern hat sich eine Frau eine Wohnung angesehen. Im Gespräch mit einem Freund vergleicht sie die neue Wohnung mit ihrer jetzigen Wohnung. Hören Sie zu und ergänzen Sie fehlende Informationen auf den Linien.

	the new flat	her flat
bedrooms		
Which floor?	____th	ground floor
How old?	____ years	____ years
price	£______ / week	£______ / month
balcony	______	no
garage	______	yes

c Folgende Wünsche hat die Frau an ihre neue Wohnung. Was davon bietet die Wohnung? Machen Sie ein Häkchen.

- ☐ one more bedroom
- ☐ a more modern flat
- ☐ a flat on a higher floor
- ☐ a balcony
- ☐ a cheaper flat
- ☐ a garage

d L2:31 Was glauben Sie – hat sie die Wohnung genommen? Hören Sie zu, dann finden Sie es heraus.

S. 185

Jetzt kann ich …

mich nach der Wohnung von jemandem erkundigen.	www: U10A1 CD-R 2: 30
meine Wohnung beschreiben.	www: U10A2 CD-R 2: 29+32
Meinungen anderer Leute zustimmen oder sie ablehnen.	www: U10A3
Vergleiche anstellen.	www: U10A4 CD-R 2: 31

Part B Hotels

Talking about hotels | How to book a hotel room | How to check out of a hotel | Superlatives

Compare a one star hotel and a five-star hotel. Which would you like to stay in? Use the adjectives: comfortable | expensive | nice | beautiful | cheap.

Unusual hotels

1a Here are pictures of three unusual hotels in the USA.

A

B

C

Find out why these hotels are unusual. Work in groups of three.
Student A: Look at page 165.
Student B: Look at page 167.
Student C: Look at page 168.

Now tell your group why your hotel is unusual and any other information you can remember about it.

150 One hundred **and** fifty.
205 Two hundred **and** five.

1b When each person in the group has told the others about his/her hotel, talk about the three hotels.
I'd like to go to the lighthouse hotel / the station hotel / the library hotel because …
I wouldn't like to go to that hotel because …
It sounds interesting / romantic / quiet / fun / …

1c Now talk together in your group. You can look back at the hotel information if you need to. Which hotel (A, B or C) is …

1 the cheapest? ☐
2 the most expensive? ☐
3 the biggest? ☐
4 the quietest? ☐
5 the noisiest? ☐
6 the most romantic? ☐
7 the best hotel for a business meeting? ☐
8 the easiest hotel to travel to from Europe? ☐

The biggest and the best

2 Grammar focus

Superlatives

Short adjectives	**The quietest / biggest** rooms are $150.
Adjectives ending with *-y*	The station hotel is **the noisiest**.
Long adjectives	**The most expensive** hotel is in Manhattan.
good / bad	I think the lighthouse hotel is **the best / the worst**.

2a With a partner, talk about these groups of three items and underline the 'superlative' one in each group.

1 Three expensive hotels: three-star, four-star, five-star.
2 Three big cities: Berlin, Bonn, New York.
3 Three long rivers: the Rhein, the Amazon, the Thames.
4 Three high mountains: the Matterhorn, the Zugspitze, Mount Everest.
5 Three rich countries: Dubai, Switzerland, France.
6 Three important travel documents: ticket, hotel reservation, map.

Compare your answers in class.

2b Complete these sentences about Great Britain with the superlative forms of these adjectives.

busy | expensive | high | old | popular | sunny

1 Ben Nevis is ______________ mountain (1,344 m).
2 Heathrow is ______________ airport (67 million passengers per year).
3 Eastbourne is ______________ town (about 2,000 hours of sunshine per year).
4 Oxford and Cambridge have ______________ universities (about 800 years old).
5 The Langham Hotel in London is ______________ hotel (£6,000 per suite per night).
6 Jack was ______________ name for baby boys from 1996 to 2007 (number one in the list of baby names).

Booking a hotel room

3 Word focus Hotel services and facilities

3a Match the icons with their meanings. Write the numbers in the boxes.

- [ ] babysitting service
- [ ] bar
- [ ] car park
- [ ] family rooms
- [ ] Internet access
- [ ] lift
- [ ] children's play area
- [ ] conference rooms
- [ ] room service
- [ ] swimming pool

3b Which of these services and facilities are the most important for you when you choose a hotel?

4a T2:25 Listen to a man phoning a hotel to book a room. How many people does he book a room for?

4b T2:26 Listen again and fill in the booking form.

Manor Hotel ***Booking form***

○ Single room ○ Double room ○ Family room

Extras: ______ *Arrival date:* ______ *Number of nights:* ______

Price: ______ *○ per night ○ per week ○ per person ○ per room*

Breakfast included? ○ Yes ○ No

5 How to book a hotel room

I'd like to book a double room / single room / family room, please.
… with a bath / shower.
… for two nights.
Is there a swimming pool / lift / bar?
Is the price per person or per room?
Is breakfast included?
What time must I check out?

5a With a partner, practise phoning a hotel to book a room.
Student A: You are the guest. Use these notes to help you.
Student B: You are the hotel receptionist. Help the guest and ask for his/her contact details.

Now change roles.

Phone Tower Hotel and book
1x single + shower
25th Feb, 2 nights
Swimming pool?
Price – incl. breakfast?
Check out?

Phone Grange Hotel
1x double + bath
1st May, 5 nights
Lift? (or room on ground floor?)

6a In Unit 1 of this book, you practised checking *into* a hotel. Here are some phrases you might say or hear when you check *out* at the end of your stay. Which phrases does the receptionist (R) say and which does the guest (G) say?

I'd like to check out, please. ☐	Everything was fine, thank you. ☐	Can I pay with this credit card? ☐
What room number, please? ☐	Did you have anything from the minibar? ☐	Could I have your keycard, please? ☐
Was everything alright? ☐	How would you like to pay? ☐	Can I help you? ☐

6b With a partner, practise checking out of a hotel. Use the phrases above. Take turns to be the guest.

Flexizone

Task Superlative Hotel Awards

a Your task is to design a hotel to win the Superlative Hotel Award. First, as a class, choose a category of hotel:

The best hotel for young people.
The best hotel for business people.
The best hotel for families with small children.

Now work in groups of three. You want to win the Superlative Hotel Award. Talk together and write your ideas here. What can your hotel offer?

Hotel name and place:

Our guests:

Our hotel is:

Our hotel has got:

Our rooms:

Extra services and facilities:

b One person from each group presents their hotel to the rest of the class.

c Which hotel is the best and wins the Superlative Hotel Award?

Your turn Hotels (→ www)

1 How to ...

a Wie Sie ein Hotel beschreiben.
Schreiben Sie die Wörter in die Lücken.

It's | It's a | There are | There's | You can

1 ________ near the airport.
2 ________ a swimming pool.
3 ________ ________ 168 rooms on eight floors.
4 ________ ________ 5-star hotel.
5 ________ ________ see the sea from all the rooms.

b Wie Sie ein Hotelzimmer buchen.
Schreiben Sie die Wörter in der richtigen Reihenfolge.

1 a double room, | to book | please | I'd like
____
2 I'd like | with | a room | to have | a shower
____
3 a room | please | Have you got | for 3 nights, | ?
____
4 is | per night | the room | How much | ?
____
5 breakfast | in the room price | Is | included | ?
____
6 in | Is there | your hotel | a lift | ?
____

c Wie Sie aus einem Hotel auschecken.
Schreiben Sie die Wörter in die Lücken.

didn't have | check out | pay | was | were

1 We'd like to ________ ________, please.
2 We ________ in room 306.
3 The room ________ very comfortable.
4 We ________ ________ anything from the minibar.
5 Can I ________ with this credit card?

L2:32 Hören Sie und überprüfen Sie Ihre Antworten.

L2:33 **Say it like this** Hören Sie und sprechen Sie nach.

2 Word focus

a Hotel rooms and facilities
Schreiben Sie die Wörter in das Kreuzworträtsel.

1 I'd like a room with a 
2 You can phone room ~ and order dinner.
3 The room is £90 ~ night.
4 There is a ~ room for 90–100 people.
5 There's a ~-sitting service.
6 A room for one person is a ~ room.
7 There's a ~ with cold drinks in every room.
8 All the rooms have Internet ~.
9 You can book theatre tickets at the ~.
10 There's a play ~ for children.
11 I'd like a room with a 
12 A room for two people is a ~ room.
13 A room with a third bed for a child is a ~ room.

				1	b						
		2	s								
				3	p						
4	c										
		5	b								
			6	s							
		7	m								
				8	a						
		9	r								
				10	a						
			11	s							
				12	d						
			13	f							

b Important travel documents
Ergänzen Sie die Vokale (a, e, i, o, u) in folgenden Wörtern.

m__p p__ssp__rt h__t__l r__s__rv__t__ __n

t__ck__t

3 Grammar focus

Superlatives

→ G19 (S. 177)

Zunächst ein Blick auf die Grammatik von Unit 10A: Und nun:

A is **cheaper than** B. A is **bigger than** B. A is **sunnier than** B.	But C is **the cheapest**. But C is **the biggest**. But C is **the sunniest**.
A is **more popular than** B.	But C is **the most popular**.
A is **better than** B. A is **worse than** B.	But C is **the best**. But C is **the worst**.

a Schreiben Sie Sätze über die Männer. Verwenden Sie jedes Mal einen Superlativ.

Mark	Paul	Tom
39 years old 1.89 metres 80 kilos fitness – excellent	45 years old 1.82 metres 88 kilos fitness – OK	40 years old 1.80 metres 89 kilos fitness: not good

1 *(old)* Paul is the ____________
2 *(short)* ____________
3 *(young)* ____________
4 *(fit)* ____________
5 *(heavy)* ____________
6 *(tall)* ____________

b Stellen Sie Fragen zu London.

1 You want to have a drink in an old pub. Ask:
Where is the oldest pub in London?
2 You want to eat in a good restaurant. Ask:
____
3 You want to go to an interesting museum. Ask:
____
4 You want to go to a big market. Ask:
____
5 You want to take a photo of a bad modern building in London. Ask:
____
6 You want go to the top floor of a very high building. Ask:
____

4 Round up

a Wann sagt ein Hotelgast folgende Sätze? Bei … der Buchung (A), der Ankunft (B) oder der Abfahrt (C)

1 ☐ Where's the lift?
2 ☐ Thank you very much. See you again next year.
3 ☐ I'm sorry, but have you got a bigger room?
4 ☐ Can you tell me the way to your hotel, please?
5 ☐ What is the earliest time we can arrive?
6 ☐ Can we leave our bags here for an hour or two? Our train is at 4.30.

b Welche Art von Hotel eignet sich am besten für Sie für einen Sommerurlaub am Meer? Machen Sie bei jeder Dreiergruppe ein Häkchen.

1	☐ big and modern	☐ small and modern	☐ small and old
2	☐ near the beach	☐ in the town centre	☐ a long way from the beach
3	☐ for families	☐ for young people	☐ for older people
4	☐ swimming pool	☐ no sports activities	☐ a lot of sports activities
5	☐ all meals always included	☐ breakfast only is possible	☐ no meals included

c L2:34 Sue erzählt von ihrem Lieblingshotel in Griechenland. Hören Sie zu und unterstreichen Sie in Übung 4b die Dinge, die sie an diesem Hotel mag.

d Meinen Sie, dass Sie zusammen mit Sue gerne einen Sommerurlaub verbringen würden?

S. 185

Jetzt kann ich …

ein Hotel beschreiben und darüber sprechen, was es bietet. ○○○ www: U10B1 CD-R 2: 33+35

ein Hotelzimmer buchen. ○○○ www: U10B2 CD-R 2: 36

aus einem Hotel auschecken. ○○○ www: U10B3

Reading Queen Mary's dolls' house

In 1920, Sir Edwin Lutyens, the best architect in Britain, designed a dolls' house for Queen Mary, King George V's wife. Over 1,500 artists and craftsmen worked on the project and made miniature furniture and models of things in Buckingham Palace and Windsor Castle. In 1924, they gave the dolls' house to Queen Mary.

Queen Mary's dolls' house shows how the royal family lived in the 1920s. There are bedrooms, bathrooms, a kitchen and a library, living rooms, a dining room, a wine cellar, a garage and a beautiful garden. And all the details are perfect. The books in the library have got Queen Mary's initials on them – and they are real books! A lot of writers, for example Rudyard Kipling *(The Jungle Book)* and Sir Arthur Conan Doyle *(Sherlock Holmes)* wrote short books for the library. Artists painted miniature pictures for the dolls' house – there is a wonderful portrait of Queen Elizabeth I in the library. And craftsmen made five perfect little bathrooms (with hot and cold water and toilets that flush!). In the wine cellar, there are bottles of wine that are about two centimetres high – and they have real wine in them. And, of course, there's a lift to take the little dolls from the cellar to the bedrooms.

You can see Queen Mary's dolls' house in Windsor Castle. It's a popular tourist attraction and it's probably the most expensive and the most beautiful dolls' house in the world.

Glossary

dining room Esszimmer | craftsmen Handwerker | furniture Möbel | castle Schloss | wine cellar Weinkeller | paint malen | flush spülen | probably vermutlich

Out and About

A family house

'My grandmother, great-grandmother and great-great-grandmother lived in this house and I was born here in 1948. The house is very old – 1703, I think. And it's very big – it's got more than 750 rooms! The garden's big, too – perfect for garden parties. The nearest underground stations are Hyde Park Corner and St. James's Park, so it's central. The only problem is the tourists in the summer … .'

What's the name of the house?

Find the solution in *Out and About*, page 42.

Getting around

Part A Transport

Different ways of travelling | How to ask for train information and buy a ticket | Object pronouns

What's the name of the public transport system in your town (e.g. BVG in Berlin)?
Is the transport system very good / quite good / alright / bad? Take a class vote.

Different ways of travelling

1 Word focus Methods of transport

1a Fill in the missing letters to make the words for different ways of travelling.

bik___ b___s ___ar m___torbi___e p___ane

t___xi tra___n t___am un___er___rou___d

1b With a partner, take turns to ask the questions and answer with a word from the list above. More than one answer is possible for some questions.
Which method of transport …

1 is the fastest?
2 is the cheapest?
3 is the most dangerous?
4 is a good way to keep fit?
5 is the most expensive in your town?
6 isn't very nice in bad weather?
7 can be fast when the roads are very busy?
8 is popular in your town?

1c Match the sentences with the same meaning. Write the numbers in the boxes.

1 I go by plane. 3 I go by bike. ☐ I drive. ☐ I fly.
2 I go by car. 4 I go on foot. ☐ I walk. ☐ I cycle.

I go **by** train | bus | tram | car | plane.
I go **on** foot.

T2:27 **Say it like this** Listen and tick the verb you hear.

1 ☐ walk ☐ work 3 ☐ walked ☐ worked
2 ☐ walking ☐ working 4 ☐ walked ☐ worked

Work with a partner. Take turns to say one of these sentences. Your partner must say which sentence it is.
a) I walked there yesterday. / b) I worked there yesterday.

2a How do these people go to work every day?

1

2

3

2b T2:28 Now listen to the people in the photos. A market research person stops them in the street and asks them how they go to work. Fill in their travel times.

1 _____ minutes 2 _____ minutes 3 _____ minutes

T2:29 Listen again to the first dialogue and write in the missing words in these two questions:

How _________ you usually _________ to work?

How _________ does it _________?

2c Work in small groups. Ask the other people in your group how they go to these places and how long it takes.

work | the town centre | the supermarket | the park | your English lesson | your best friend's house

How do you usually go to …?

How long does it take?

Mum's taxi

3a Look at this keyring. What do you think *Mum's taxi* is?

T2:30 Listen to a mother and fill in her calendar with the activities that her children, Anna and Sam, do.

3b Read these sentences that the mother says about her week. Replace the words for the people in brackets with the right word from the list below.

him | her | us | them

1 I drive __________ (my daughter) to the leisure centre.

2 I take __________ (my son) to football.

3 I take __________ (my children) to the music school.

4 They can drive __________ (my husband and me) everywhere.

T2:31 Listen again and check your answers.

4 Grammar focus

Object pronouns

Can you take **me** to the leisure centre, please?
I can take **you** to the leisure centre, if you like.
I take **him** to football.
I take **her** to kickboxing.
They bought **it** for me.
They can drive **us** everywhere.
I take **them** to their drama group.

4a Complete these sentences with the right word:

her | him | it | me | them | us

1 My car was at the garage yesterday, so my neighbour took __________ to work.

2 My son goes to school and I take __________ there every morning.

3 When my parents go on holiday, I usually drive __________ to the airport.

4 My wife hasn't got a car, so I take __________ to work.

5 When my car is dirty, my son washes __________.

6 Our boss often invites __________ all to his house.

Check your answers with a partner.

4b Now fill in **one** of these sentences about your life and tell the class.

My __________ *hasn't / haven't* got a car, so I take *him / her / them* to __________.

I / we haven't got a car, so my __________ takes *me / us* to __________.

At the station

5a Look at this departures board at Paddington station in London. What time of day is it – morning, afternoon or evening?

18:57	**Plymouth**	Platform 4	(arr Plymouth 22:30)	ON TIME
19:03	**Swansea**	Platform 8	(arr Swansea 23:11)	ON TIME
19:10	**Heathrow**	Platform 6	(arr Heathrow 19:33)	ON TIME
19:22	**Newbury**	Platform 11	(arr Newbury 20:34)	EXPECTED 19:40
19:44	**Oxford**	Platform 9	(arr Oxford 21:25)	ON TIME

We usually use the 24 hour clock for timetables.
18:45 – eighteen forty-five 20:05 – twenty oh five

5b Are these sentences true (T) or false (F)?

1 ☐ The train to Newbury leaves from platform 8.
2 ☐ The 19:03 usually arrives in Swansea at 23:11.
3 ☐ The 18:57 goes to Oxford.
4 ☐ The train to Heathrow airport is late.
5 ☐ The train to Newbury is on time.

Check your answers with a partner. Then work together and correct the false statements, e.g. *The train to Newbury leaves from platform 11.*

I'd like a single to London zoo, please.

6 How to ask for train information and to buy a ticket

When's the next train to (town)?
Which platform?
Is the train on time?
How much is a single / return / day return?
I'd like a single / return, please.

If you have problems, just ask for help:
Excuse me.
Can you help me, please?
I don't understand (the timetable / the information / the ticket system).

6a With a partner, take turns to be the passenger and the train information person. Student A: You want to go to Plymouth. Student B: You want to go to Newbury. Use the departures board in exercise 5 to ask and answer questions, and then buy a ticket.

Flexizone

A Write a sentence about yourself, your family or friends with *like, help, love, work with, do sport with,* with object pronouns, e.g. *I like her. / He helps me.* Read your sentence to the class and they can guess who the people in your sentence are, e.g.
I like her. → *I think it's your boss. Or is it your sister?*
He helps me. → *I think it's your brother. Or is it your neighbour?*

B Talk in small groups. What do you do when you travel? *When I drive, I always listen to music. When I go by tram, I usually look out of the window. What about you?*

Your turn Transport (→ www)

1 How to ...

Schreiben Sie die Wörter in die Lücken.

a Wie Sie über Reisen sprechen.

by | Do | How | How often | on | on holiday | go | very

1 How do you ________ to work? – I go ________ bus.

2 ________ do you usually go ________ ________? – I usually fly.

3 ________ you go to the supermarket by car? – No, I don't. I go ________ foot.

4 ________ ________ do you travel by train? – Not ________ often.

b Wie Sie über Fahrpläne sprechen.

19:10	Heathrow	Platform 6	(arr Heathrow 19:33)	ON TIME
19:22	Newbury	Platform 11	(arr Newbury 20:34)	EXPECTED 19:40

at | from | late | on | to

1 The 19.10 goes ________ Heathrow.

2 It leaves ________ platform 6.

3 It arrives ________ 19.33.

4 It is ________ time.

5 The train to Newbury is more than an hour ________.

c Wie Sie Auskünfte zu Zügen einholen.

How long | platform | What time | When | Which

1 ________ is the next train to Newbury?

2 ________ ________ is the fast train to Newbury?

3 Which ________ does it leave from?

4 ________ platform does it arrive at?

5 ________ ________ does it take?

L2:35 Hören Sie und überprüfen Sie Ihre Antworten.

L2:36 **Say it like this** Hören Sie und sprechen Sie nach.

2 Word focus

a Methods of transport

Schreiben Sie die Wörter für die Verkehrsmittel.

1 
b ________

2 
p ________

3 
t ________

4 
t ________

5 
t ________

6 
u ________

b At the station

Schreiben Sie die Wörter in das Kreuzworträtsel.

1 The train leaves from ~ 3.
2 If you don't understand, ask for ~.
3 The times of the trains are in the ~.
4 When you are on the train, you're a ~.
5 A ticket to go there and back is a ~ ticket.
6 The ~ train to London only takes half an hour.
7 The train isn't early or on time, it's ~.
8 Buy a ~ before you get on the train.
9 Look at the departure ~ for information.
10 To go there and not come back by train – buy a ~ ticket.

1 p
2 h
3 t
4 p
5 r
6 f
7 l
8 t
9 b
10 s

3 Grammar focus

3.1 Object Pronouns

➔ G3 (S. 171)

She takes **me** to the supermarket every Friday.
Can I phone **you** tomorrow?
I phoned **him** yesterday.
They see **her** every weekend.
She bought **it** last week.
They gave **us** a lot of books for the school library.
I saw **you** two at the station this morning.
We asked **them** a lot of questions.

Pronomen im Objektfall verändern sich im Englischen nie:
me = *mir* und *mich*,
you = *dir* und *dich* usw.

a Welches Bild passt zu welchem Satz? Schreiben Sie die Buchstaben in die Kästchen.

- [ ] She gave her a drink.
- [ ] She ate it at lunchtime.
- [ ] She ate them at lunchtime.
- [ ] She gave him a drink.
- [ ] She saw him yesterday.
- [ ] She saw her yesterday.

b Beantworten Sie folgende Fragen. Ersetzen Sie die kursiv gesetzten Wörter mit einem Objektpronomen aus der Grammatikbox oben.

1 Where did he buy *his shoes*? (in Italy)
He ______
2 When did she last see *her mother*? (yesterday evening)
______
3 Where did they park *their car*? (in the street)
______
4 What did they give *their father* for Christmas? (some socks)
______
5 What did she ask *you and the other students* in your class? (a lot of questions)
______

3.2 *By* or *on*?

➔ G21 (S. 178)

I went **by** train / bike / car / plane / … | I went **on** foot.

Schreiben Sie Sätze mit *by* oder *on*, die das Gleiche bedeuten wie die vorgegebenen Sätze.

1 He flew to Paris. ➔ He went ______
2 She drove to work. ➔ She ______
3 They walked to the pub. ➔ They ______

4 Round up

a L2:37 Hören Sie die Ansagen und Gespräche. Wo haben sie stattgefunden? Schreiben Sie die Zahlen in die Kästchen.

the airport ☐ ☐ the station ☐ ☐ a bus stop ☐ ☐

b Beantworten Sie die Fragen zu folgender Zugkarte.

Wenn Sie die Information auf einer Zugkarte verstehen müssen, schauen Sie zuerst auf das, was Sie leicht erkennen können – Daten, Preise, andere Zahlen usw.

1 When did the passenger travel? ______
2 Where did the passenger travel from? ______
3 Where did the passenger travel to? ______
4 Was the ticket for a child? ______
5 How much was the ticket? ______

S. 186

Jetzt kann ich …

über Reisen sprechen.	○○○	www: U11A1 CD-R 2: 39+43
über Fahrpläne sprechen.	○○○	www: U11A2
Auskünfte zu Zügen einholen.	○○○	www: U11A3
Informationen auf einer Zugkarte verstehen.	○○○	www: U11A4

Part B Going the right way

Warnings and instructions | Signs and symbols | Asking for and giving directions | Imperatives

Which of these do *you* use to help you find the way: a map or street plan, a compass, an online route planner, satellite navigation (sat nav)? Or do you ask someone for directions?

Warnings and instructions for travellers

1a Look at this photo of a warning sign. Can you guess the meaning of the opposite adjectives *wide* and *narrow*?

1b Now read about it.

> **Warning – sat nav!**
>
> The village of Exton has got a new warning sign. It warns drivers: *Don't follow your sat nav!*
>
> Because there's a mistake in the electronic information system, the satellite navigation (sat nav) system in cars sends drivers along Beacon Hill Lane, a very narrow road. And then big, wide cars get stuck.
>
> The people in Exton hope that the signs will stop drivers before they go into the lane. 'We didn't have a problem before everyone got sat nav,' said one villager.
>
> Exton's message to drivers is: *Stop! Look! Think! If a lane is only six feet* wide, don't try to drive along it!*
>
> * 1.80m

What does the article tell us? Tick the correct box in each pair.

1 ☐ Sat navs always give good directions.
☐ Sat navs don't always give good directions.

2 ☐ Big cars have problems in Beacon Hill Lane.
☐ Motorbikes have problems in Beacon Hill Lane.

3 ☐ The people in Exton want to help drivers.
☐ The people in Exton don't like drivers.

4 ☐ Don't use your sat nav.
☐ Use your sat nav – but use your head, too.

2 **Grammar focus**

Imperatives

Stop! Look! Think!
Don't follow your sat nav!
Don't try to drive along a very narrow lane!

2a Here are some more signs for drivers and other travellers. Match the signs to the imperatives and write the numbers in the boxes.

☐ don't walk	☐ stop
☐ do not enter	☐ wait here for the bus
☐ drive slowly	☐ walk
☐ go in here	☐ walk on the left, cycle on the right
☐ go left	☐ walk on the left, stand on the right

2b Fill in the gaps with the right imperatives in these warnings and instructions for driving in Britain.

Drive | Stop | Take | Don't drink | Don't park | Don't use

1 ______________ alcohol before you drive.
2 ______________ at a red light.
3 ______________ on a double yellow line.
4 ______________ your mobile.
5 ______________ a break when you're tired.

And the most important instruction for driving in Britain:

6 ______________ on the left!

Directions

3 Word focus Things on a map

3a Fill in the missing letters to make the names of the things you find on a map or street plan.

1
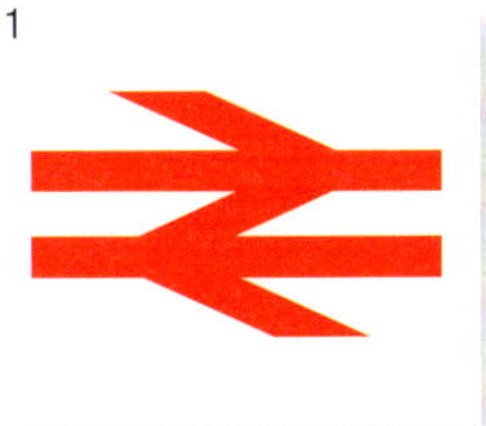
s _ t _ _ _ _

2

un _ _ _ _ _ _ o _ d

3

b _ _ s _ _ _

4

c _ _ _ _ h

5

t _ _ _ _ re

6

h _ _ p _ _ _ l

7

z _ o

8

c _ _ p _ _ _

9

t _ _ i st _ _ d

10

f _ _ _ _ _ _ _ l
s _ a _ ium

11

c _ stle

12
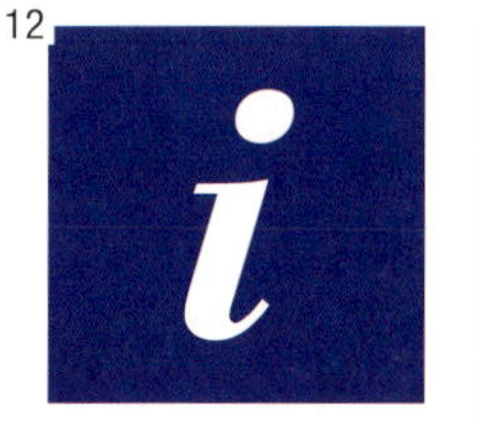
t _ _ ris _
i _ f _ _ _ _ _ _ _ _ _ _
off _ c _

Check your answers in class.

3b With a partner, take turns to ask and answer these questions:

Where in a town can you …

1 find a taxi?
2 get information about the town?
3 buy a train ticket?
4 see a musical?
5 watch a football match?
6 see an elephant?

Where can you buy a train ticket?
At the station.

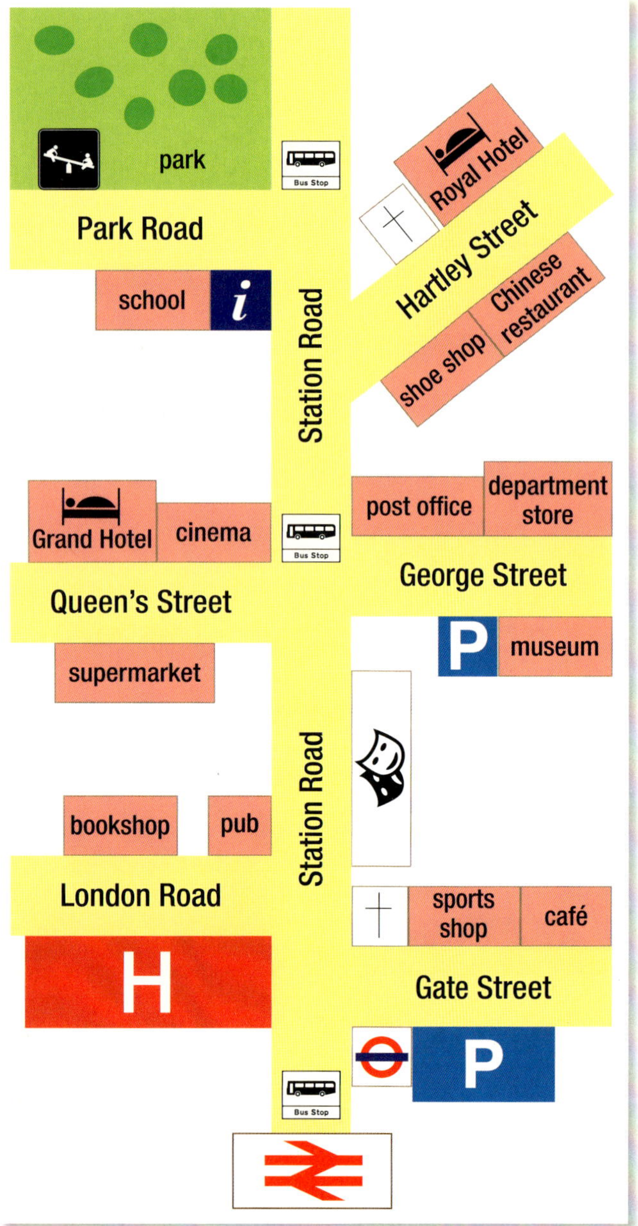

4a Look at this street plan. With a partner, answer the questions about the town.

1 How many churches are there?
2 How many bus stops are there in Station Road?
3 What's next to the school?
4 What's opposite the bookshop?
5 What's on the corner of Station Road and George Street?
6 Where's the underground station?
7 Where's the supermarket?
8 Where's the museum?

4b T2:32 Three passengers arrive at the station. They all ask for directions. Listen and follow the directions. Where does each person want to go?

1 ____________________
2 ____________________
3 ____________________

4c Look at the directions to the department store and fill in the missing words.

along | left | past | right | second

Go __________ Station Road.

Take the __________ street on the __________.

That's George Street.

Go along George Street.

Go __________ the post office, and the store is on the __________.

T2:33 Listen again to the first dialogue and check your answers.

5 How to ask for and give directions

Excuse me. Can you tell me the way to the department store, please?
Go along Station Road.
Take the first / second / third street on the left / right.
Go left / right into George Street.
Go past the post office.
The store is on the left / right.

To check that you understand, say:
Can I repeat that, to check?

5a With a partner, practise asking for and giving directions from the station to other places on the street plan.

5b With a different partner, take turns to ask for and give directions from different starting points on the street plan.
Can you tell me the way from (the museum) to (the bookshop) please?

Flexizone

Task Transport questionnaire

Fill in the gaps to make questions about transport.

Do you like going on holiday by car ?

I love it.	I like it.	I don't like it.	I never go on holiday by car.

How often do you ______________________________ ?

Every day.	Once or twice a week.	Not very often.	Never.

How did you ______________________________ last week?

By car.	By bike.	By public transport.	I walked.

When did you last ______________________________ ?

Earlier today.	Yesterday.	Last week.	A long time ago.

Now walk around the class and ask your questions to five other students. Tick (✔) their answers.

Then sit down and tell the class one of your results, e.g.
Two people like going on holiday by car, two people don't like it and one person loves it.

Your turn Going the right way (→ www)

1 How to …

Schreiben Sie die Wörter in die Lücken.

a Wie Sie nach dem Weg fragen.

can you | is there | know | near | the nearest | the way

1 Excuse me, __________ __________ tell me __________ __________ to the station, please?

2 Excuse me, do you __________ where __________ __________ bus stop is?

3 Excuse me, __________ __________ a post office __________ here?

b Wie Sie den Weg beschreiben.

Schreiben Sie die Wörter in der richtigen Reihenfolge.

along | Go | into | left | on | past | right | Take

1
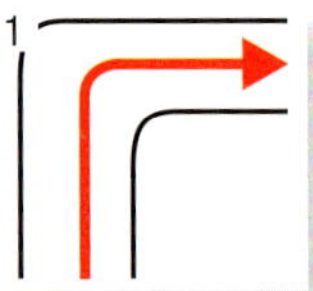

2
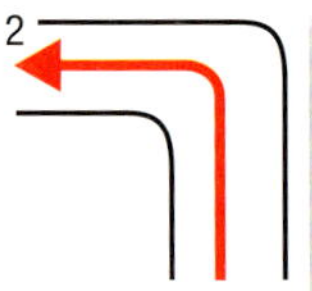

3
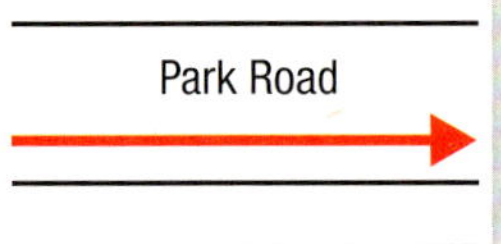

4
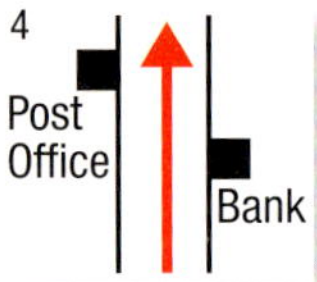

5

6
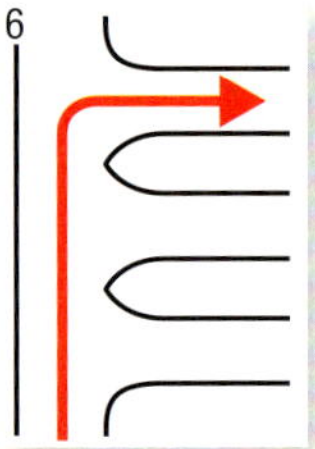

1 Go __________.

2 Go __________.

3 Go __________ Park Road.

4 Go __________ the bank.

The Post Office is __________ the left.

5 __________ right __________ Station Road.

6 __________ the third street on the right.

L2:38 Hören Sie und überprüfen Sie Ihre Antworten.

L2:39 **Say it like this** Hören Sie und sprechen Sie nach.

2 Word focus

Places in my town

Wo gibt es Folgendes in der Stadt? Schreiben Sie die Wörter auf die Zeilen.

1 I can buy a stamp here: the _ _ _ _ _ _ _ _ _ _

2 I can see a musical here: the _ _ _ _ _ _ _

3 I can get a street plan here: the _ _ _ _ _ _ _ _ _ _ _ _ _ _ _ _ _ _ _ _ _ _ _ _

4 I can drink a beer here: the _ _ _

5 I can sleep here: the _ _ _ _ _

6 I can see a doctor here: the _ _ _ _ _ _ _ _

7 I can watch a football match here: the _ _ _ _ _ _ _ _ _ _ _ _ _ _ _

8 I can get married here: the _ _ _ _ _ _

9 I can have dinner here: the _ _ _ _ _ _ _ _ _ _

10 I can see a film here: the _ _ _ _ _ _

11 I can leave my car here: the _ _ _ _ _ _ _

12 I can see a giraffe here: the _ _ _

13 I can buy some roses here: the _ _ _ _ _ _ _ _ _ _

14 I can buy a train ticket here: the _ _ _ _ _ _ _

15 I can buy fresh fruit and vegetables here: the _ _ _ _ _ _

16 I can have a picnic here: the _ _ _ _

17 I can buy some US dollars here: the _ _ _ _

18 I can find a taxi here: the _ _ _ _ _ _ _ _ _

19 I can buy a dictionary here: the _ _ _ _ _ _ _ _

20 I can buy all our food here: the _ _ _ _ _ _ _ _ _ _ _

21 I can do some sports here: the _ _ _ _ _ _ _ _ _ _ _ _ _

22 I can get on a bus here: the _ _ _ _ _ _ _

3 Grammar focus

3.1 Imperatives

→ G20 (S. 177)

Use the sat nav.	**Park** your car in the car park.
Don't use a map.	**Don't park** your car in the street.

Die Befehlsform ist immer gleich – egal, ob Sie mit einer Person oder mit mehreren Personen sprechen.

a Ein Teilnehmer eines Englischkurses hat ein paar Probleme mit Englisch. Was können die anderen ihm raten? Schreiben Sie die Verben in die Sätze.

Ask | Buy | Come | Do | Read | Speak | Watch

1 ____________ your *Compass* book at home.

2 ____________ to your English neighbour in English.

3 ____________ your DVDs in English.

4 ____________ your homework every week.

5 ____________ to the lesson every week.

6 ____________ an English newspaper once a week.

7 ____________ the others in the class for help.

b Was sagen ihm die anderen Kursteilnehmer, was er **nicht** tun soll? Schreiben Sie verneinte Befehle in die Sätze.

be | speak | worry

1 ____________ ____________ about mistakes.

2 ____________ ____________ nervous in class.

3 ____________ ____________ German in the lesson.

3.2 Prepositions

→ G21 (S. 178)

Folgende Präpositionen können Sie verwenden, um über Dinge in der Stadt zu sprechen.

at | in | on | opposite | to

Schreiben Sie sie in die Antworten. Verwenden Sie jede Präposition einmal.

1 Where did you see him? – ____________ the bus stop.

2 Where's the shoe shop? – ____________ the corner of Park Road and Station Road.

3 Where did you go yesterday evening? – ____________ the theatre.

4 Where's the tourist information office? – ____________ the bank.

5 Where did you meet your friends? – ____________ the pub.

4 Round up

a Beantworten Sie die Fragen zum Zentrum von Wantage.

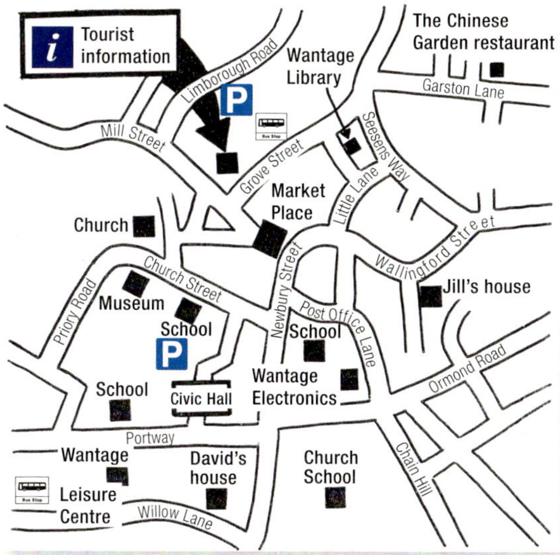

1 Where is Wantage Electronics?

It's ____________.

2 Where does David live? ____________.

3 Does Jill live in the same street? ____________.

b L2:40 Hören Sie, wie Jill zwei Leuten den Weg beschreibt. Wohin wollen sie? Sie befinden sich bei der Bushaltestelle in Grove Street in der Nähe der Touristeninformation.

1 The woman wants to go to the ____________.

2 The man wants to go to the ____________.

Sie sind im Museum und jemand fragt Sie nach dem Weg zu Wantage Electronics. Notieren Sie die Wegbeschreibung.

Go out of the museum and go ____________

S. 186

Jetzt kann ich ...

nach dem Weg fragen und Wegbeschreibungen verstehen.	www: U11B1 CD-R 2: 45
den Weg beschreiben.	www: U11B2 CD-R 2: 44
über Orte in der Stadt und auf einem Stadtplan sprechen.	www: U11B3

Reading Ten facts about the Tube

1. The London underground (the Tube) opened on January 10th, 1863.
2. Over 50% of the network is not underground, it's above ground.
3. It's ten degrees hotter on the underground than above ground.
4. The London underground has got 268 stations and about 400 km of tracks.
5. About 3 million people travel on the underground every day.
6. Victoria is the busiest station with 85 million passengers each year.
7. There's only 0.25 km between Leicester Square and Covent Garden – it can be quicker to walk!
8. Earl's Court had the first escalator on the underground (1911) – there are now 409 escalators and 112 lifts.
9. About half a million mice live in the London underground.
10. Only one baby was born in the underground and that was in 1924. Her name? **T**helma **U**rsula **B**eatrice **E**leanor.

Glossary
above oberhalb | degree Grad | track Gleis | passengers Passagiere | between zwischen | escalator Rolltreppe | mice Mäuse

Out and About
Transport quiz

1 Which is the oldest underground train system?
a) ☐ the Métro in Paris b) ☐ the Subway in New York c) ☐ the Tube in London

2 Who was the first president of the Ford Motor Company?
a) ☐ Gerald Ford b) ☐ Harrison Ford c) ☐ Henry Ford

3 Where must you drive on the left?
a) ☐ In Canada b) ☐ In Japan c) ☐ In Sweden

4 Where is Schipol airport?
a ☐ Amsterdam b) ☐ Brussels c) ☐ Vienna

5 Which train station can you see in the Harry Potter films?
a) ☐ Euston b) ☐ King's Cross c) ☐ Paddington

Find the solution in *Out and About*, page 48.

Making plans

Part A Plans for different seasons

The seasons and the weather I Talking about plans for the future (1) I How to make small talk I *going to* future (1), positive sentences

Which of these are the best and worst subjects for small talk when you meet someone new at a party?
family I work I politics I personal problems I sport I religion I money I the weather

The seasons and the weather

1 Word focus The seasons

Match the names of the seasons to the pictures. Write the numbers in the boxes.
1 autumn I 2 spring I 3 summer I 4 winter

2 Word focus The weather

Match the weather icons to the sentences. Write the numbers in the boxes.

1
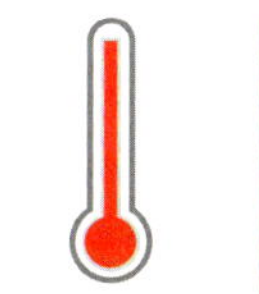
2
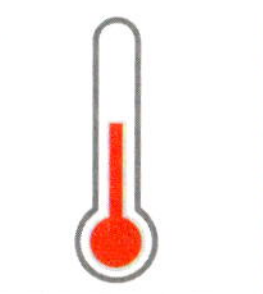
3
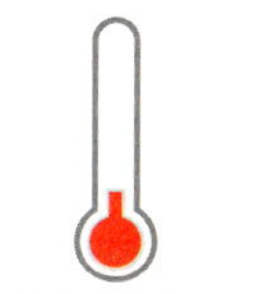
4

5

6
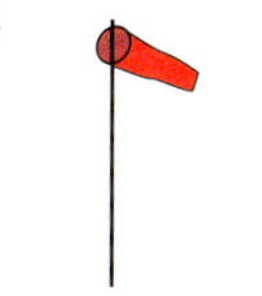
7

8

☐ It's often cloudy. ☐ It's often sunny. ☐ It's often windy. ☐ It rains a lot.
☐ It's often cold. ☐ It's often warm. ☐ It's often hot. ☐ It snows a lot.

3 How to talk about the weather and the seasons

What's the weather like in the (autumn)?
It's often (cold).
It's sometimes (warm).
It rains / snows a lot.

3a Walk around the class and ask the other students *What's your favourite season?* and make a group with the other students who like the same season as you.
Then talk together in your group about your favourite season – the weather, the festivals, the food and the different activities you like doing. Then tell the class.

Plans for the weekend

4a T2:34 Listen to David and Jill at work, on four different Friday afternoons in the year. They talk about their plans for the weekend. What season is it in each dialogue? Write the numbers of the dialogues in the boxes.

☐ spring ☐ summer ☐ autumn ☐ winter

4b T2:35 Listen again and write the missing words in these sentences:

1 a Jill's going to c__________ her house.
b She's going to o__________ all the windows.

2 a David's going to s__________ some time with his wife.
b They're going to s__________ at home.

3 a Jill's going to s__________ under a tree.
b She's going to d__________ iced tea.

4 a David and Mel are going to w__________ in the garden.
b Their friend's going to m__________ cider with the apples.

5 Grammar focus

going to future (positive sentences)

I'm going to sit in the garden tomorrow.
She's going to drink iced tea at the weekend.
We're going to eat Chinese food on Sunday.

going to + the verb *go*
going to go to is a bit long and difficult to say, so we usually just say *going to*.
We're going to go to a restaurant tomorrow. →
We're going to a restaurant tomorrow.

T2:36 **Say it like this** Listen and repeat these words:
winter, weather, warm, windy

Now listen to this:
Next week we're going to Wales with our friends, William and Wendy. We're going to walk along the west coast. We want the weather to be windy because we're going to have a windsurfing lesson on Wednesday.

Take turns with a partner to read the paragraph out loud.

5a Read these sentences and tick any that are true about your plans for the next few days.

1 ☐ I'm going to do something relaxing.
2 ☐ I'm going to spend a lot of time outside.
3 ☐ I'm going to do something very active or sporty.
4 ☐ I'm going to do something creative.
5 ☐ I'm going to do my English homework.
6 ☐ I'm going to work hard.

5b Think about *when* you're going to do these things.

tomorrow
tonight
on Sunday
next week
at the weekend

I'm going to do something relaxing tonight. I'm going to watch my favourite TV programme.

Now tell a partner what you're going to do and when you're going to do it.

5c There are six students in an afternoon class. Each student has got plans for after the class. Talk to your partner. Where are the students going after the class and what are they going to do there?

She's going to the supermarket and she's going to buy some food.

1 Nina's got a shopping list.
2 Trudy's got her tennis bag.
3 Ludovic's got the cinema page from the local newspaper.
4 Sebastian's got a letter, but it hasn't got a stamp.
5 Kirsty's got a photo of a man and the address of a café.

What are you going to do after your English class today?

Making small talk

6a T2:37 Listen to a doctor called Giulia Lunardi, from Rome. She's at a conference in Amsterdam. She makes small talk with some of the other doctors at the conference. Tick the subjects they talk about in each dialogue.

Dialogue 1 (Giulia and Josh)
- ☐ a person they both know
- ☐ their plans for the weekend
- ☐ the weather

Dialogue 2 (Giulia and Dina)
- ☐ the last time they met
- ☐ the conference
- ☐ the city of Amsterdam

Dialogue 3 (Giulia and Tahira)
- ☐ the weather
- ☐ the city of Amsterdam
- ☐ their plans for the weekend

6b Match the halves of the sentences they say.

1 I think you know	☐ today!
2 It's very warm	☐ first visit to Amsterdam?
3 I think we met in	☐ my colleague, Professor Lamarr.
4 It's a very	☐ London last year.
5 Is this your	☐ plans for the weekend?
6 Have you got any	☐ good conference.

T2:38 Listen and check your answers.

7 How to make small talk

It's very warm / hot / cold today.
I think we met …
I think you know my colleague, (name).
It's a good conference / a great party.
Is this your first visit to (town)?

Where are you from in (country)?
Have you got any plans for the weekend / later?

Yes, it is. Much better / colder than yesterday.
Yes, we did. We …
Yes, I do. He's/She's …
Yes, it is. It's …
Yes, it is. / No, it isn't. I came here …

Maybe you can't understand every word of a conversation but to show that you're interested, say: *Really? That's interesting.*

7a You're at a conference in Scotland. Walk around the classroom and meet the other guests. Introduce yourself (look back at Unit 1 if you need help) and make small talk. After a minute, your teacher will give a signal for you to find a new person to talk to.

Flexizone

A Play a game round the class. The first student says *Tomorrow I'm going to (get up at six o'clock).* The next student says *Tomorrow I'm going to get up at six o'clock and then I'm going to (have breakfast).* Continue round the class, until you come back to the first student. He/She must try to remember the list for the full day.

B Work in small groups. Think of things you could say to make small talk with an American visitor to your town, a friend's new partner, a new student in the class, a new neighbour, the person next to you on a plane.

Your turn Plans for different seasons (→ www)

1 How to …

Schreiben Sie die Wörter in die Lücken.

a Wie Sie über das Wetter sprechen.

cold | like | snows | today | weather | yesterday

1 What's the ______________ usually ______________ there?

2 It's often ______________ .

3 It usually ______________ a lot in winter.

4 What's the weather like there ______________ ?

5 What was the weather like there ______________ ?

b Wie Sie über Pläne für die Zukunft sprechen.

after | at | next | on | tomorrow evening | tonight

We're going to visit them …

______________ the class ______________ .

______________ ______________ .

______________ Friday 22nd.

______________ the weekend.

______________ winter.

c Wie Sie bei einer Konferenz Smalltalk-Gespräche führen.

are you | first | from | great | know | very good

1 It's a ______________ conference.

2 The speakers are ______________ ______________ .

3 I think you ______________ my colleague, Ben.

4 Is this your ______________ conference here?

5 Where ______________ ______________ ______________ ?

Finden Sie die richtigen Antworten für die Sätze 1–5.

☐ Yes, they are.
☐ No, it's my third or fourth, I think.
☐ A very small place near Manchester.
☐ Yes, it's really interesting.
☐ Oh yes, I know him very well.

L2:41 Hören Sie und überprüfen Sie Ihre Antworten.

L2:42 **Say it like this** Hören Sie und sprechen Sie nach.

2 Word focus

a The weather

Ergänzen Sie die Vokale (a, e, i, o, u) in den Wetterwörtern.

c l __ __ d y	s n __ w
c __ l d	s __ n n y
h __ t	w __ r m
r __ __ n	w __ n d y

L2:43 Hören Sie, wie das Wetter heute ist, und entscheiden Sie, welches der Adjektive von oben passt.

1 ______________ 4 ______________

2 ______________ 5 ______________

3 ______________ 6 ______________

b The seasons

Ergänzen Sie die Wörter für die anderen Jahreszeiten in England und in Neuseeland.

	England	New Zealand
Dec-Feb	winter	
March-May		
June-Aug		winter
Sept-Nov		

Welche der Aussagen beschreiben England (E), welche Neuseeland (NZ)? Kreisen Sie ein. Über welche Jahreszeit wird jeweils gesprochen?

1 People go to the beach a lot and sometimes have their Christmas dinner on the beach. E NZ ______________

2 The trees are beautiful reds and browns. Only one of the months has got 31 days. E NZ ______________

3 It's never warm and the shortest month of the year is in this season. E NZ ______________

4 It rains a lot and is cold and grey. Two of the months have only four letters in their names. E NZ ______________

3 Grammar focus

3.1 *Going to* future (positive sentences) → G22 (S. 178)

I'm going to see her at the weekend.
You're going to finish your work tomorrow.
She's/He's going to stay at home tonight.
It's going to rain on Sunday.
We're/You're/They're going to buy a house next year.

a Schreiben Sie Sätze über Jills Pläne nächste Woche. Ordnen Sie sie den Kategorien *at home*, *in town* oder *in her office* zu.

buy	a special dinner
cook	some shoes
have a meeting	her friends
meet	in the garden
send	some emails
read a book	with her boss

at home
1 She's going to ______
2 ______

in town
3 ______
4 ______

in her office
5 ______
6 ______

3.2 *Going to* future (positive sentences) → G22 (S. 178)

Going to go klingt etwas schwerfällig. Deshalb wird *to go* weggelassen: *We're going ~~to go~~ to Paris next weekend.*

They're going to the theatre on Saturday.
They're going to see a musical.

Schreiben Sie über John.
1 pub / Friday evening – meet some friends

______

Schreiben Sie über sich und die anderen Kursteilnehmer.
2 lesson / next *(day?)* – speak English

______

4 Round up

a L2:44 Heute Abend bleiben John und Sue zu Hause. Hören Sie zu und wählen Sie die korrekte Information.

1 They're going to
a) ☐ visit some friends in Wales.
b) ☐ visit some friends in France.
c) ☐ stay at home.

2 They're going to
a) ☐ travel by train.
b) ☐ drive to Wales.
c) ☐ travel a bus.

3 It's going to
a) ☐ be very warm.
b) ☐ rain.
c) ☐ be cloudy.

4 Their friends are going to return to France
a) ☐ next summer.
b) ☐ at Christmas.
c) ☐ in the spring.

5 Sue's going to
a) ☐ be very happy when her friends go back to France.
b) ☐ be very unhappy when her friends go back to France.
c) ☐ visit her friends every year in France.

b Schreiben Sie auf, was Sie tun werden:

tomorrow morning: ______

tomorrow evening: ______

at the weekend: ______

S. 186

Jetzt kann ich ...

über das Wetter sprechen. — www: U12A1, CD-R 2: 48

über meine Pläne in der Zukunft sprechen. — www: U12A2, CD-R 2: 49

an einem Smalltalk-Gespräch teilnehmen. — www: U12A3, CD-R 2: 51

Part B A weekend away

Talking about plans for the future (2) | How to make an informal phone call | *going to* future (2) negative sentences and questions

What are you going to do next weekend? Is it going to be a special weekend (e.g. a birthday or a wedding anniversary) for anyone in the class?

Plans for a special weekend

1a Look at this advert for a hotel. Talk to a partner. What has the hotel got? Would you like to stay there? Why / why not?

Linton Court Hotel and Spa ****

- Indoor pool
- Sauna
- Massages – aromatherapy, reiki, shiatsu, hot stone therapy, Indian head massage
- Beauty salon
- Large gardens and parkland
- Golf
- Restaurant
- Cocktail bar
- Free bottle of champagne per room.

1b T2:39 David is going to the hotel with his wife, Mel. Jill, his PA, sees the brochure.
Listen and cross out the wrong information.

1 David and Mel are going to celebrate *his 50th birthday / their 20th wedding anniversary.*
2 David and Mel like doing *the same things / different things.*

1c T2:40 Listen again. Tick (✓) the things that David and / or Mel are going to do this weekend and put a cross (✗) for the things they aren't going to do.

	David	Mel
have a massage	☐	☐
have a manicure	☐	☐
play golf	☐	☐
relax	☐	☐
talk about his/her job	☐	☐

Now talk to a partner and say what they are / aren't going to do.

She's going to … — *She isn't going to …*
He's going to … — *He isn't going to …*
They're going to … — *They aren't going to …*

2 Grammar focus

going to future (questions and negative sentences)

What are you going to do next weekend?
Are you going to celebrate?
I'm not going to have a manicure.
She isn't going to play golf.
They aren't going to talk about their jobs.

2a What are you going to do later today, after your English class? Work with a partner. Take turns to ask and answer the questions. Tick (✓) the things your partner is going to do and put a cross (✗) for the things he/she isn't going to do.
Are you …

- ☐ going to cycle home?
- ☐ going home by public transport?
- ☐ going to cook a meal?
- ☐ going to do your English homework?
- ☐ going to use a computer?
- ☐ going to the supermarket?
- ☐ going to watch television?

Tell the class one thing your partner is going to do and one thing he/she isn't going to do.

2b With a partner, write three questions starting with *Are you going to …?* to ask your teacher about his/her plans for after the class and/or for next weekend. Ask your teacher your questions. At the end, each student must say one thing that the teacher is or isn't going to do.

A phone call

3a It's Sunday evening. David and Mel are at home again after their anniversary weekend. Do you think they enjoyed it? What do you think happened? Talk in small groups and write three sentences. Then read them to the class.

played / didn't play
drank / didn't drink
had / didn't have
relaxed / didn't relax
talked / didn't talk

We think that David …
We think that Mel …
We think that David and Mel …

3b T2:41 Listen to a phone call and check your answers. Which group had the most correct sentences?

3c T2:42 Listen again and put these phrases in the order they come in the phone call. Write the numbers 1–6 in the boxes.

- ☐ See you tomorrow. Bye!
- 1 Hello?
- ☐ Yes, just a minute, please.
- ☐ It's Jill here, from David's office.
- ☐ Is David there, please?
- ☐ Thanks for phoning.

4 **How to** make an informal phone call.

Hello. It's (name) here, from (place).
Is (name) there, please?
Just a minute, please.
Thanks for phoning.

English speakers don't usually give their name when they answer the phone at home or their personal mobile. They just say *Hello?*

4a Work in groups of three. Take turns to phone each other and have a short conversation. First, Student A wants to speak to Student B, but Student C answers the phone. Then change roles.

Here are some ideas for reasons to call:
To ask about his/her plans for next weekend.
To organise a meal in a restaurant for the class at the end of this course.
To ask for help with your English homework.
To invite him/her to a party.

Compass characters

Make two teams. In your team, write sentences about the characters in this course book. Some of the sentences must be true, and some must be false. You need at least one sentence per player.

- ______________________
- ______________________
- ______________________
- ______________________
- ______________________
- ______________________

Take turns to ask your questions to the other team. Give a point for each correct answer.

Flexizone

Game Compass puzzle

- Make four teams: North, South, East and West.
- In your team, write words from this course in the spaces in your point of the compass. You can use the word lists at the back of the book (pages 194–221) to help you. You can also use other forms of the words e.g. plurals, comparatives, superlatives, adverbs, past tenses, *-ing* forms.
- Write a sentence for each of your words. It can be a statement, a question, a phrase from a dialogue – anything from the course.
  e.g. The South team choose the word SEE. They can write:
  What did you (SEE) at the cinema last night? or
  You can (SEE) Mount Fuji from the top of the Landmark Tower.
- Talk to someone from another team.
- Read your sentences to the other player, so that he/she can guess your words.
- Listen to the other player's sentences and guess his/her words. When you get a correct answer, write the word in the grid.
- When you've both got all five answers, find a new partner from another team.
- The winner is the first person to fill his/her Compass puzzle.

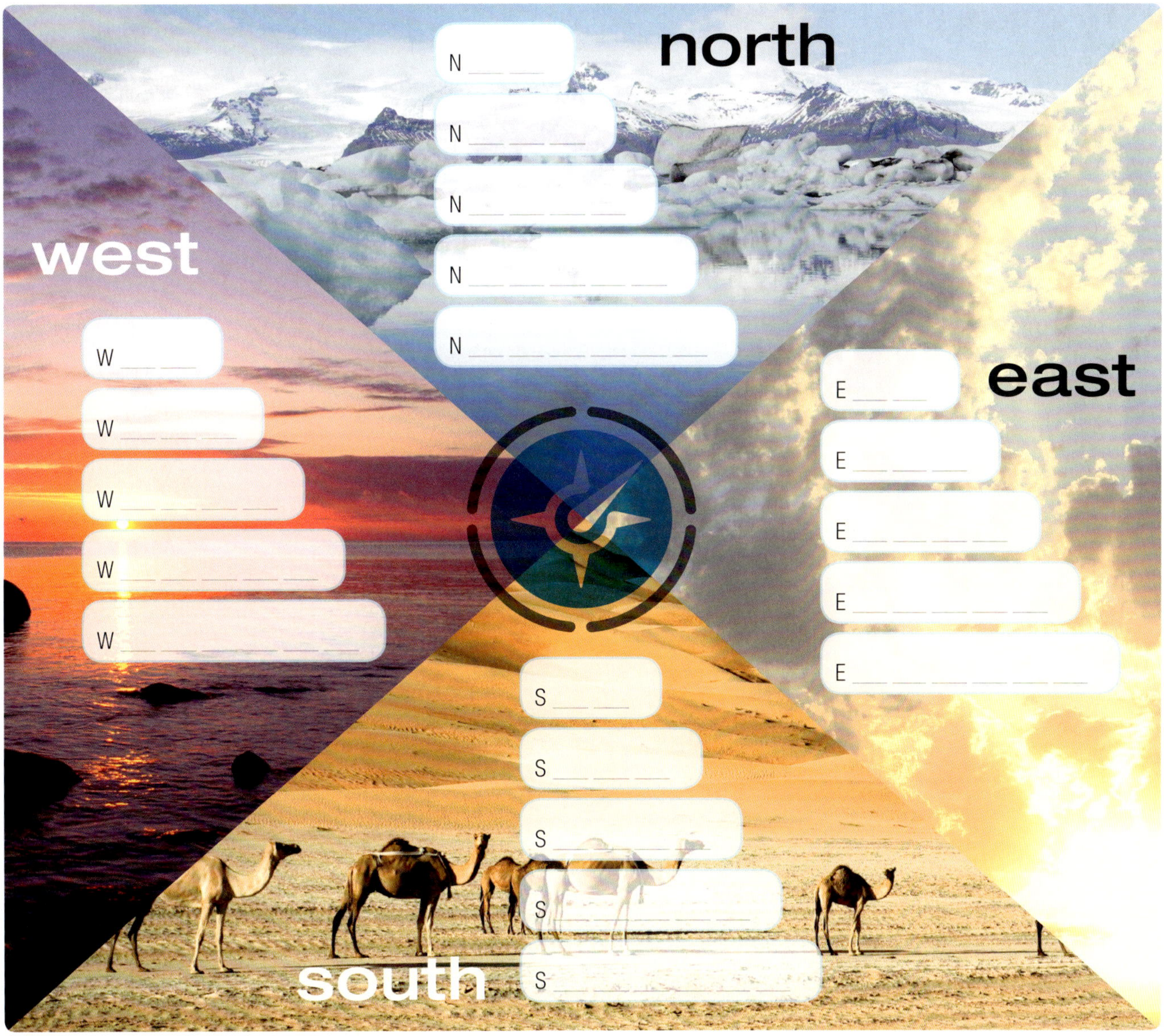

Your turn A weekend away (→ www)

1 How to …

Schreiben Sie die Wörter in die Lücken.

a Wie Sie über einen Wochenendkurzurlaub sprechen.

Are | away | going | going to | next weekend | to stay | We're

1 We're ____ to Liverpool ____ ____.

2 We're going ____ ____ in a spa hotel.

3 ____ ____ ____ celebrate our wedding anniversary.

4 ____ you going ____ next weekend?

b Wie Sie ein privates Telefongespräch führen.

fine | how | is John there | it's Kath here | minute | you

Sue: Hello.
Kath: Hello, ____ ____ ____.

Sue: Hello Kath, ____ are you?

Kath: I'm ____ thanks, and ____?
Sue: I'm fine, too.

Kath: Sue, ____ ____ ____, please?

Sue: Yes, he is. Just a ____.
…

Bye | for calling | See you | welcome

John: Hello, Kath.
Kath: Hi, John.
John: Is there a problem with tomorrow?
Kath: No, but we're going to leave an hour later, at ten.

John: Oh that's good. Thanks ____ ____.

Kath: You're ____. ____ ____ tomorrow. Bye.

John: ____.

L2:45 Hören Sie und überprüfen Sie Ihre Antworten.

L2:46 **Say it like this** Hören Sie und wiederholen Sie die Sätze in a. Hören Sie dann Dialog b und lesen Sie Kaths Teil des Telefongesprächs mit.

2 Word focus David and Mel's weekend in a spa hotel

Welche der blauen Wörter passen zu den roten? Schreiben Sie die Nummern in die Kästchen.

1 play	5 a wedding	☐ bar	☐ television
2 watch	6 a beauty	☐ massage	☐ of champagne
3 a head	7 a cocktail	☐ golf	☐ a manicure
4 have	8 a free bottle	☐ salon	☐ anniversary

3 Grammar focus

***Going to* future** → G22 (S. 178)

Are you going to stay at home next weekend?	No, **I'm not going to stay** at home. **I'm going to visit** my sister.
Is your brother going to be there, too?	No, **he isn't going to be** there. **He's going to stay** at home.
Are your friends going to have a holiday? What **are they going to do**?	No, **they aren't going to have** a holiday. **They're going to work** all summer.

Ergänzen Sie die Verben: positiv (+), negativ (–) und Fragen (?)

1 (–) She ____ ____ ____ come to the lesson next week.

2 (?) ____ she ____ ____ phone us?

3 (+) She' ____ ____ ____ phone next Friday.

4 (?) ____ they ____ ____ drive here?

5 (–) They ____ ____ ____ drive here.

6 (+) They' ____ ____ ____ walk.

S. 187

Jetzt kann ich …

über einen Wochenend-kurzurlaub sprechen.	www: U12B1
ein privates Telefon-gespräch führen.	www: U12B2 CD-R 2: 55+56
Fragen zu Plänen für die Zukunft stellen.	www: U12B3 CD-R 2: 52+53+54

4 Round up **All about me!**

Jetzt am Ende von Compass A1 können Sie schon viel über sich und Ihr Leben sagen. Vervollständigen Sie die Sätze … über sich.

Ich kann persönliche Informationen geben:

I'm from ______________________.

I work ______________________.

My address is ______________________.

My phone number is ______________________.

My birthday is on ______________________.

Ich kann mich selbst beschreiben:

I've got ______________________ eyes.

I've got *long / short* hair. I'm *very tall / tall / not very tall.*

Ich kann sagen, was ich mag und nicht mag:

I like ______________________.

______________ I don't like ______________

______________________.

Ich kann über die Stadt, in der ich lebe, sprechen:

I live in ______________. There are a lot of ______________ in my town. There's a ______________________ in my town.

There isn't a ______________ in my town.

Ich kann sagen, wie oft ich etwas tue:

I *usually / often / sometimes / never* drink wine at lunchtime. I eat in a restaurant *every day / once a week /* ______________________.

Ich kann meine Wohnung beschreiben:

I live in a ______________. I haven't got a ______________.

There are ______________________ in my *house / flat.*

My *house / flat* is very ______________________.

Ich kann über meinen letzten Urlaub sprechen:

I went to ______________________.

I stayed ______________________.

The weather was ______________. I *saw / bought / liked* ______________________.

Ich kann über meine Familie sprechen:

I'm from a *big / small* family. I've got a ______________________. I haven't got any ______________________.

Ich kann über meine Pläne für die Zukunft sprechen:

I'm going to ______________________ this evening. I'm not going to ______________________ tomorrow. My friend(s) and I are going to ______________________ at the weekend.

Gut gemacht! Viel können Sie schon über sich sagen, nicht wahr?

Reading Going to Sydney

Sydney, New South Wales, Australia

Climate:	Average summer temperature: 25°
Population:	4,000,000
Tourist highlights:	Sydney Opera House, Sydney Harbour
Beaches:	70, including Bondi beach

A young English couple, Emma Nunn of Kent and Raoul Christian of London, both 19, wanted to have a holiday in Australia. They bought their tickets on the Internet – two tickets to Sydney. They were happy to find cheap tickets for £740 each.

They flew from Heathrow airport and, after six hours, they landed in Nova Scotia, Canada. Then they changed planes and flew on to Sydney. But when the plane landed in Sydney, Emma and Raoul realised it was the wrong Sydney! They were in Sydney, Canada, not Sydney, Australia!

Sydney, Nova Scotia, Canada

Climate:	Mild, 80 foggy days per year
Population:	26,083
Tourist highlights:	Museums, churches, parks
Beaches:	150m long Mira Gut Beach – 14 km south of the city

An airline spokesperson said, 'Mistakes like this happen more often than you think. I know one man who wanted to go to Dhaka in Bangladesh – and he bought a ticket to Dakkar in West Africa! Then there was a woman at Heathrow airport who wanted to go to Turkey – and they gave her directions to Torquay in south-west England! And in Germany, a travel agent confused Bayreuth with Beirut! You really must be careful when you book tickets.'

Glossary

average durchschnittlich I population Bevölkerung I harbour Hafen I including einschließlich I flew on flogen weiter I realise erkennen I foggy neblig I airline spokesperson Sprecher der Fluggesellschaft I travel agent Reisebüro

Out and About

What's the word?

Write the letters on the lines.

The first letter's in WARM but isn't in RAIN. W M
The second's in WINTER but isn't in SPRING.
The third letter's in MAY but not in JULY.
The fourth's in SEPTEMBER but not in NOVEMBER.
The fifth is in HOT but isn't in COLD.
The sixth is in SUMMER but isn't in AUTUMN.
The last letter's in RAIN but isn't in WINDY.

Find the solution in *Out and About*, page 51.

Diese Testübungen orientieren sich an den Aufgabenformaten der Prüfung *telc English A1*. Bitte markieren Sie Ihre Antworten mit einem Querbalken (–) in den Antwortabschnitten rechts neben den Aufgaben.

1 Language elements

Markieren Sie (–) die richtige Antwort **a)** oder **b)** im Antwortabschnitt.

My new flat is ___1___ the second floor. It is more ___2___ than my old flat but it's wonderful. I ___3___ have a balcony before and there ___4___ a garage for my car ... and now I've got a balcony and a garage and the flat is ___5___ than my old one. I ___6___ for a flat for six months and this flat was the ___7___ one I saw. I'm ___8___ to have a party next weekend. Would you ___9___ to come? Please come, but please ___10___ bring a present! I've got everything I need.

1 a) in b) on
3 a) don't b) didn't
5 a) big b) bigger
7 a) good b) best
9 a) like b) please

2 a) expensive b) cheap
4 a) was b) wasn't
6 a) looked b) look
8 a) want b) going
10 a) you b) don't

Nun noch ein paar Informationen zu der Wohnung. Markieren Sie (–) die richtige Antwort **a)** oder **b)** im Antwortabschnitt.

The flat is in the ___11___ popular part of town.
The living room is the ___12___ room.
___13___ flat is it? – It's my friend's.
When did your friend buy ___14___?
The best thing is that it's ___15___ a great restaurant.

11 a) more b) most
12 a) sunny b) sunniest
13 a) Whose b) Who
14 a) them b) it
15 a) next b) opposite

1

Language elements

	a)	b)
1		
2		
3		
4		
5		
6		
7		
8		
9		
10		
11		
12		
13		
14		
15		

= ______ / 15

2 L2:47 Listening comprehension

Lesen Sie zunächst die Situationen und die Aussagen, die ihnen folgen. Hören Sie dann die Aufnahme. Markieren Sie (–) die richtige Antwort **True (T)** oder **False (F)** im Antwortabschnitt.

16 *Situation:*
The man is at the hotel reception.
This is the last day of his holiday.

17 *Situation:*
You are at the station to meet a friend from London.
Your friend's train is on time.

18 *Situation:*
A woman is on the phone to a man who wants a new flat.
The man wants to buy a flat.

19 *Situation:*
Your friend came home from her holiday yesterday.
She had a wonderful holiday.

20 *Situation:*
You are in London. You ask a man where the bus to Heathrow Airport leaves from.
Now you know where the bus stop is.

2

Listening comprehension

	T	F
16		
17		
18		
19		
20		

= ______ / 5

3 Situational responses

Part A L2:48

Sehen Sie sich zunächst die Erwiderungen **a) – d)** an.
Hören Sie dann die Aufnahme.
Markieren Sie (–) die richtige Erwiderung **a)**, **b)**, **c)** oder **d)** im Antwortabschnitt.

21 ______
22 ______
23 ______

a) His name's Johnson, I think.
b) Yes, I think so, too.
c) He's on holiday this week.
d) I'm fine thanks, and you?

Part B L2:49

Sehen Sie sich zunächst die Erwiderungen **e) – h)** an.
Hören Sie dann die Aufnahme.
Markieren Sie (–) die richtige Erwiderung **e)**, **f)**, **g)** oder **h)** im Antwortabschnitt.

24 ______
25 ______
26 ______

e) It's here, on the right.
f) A single or a return?
g) For three nights.
h) A single or a double?

3 Situational responses

Part A				
21	a)	b)	c)	d)
22	a)	b)	c)	d)
23	a)	b)	c)	d)
Part B				
24	e)	f)	g)	h)
25	e)	f)	g)	h)
26	e)	f)	g)	h)

= ______ / 6

4 Reading comprehension

Lesen Sie zunächst die Fragen 27 – 30. Lesen Sie dann die E-Mail von Ihren Freunden aus Rom.
Markieren Sie (–) die richtige Antwort **True (T)** oder **False (F)** im Antwortabschnitt.

Hello from Rome!

It's great here - and I'm happy to see a new city ... Jack came here about 10 years ago, but I didn't come with him.

We arrived yesterday. The flight wasn't very good. The weather was bad when we left London - very cold and windy. But when we arrived here it was sunny and warm!

We've only got three more days - and there is a lot to see here. We're off to see the Sistine Chapel this morning.

The hotel is fine - a bit expensive for what it is. But it's right in the centre of everything and so we can walk to a lot of the tourist attractions ... so that's OK.

See you next week.

Love,
Sabine

27 This is Sabine's first visit to Rome.

28 The weather in London was better than in Rome.

29 Jack and Sabine are in Rome for a week.

30 Their hotel is much too expensive.

4 Reading comprehension

	T	F
27		
28		
29		
30		

= ______ / 4

total

= ______ / 30

S. 187

Unit 1 Part B Exercise 7b (Page 16)

Student A: Stellen Sie Ihrem Partner / Ihrer Partnerin Fragen und tragen Sie die Informationen ein.

Surname: ______________________

First name: ______________________

First name: ______________________

Nationality: ______________________

Berichten Sie nun Ihrem Partner / Ihrer Partnerin.

This is Melina and Corey Johnson. They're from Dallas, Texas.

Unit 6 Part A Exercise 6 (Page 73)

Student A: Lesen Sie den Text über eine ungewöhnliche Bar.

Remote lounge, Manhattan, New York.

With 60 video cameras and 120 television screens, this bar is the perfect place to watch people. You can control the cameras and watch the other guests on the screen at your table – and they can watch you, too! There's a phone on each table, so you can call the guests at other tables.

+++ **Good for:** voyeurs, flirting, meeting people, cocktails.

Berichten Sie den Mitgliedern Ihrer Gruppe über die Bar.

Nachdem jede Person in der Gruppe von seinem/ihrem Restaurant oder von seiner/ihrer Bar erzählt hat, sprechen Sie gemeinsam in der Gruppe. Wohin würden Sie gerne gehen?

I'd like to go to that restaurant because …
I wouldn't like to go to that restaurant because …
It sounds interesting / silly / fun / good / bad.
Would you like to go there, Ben?

Unit 1 Part B Exercise 7b (Page 16)

Student B: Berichten Sie Ihrem Partner / Ihrer Partnerin.

This is Eileen and Frank Howden.
They're from Melbourne, Australia.

Stellen Sie Ihrem Partner / Ihrer Partnerin nun Fragen und tragen Sie die Informationen ein.

Surname: ______________________

First name: ______________________

First name: ______________________

Nationality: ______________________

Unit 6 Part A Exercise 6 (Page 73)

Student B: Lesen Sie den Text über ein ungewöhnliches Restaurant.

La Locanda dei Girasoli, Rome.

Good quality Italian food – pizzas, pasta, salads, meat and fish. This 100-seat restaurant is an initiative to give work to people with Down's syndrome. These friendly young people do a very good job and enjoy the contact with the customers.

+++ **Good for:** great food and friendly service.

Berichten Sie den Mitgliedern Ihrer Gruppe über das Restaurant.

Nachdem jede Person in der Gruppe von seinem/ihrem Restaurant oder von seiner/ihrer Bar erzählt hat, sprechen Sie gemeinsam in der Gruppe. Wohin würden Sie gerne gehen?

I'd like to go to that restaurant because …
I wouldn't like to go to that restaurant because …

It sounds interesting / silly / fun / good / bad.
Would you like to go there, Ben?

Unit 6 Part A Exercise 6 (Page 73)

Student C: Lesen Sie den Text über eine ungewöhnliche Bar.

Absolut Icebar, Mayfair, London.

London's coolest bar! In a normal bar, the barman asks 'Would you like ice in your drink?' Here, your drink is *in* the ice. Everything here is made of ice – the bar, the tables, and even the glasses. It can be a hot day in London, but the temperature is always minus five in the Icebar.

+++ **Good for:** cool atmosphere

Berichten Sie den Mitgliedern Ihrer Gruppe über die Bar.

Nachdem jede Person in der Gruppe von seinem/ihrem Restaurant oder von seiner/ihrer Bar erzählt hat, sprechen Sie gemeinsam in der Gruppe. Wohin würden Sie gerne gehen?

I'd like to go to that restaurant because …
I wouldn't like to go to that restaurant because …
It sounds interesting / silly / fun / good / bad.
Would you like to go there, Ben?

Unit 7 Part A Exercise 2b (Page 85)

Student A: Fragen Sie Student B nach dem Preis des Koffers, der Sonnencreme und der Stifte. Schreiben Sie die Preise auf die Etiketten.
How much is / are …?

Unit 6 Part A Exercise 6 (Page 73)

Student D: Lesen Sie den Text über ein ungewöhnliches Restaurant.

Colonial tramcar restaurant, Melbourne.

A first class restaurant – in a tram! Have dinner and a tour of the city at the same time. The trams have one-way glass windows, so you can see out, but people in the street can't see in. The atmosphere is formal but friendly and the decor is elegant in a colonial style.

+++ **Good for:** elegant sightseeing.

Berichten Sie den Mitgliedern Ihrer Gruppe über das Restaurant.

Nachdem jede Person in der Gruppe von seinem/ihrem Restaurant oder von seiner/ihrer Bar erzählt hat, sprechen Sie gemeinsam in der Gruppe. Wohin würden Sie gerne gehen?

I'd like to go to that restaurant because …
I wouldn't like to go to that restaurant because …

It sounds interesting / silly / fun / good / bad.
Would you like to go there, Ben?

Unit 7 Part A Exercise 2b (Page 85)

Student B: Fragen Sie Student A nach dem Preis des T-Shirts, der Handtücher und der Postkarten. Schreiben Sie die Preise in die Etiketten.
How much is / are …?

Unit 8 Part B Exercise 4 (Page 103)

Gruppe A: Vervollständigen Sie die Fragen mit den Wendungen: *Is there* | *do you watch* | *Do you buy* | *Did you watch*

Do you love television?

__________ a television in your bedroom? Yes ☐ No ☐

__________ a TV magazine every week? Yes ☐ No ☐

How often __________ ...

- documentaries? Often ☐ Sometimes ☐ Never ☐
- detective series? Often ☐ Sometimes ☐ Never ☐
- romantic films or series? Often ☐ Sometimes ☐ Never ☐
- other drama series? Often ☐ Sometimes ☐ Never ☐
- talk shows? Often ☐ Sometimes ☐ Never ☐

__________ television after 11 o'clock last night? Yes ☐ No ☐

Suchen Sie sich einen Partner / eine Partnerin aus Gruppe B. Stellen Sie ihm/ihr Fragen und vermerken Sie die Antworten im Fragebogen. Beantworten Sie dann seine/ihre Fragen. Ermitteln Sie nun das Ergebnis.

Yes / Often = 2 points ☐
Sometimes = 1 point ☐
No / Never = 0 points ☐
Your partner's score ☐

Scores

0–5 You don't watch much television. You do other things in your free time.

6–12 You enjoy watching television, but you only watch programmes that interest you.

13+ You *love* watching television!

Unit 10 Part B Exercise 1 (Page 128)

Student A: Lesen Sie den Text über ein ungewöhnliches Hotel.

The East Brother Light Station Hotel

This hotel is on an island near San Francisco. It's an active lighthouse.

A stay at the 130-year-old lighthouse includes champagne when you arrive (after a 10 minute boat trip to the island), dinner with wine, and a full breakfast the next morning.

There is also a tour of the island, so you can learn about the work of this wonderful building. Guests can stay in one of five double rooms. Listen to the sea and relax!

Rooms: US$250 – US$350 per night

Gehen Sie zurück zu S. 128 und erzählen Sie Ihrer Gruppe von diesem Hotel.

Unit 8 Part B Exercise 4 (Page 103)

Guppe B: Vervollständigen Sie die Fragen mit den Wendungen: *Is there* | *do you watch* | *Did you watch* | *Do you spend*

Do you love television?

______________ a television in your kitchen? Yes ☐ No ☐

______________ more than four hours in front of the TV every day? Yes ☐ No ☐

How often ______________ …

• sport?	Often ☐	Sometimes ☐	Never ☐
• action films or series?	Often ☐	Sometimes ☐	Never ☐
• comedy films or series?	Often ☐	Sometimes ☐	Never ☐
• reality shows?	Often ☐	Sometimes ☐	Never ☐
• the news?	Often ☐	Sometimes ☐	Never ☐

______________ television at breakfast this morning? Yes ☐ No ☐

Suchen Sie sich einen Partner / eine Partnerin aus Gruppe A. Beantworten Sie seine/ihre Fragen. Dann stellen Sie ihm/ihr Ihre Fragen und vermerken Sie die Antworten im Fragebogen. Ermitteln Sie nun das Ergebnis.

Yes / Often = 2 points ☐
Sometimes = 1 point ☐
No / Never = 0 points ☐
Your partner's score ☐

Scores

0–5 You don't watch much television. You do other things in your free time.
6–12 You enjoy watching television, but you only watch programmes that interest you.
13+ You *love* watching television!

Unit 9 Part B Game (Page 117)

From the top of the Landmark Tower you can see Mount Fuji.

Unit 4 Part A Exercise 5 (Page 49)

Student B: Beantworten Sie diese Fragen und ermitteln Sie das Ergebnis. Haken ✓ Sie die Kästchen ab, wenn Ihre Antwort *ja* ist.

Are you a lark?

	You	Your partner
Do you get up before 9 o'clock on Sundays?		
Do you feel tired in the evening?		
Do you have a good breakfast?		
Do you leave parties before the end?		
Do you wake up before your alarm?		
Score:		

Student A wird Ihnen nun seine/ihre Fragen stellen. Geben Sie eine Kurzantwort *Yes, I do* oder *No, I don't.*

Stellen Sie jetzt Student A Ihre Fragen und ermitteln Sie das Ergebnis.

Vergleichen Sie Ihre Ergebnisse für beide Fragenblöcke und entscheiden Sie, ob Sie und Ihr Partner / Ihre Partnerin „Nachteulen" oder „Lerchen" sind. Wie viele Kursteilnehmer sind „Lerchen" und wie viele „Nachteulen"?

Unit 10 Part B Exercise 1 (Page 128)

Student B: Lesen Sie den Text über ein ungewöhnliches Hotel.

The Historic Union Station Hotel, Indianapolis

This hotel is in an old train station, America's First 'Union Station' in Indianapolis. The building is still an active station and guests can often hear trains.

It has 275 bedrooms, including 26 rooms in Pullman sleeper cars. Guests can also enjoy the Grand Hall, the restaurant and bar, the swimming pool and fitness room.

The hotel is popular with business people and has meeting rooms and conference facilities.

Rooms: US$150 – US$250 per night

Gehen Sie zurück zu S. 128 und erzählen Sie Ihrer Gruppe von diesem Hotel.

Unit 4 Part A Exercise 5 (Page 49)

Student A: Beantworten Sie diese Fragen und ermitteln Sie das Ergebnis. Haken ✓ Sie die Kästchen ab, wenn Ihre Antwort *ja* ist.

Student B wird Ihnen nun seine/ihre Fragen stellen. Geben Sie eine Kurzantwort *Yes, I do* oder *No, I don't.*

Stellen Sie jetzt Student B Ihre Fragen und ermitteln Sie das Ergebnis.

Vergleichen Sie Ihre Ergebnisse für beide Fragenblöcke und entscheiden Sie, ob Sie und Ihr Partner / Ihre Partnerin „Nachteulen" oder „Lerchen" sind. Wie viele Kursteilnehmer sind „Lerchen" und wie viele „Nachteulen"?

Are you an owl?	You	Your partner
Do you go to bed after 11 o'clock on weekdays?		
Do you feel tired in the morning?		
Do you work better after lunch?		
Do you need strong coffee in the morning?		
Do you watch late night films on television?		
Score:		

Unit 10 Part B Exercise 1 (Page 128)

Student C: Lesen Sie den Text über ein ungewöhnliches Hotel.

The Library Hotel, New York

The Library Hotel in Manhattan has ten floors, 60 rooms and 6,000 books.

Each of the bedrooms has books on a different subject, from Astronomy to Zoology. Guests with a special interest can book the room for their special subject, or you can take a chance and maybe find a new interest.

Have a coffee and read or write in the quiet public rooms or in the garden.

Rooms: US$350 – US$500 per night

Gehen Sie zurück zu S. 128 und erzählen Sie Ihrer Gruppe von diesem Hotel.

GO Grammar terms Grammatikbezeichnungen

Englisch	Deutsch / Lateinisch
Adjective	Eigenschaftswort / Adjektiv
Adjective of manner	Eigenschaftswort der Art und Weise
Adverb	Umstandswort / Adverb
Adverb of frequency	Umstandwort der Häufigkeit
Adverb of manner	Umstandwort der Art und Weise
Article	Geschlechtswort / Artikel
Comparative	1. Steigerungsstufe / Komparativ
Consonant	Mitlaut / Konsonant
Countable noun	Zählbares Hauptwort/Nomen/Substantiv
going to future	Zukunft mit *going to*
Imperative	Befehlsform / Imperativ
Infinitive	Grundform / Infinitiv
Irregular verb	Unregelmäßiges Zeitwort/Verb
Negative sentence	Verneinter Satz
Noun	Hauptwort / Nomen / Substantiv
Object pronouns	Persönliches Fürwort / Personalpronomen / Objektpronomen
Past simple	Einfache Form der Vergangenheit / Imperfekt / Präteritum
Personal pronoun	Persönliches Fürwort / Personalpronomen
Plural	Mehrzahl / Plural
Positive sentence	Aussagesatz / bejahter Satz
Possessive pronoun	Besitzanzeigendes Fürwort / Possessivpronomen
Possessive 's (Genitive)	Besitzanzeigendes 's / Besitzfall / Genitiv
Preposition	Verhältniswort / Präposition
Present simple	Einfache Form der Gegenwart / Präsens
Pronoun	Fürwort/ Pronomen
Question	Frage
Regular verb	Regelmäßiges Zeitwort/Verb
Short answer	Kurzantwort
Singular	Einzahl / Singular
Subject pronoun	Persönliches Fürwort / Personalpronomen / Subjektpronomen
Superlative	2. Steigerungsstufe / Superlativ
Uncountable noun	Nicht zählbares Hauptwort/Nomen/Substantiv
Verb	Zeitwort / Verb
Vowel	Selbstlaut / Vokal

G1 Present simple: *be* Einfache Form der Gegenwart: *be* ↺ U1A, U1B

a) question	b) positive sentences	c) negative sentences
Am I late?	**I'm** late	**I'm not** late.
Are you German?	**You're** German.	**You aren't** German.
Is he French?	**He's** French.	**He isn't** French.
Is she nice?	**She's** nice.	**She isn't** nice.
Is it a French car?	**It's** a French car.	**It isn't** a German car.
Are we OK?	**We're** OK.	**We aren't** OK.
Are you English?	**You're** English.	**You aren't** American.
Are they Greek?	**They're** Greek.	**They aren't** Turkish.
	'm = am 're = are 's = is	'm not = am not aren't = are not isn't = is not

	d) short answers	
Are you German?	Yes, **I am**.	No, **I'm not**.
Is he nice?	Yes, **he is**.	No, **he isn't**.
Are you English?	Yes, **we are**.	No, **we aren't**.
Are they from Berlin?	Yes, **they are**.	No, **they aren't**.

Kurzantworten sind höflicher, als nur mit *Yes* oder *No* zu antworten: *Is she English? – Yes, she is.*
Bei bejahten Kurzantworten verwendet man nie Kurzformen. Beispiel: *Yes, I am* **nicht** ~~*Yes, I'm*~~.

G2 The artikel Der Artikel ↺ U2A

2a *A/an* ein/eine

a stamp, **a s**tudent	**an E**nglish stamp, **an A**merican student

a steht vor Wörtern, die mit Mitlauten (b, c, d, f, g …) beginnen, *an* steht vor Wörter, die mit Selbstlauten (a, e, i, o, u) beginnen.
Bei Berufsangaben verwendet man *a/an*: *He's a teacher.*

2b *The* der/die/das

the book, **the** school	**the** English book, **the** American school

Das Wort *the* wird immer gleich geschrieben, nur die Aussprache ändert sich.
Vor Mitlauten; *the* [ðə] *book.* Vor Selbstlauten: *the* [ði] *English book.*
Allgemein gilt: Kein *the* vor Personen- und Straßennamen: *Peter lives in Bridge Road.*

G3 Pronouns Fürwörter

a) subject (wer) ⮌ U1A, U1B	b) object (wen/wem) ⮌ U11A	c) possessive (wessen) ⮌ U1A, U1B
I am from Manchester.	He phoned **me**.	**My** phone number is 0161 4236019.
You are from Austria.	I know **you**.	**Your** name is Schmitz.
He is from London.	We like **him**.	**His** name is Andrew.
She is from Paris.	I saw **her** in Paris.	**Her** house is in Paris.
It is a nice dog.	We like **it**.	**Its** name is Fido.
We are English.	They met **us** in London.	**Our** name is Thompson.
You are American.	She teaches **you** German.	**Your** teacher is nice.
They are from Athens.	I met **them** in Greece.	**Their** house is in Athens.

I schreibt man immer groß.
Die Form *you* benutzt man für die 2. Person Einzahl (Deutsch „du") und Mehrzahl (Deutsch „ihr"). Im Englischen gibt es keine Sie-Form.
Persönliche Fürwörter (Objekt) sind unveränderlich im Englischen: *me* = *mir* und *mich*, *you* = *dir* und *dich* usw.

G4 *Is there a/an …? There is a/an … – Are there any …? There are some …* ⮌ U2A, U2B

Is there a bank near here?	**Yes, there is.**	**There's a** bank in West Street.
Is there an Italian café in your town?	**No, there isn't.**	**There isn't an** Italian café near here.
Are there any good restaurants?	**Yes, there are.**	**There are some** good restaurants in the town centre.
	No, there aren't.	**There aren't any** really good restaurants here.
		there's = there is

There is … / There are … = Es gibt …
a steht vor Hauptwörtern in der Einzahl, die mit Mitlauten beginnen: b, c, d, f … .
an steht vor Hauptwörtern in der Einzahl, die mit Selbstlauten beginnen: a, e, i, o, u.
some steht vor Hauptwörtern in der Mehrzahl in bejahten Sätzen.
any steht vor Hauptwörtern in der Mehrzahl in verneinten Sätzen und in Fragen.

G5 Countable and uncountable nouns

Zählbare und unzählbare Hauptwörter ⮌ U6B

Things you can count	Things you can't count
Have you got **any** cakes?	Have you got **any** orange juice?
We haven't got **any** cakes.	We haven't got **any** orange juice.
We've got **some** sandwiches.	We've got **some** apple juice.
How many ham sandwiches have you got?	**How much** apple juice have you got?
Not many ham sandwiches.	**Not much** apple juice.
We've got **a lot of** cheese sandwiches.	We've got **a lot of** mineral water.
How many = Wie viele	How much = Wieviel

any steht vor a) Hauptwörtern in der Mehrzahl in verneinten Sätzen und Fragen,
b) unzählbaren Hauptwörtern in verneinten Sätzen und Fragen

G6 Nouns: singular and plural

Hauptwörter: Einzahl und Mehrzahl ⮌ U2B

	singular	plural
regular	park, house, church, city	park**s**, house**s**, church**es**, cit**ies**
irregular	person, child, man	**people**, child**ren**, **men**

Die Mehrzahl bildet man normalerweise durch anhängen von **s**: *book**s***.
Bei Wörter mit der Endung *s*, *ss*, *sh*, *ch*, oder *x*, wird ***es*** eingefügt: *bus**es***.
Bei Wörter mit der Endung *Konsonant* + *y* wird *y* zu ***ies***: *city* – *cit**ies***.
Manche Wörter sind Sonderfälle! *Child* – ***children***.

Manche Wörter, die man auf Deutsch in der Einzahl verwendet sind im Englischen Mehrzahl:
My trousers are blue. *Meine Hose ist blau.*
My glasses are neu. *Meine Brille ist neu.*

G7 *Have got* ⮌ U3A

a) question	b) positive sentences	c) negative sentences
Have I got your address?	**I've got** your address.	**I haven't got** your address.
Have you got a pen?	**You've got** a pen.	**You haven't got** a pencil.
Has he got a sister?	**He's got** a sister.	**He hasn't got** a brother.
Has she got a brother?	**She's got** a brother.	**She hasn't got** a sister.
Has it (the house) **got** a balcony?	**It's got** a balcony.	**It hasn't got** a garden.
Have we got your phone number?	**We've got** your phone number.	**We haven't got** your phone number.
Have you got any cousins?	**You've got** a lot of cousins.	**You haven't got** any cousins.
Have they got an English car?	**They've got** an English car.	**They haven't got** an American car.
	've got = have got 's got = has got	haven't = have not hasn't = has not

	d) short answers	
Have you got a cat?	Yes, **I have**.	No, **I haven't**.
Has he got a car?	Yes, **he has**.	No, **he hasn't**.
Have you got a garage?	Yes, **we have**.	No, **we haven't**.
Have they got a house?	Yes, **they have**.	No, **they haven't**.

Im britischen Englisch wird *have got* wie das deutsche „haben" gebraucht: *I've got a question.*
Im amerikanischen Englisch wird *have* statt *have got* verwendet: *I have a question.*

G8 Possessive *'s* Besitzfall ⮌ U3A

Whose book is this?	It's Ben**'s** book.
Who is Janet?	She's my mother's sister.

Ben**'s** book (= das Buch gehört Ben)

G9 *Can* and *can't* ↺ U3B

a) question	b) positive sentence	c) negative sentence
Can I make tea? **Can you/he/she/it/** see me? **we/you/they** speak German?	**I can** make tea. **You/He/She/It/** can see me. **We/You/They can** speak German.	**I can't** make coffee. **You/He/She/It/** can't see me. **We/You/They can't** speak Chinese.
		can't = can not

	d) short answers	
Can you sing?	Yes, **I can**.	No, **I can't**.

Can und *can't* haben für alle Personen in der Einzahl und der Mehrzahl dieselbe Form.
Can't = cannot (Vollform)
Vorsicht! Mit *can* müssen Sie immer ein Verb verwenden: *Can you speak English?*

G10 Present simple Einfache Form der Gegenwart ↺ U4A, U4B, U5A

a) questions	b) positive sentences	c) negative sentences
Do I speak good German?	**I speak** good English.	**I don't speak** good French.
Do you play chess?	**You play** chess.	**You don't play** Chess.
Does he speak Italian?	**He speaks** Italian.	**He doesn't speak** English.
Does she phone you?	**She phones** you.	**She doesn't phone** me.
Does it (the cat) **drink** milk?	**It drinks** milk.	**It doesn't drink** milk.
Do we speak good German?	**We speak** good German.	**We don't speak** good Italian.
Do you play tennis?	**You play** tennis.	**You don't play** football.
Do they go skiing?	**They go** skiing.	**They don't go** walking.
		don't = do not doesn't = does not

	d) short answers	
Do you live in Vienna?	Yes, **I do**.	No, **I don't**.
Does she speak German?	Yes, **she does**.	No, **she doesn't**.
Do you live in Germany?	Yes, **we do**.	No, **we don't**.
Do they like Paris?	Yes, **they do**.	No, **they don't**.

He, she, it: das 's' muss mit.

In der 3. Person Einzahl (he/she/it wird ein *-s* an das Zeitwort gehängt: *work works*
Bei Fragen in der 3. Person Einzahl verwendet man *does*: ***Does** he like it?*
In verneinten Sätzen in der 3. Person Einzahl verwendet man *doesn't*. *He **doesn't** like it.*

Mit dem *present simple* spricht man über Dinge, die sich wiederholen oder die immer gelten:
I go to work at 8 o'clock. The bank opens at 9 o'clock.

G11 Adverbs of frequency Umstandswörter der Häufigkeit ↺ U5B

How often are you late for work?
I'm not **often** late.
She **usually** goes to work at 8 am – but she **sometimes** arrives late!
They **always** walk to work and they're **never** late

Umstandswörter der Häufigkeit stehen vor dem Zeitwort: *I **usually walk** to work.*
Nur beim Zeitwort **be** stehen sie dahinter: *She **is always** on time, she**'s never** late.*

G12 *Would you like a/an …? Would you like to …?* ↺ U6A

Would you like a sandwich?	**Yes, please.**
Would you like to have a glass of wine?	**No, thank you.**

I'd like … = Ich hätte gerne …
I'd like to … = Ich würde gerne …

G13 Past simple of *be (was / were)*

Einfache Form der Vergangenheit von *be* ↺ U7A

a) question	b) positive	c) negative
Where **was I** last week?	**I was** on holiday.	**I wasn't** at work.
Where **were you** yesterday?	**You were** at work.	**You weren't** on holiday.
Where **was he** on Monday?	**He was** at home.	**He wasn't** at work.
Where **was she** yesterday?	**She was** in Paris.	**She wasn't** in London.
Where **was the party**?	**It was** at my office.	**It wasn't** at my house.
Where **were we** yesterday?	**We were** at the cinema.	**We weren't** at home.
Where **were you** last Saturday?	**You were** at the park.	**You weren't** at the club.
Where **were they** yesterday?	**They were** at the pub.	**They weren't** at café.

wasn't = was not
weren't = were not

	d) short answers	
Were you at work yesterday?	Yes, **I was**.	No, **I wasn't**.
Was it Friday yesterday?	Yes, **it was**.	No, **it wasn't**.
Were they in London yesterday?	Yes, **they were**.	No, **they weren't**.

G14 *was / were born* ↺ U8A

a) question	b) positive	c) negative
Where **were you born**?	**I was born** in Canada.	**I wasn't born** in America.
	d) short answers	
Were you born Ontario?	Yes, **I was**.	No, **I wasn't**.

G15 Past simple Einfache Form der Vergangenheit ↺ U7B, U8A, U8B

a) question	b) positive	c) negative
What **did I do** yesterday? What **did you/he/she/it/we/you/they do** yesterday?	**I played** football. **You/He/She/It/We/You/They played** with my nephews.	**I didn't play** tennis. **You/He/She/We/You/They didn't play** with my nieces.
		didn't = did not
	d) short answers	
Did he have lunch at 12? **Did they go** home early?	Yes, **he did**. Yes, **they did**.	No, **he didn't**. No, **they didn't**.

Die Formen der Zeitwörter im *past simple* sind für alle Personen gleich.
Die Verneinung bildet man mit *didn't*: *He **didn't** go to work.* Fragen bildet man mit *Did*: ***Did** he go to town?*

e) regular and irregular past simple forms regelmäßige und unregelmäßige Formen des *past simple*	
regelmäßig – Endungen: *-d* oder *-ed*:	dance – dance**d**, walk – walk**ed**, start – start**ed**
einige unregelmäßige Formen:	come – **came**, eat – **ate**, go – **went**, see – **saw**

Mit dem *past simple* spricht man über Dinge, die zu einem bestimmten Zeitpunkt in der Vergangenheit passiert sind.
Oft steht eine Zeitangabe dabei, z. B.: *an hour ago, yesterday, last week, two years ago.*
Eine Liste mit unregelmäßigen Verben finden Sie auf S. 179.

G16 Adjectives and adverbs of manner

Eigenschaftswörter und Umstandswörter der Art und Weise ↩ U9A

adjectives	
nice	It's a **nice** car.
good	This book is really **good**.
happy	The children are **happy**.

Eigenschaftswörter bestimmen Menschen und Dinge näher. Sie stehen vor dem Hauptwort: *It's a nice car* oder nach dem Verb *be*: *It is nice.* Die Form des Eigenschaftsworts ändert sich im Englischen nie.

adjectives	regular adverbs
nice	He sings **nicely**.
slow	She speaks **slowly**.
happy	They played **happily**.

Umstandswörter der Art und Weise geben an, wie jemand etwas macht. Regelmäßige Umstandswörter enden auf *ly*: *He drives badly.*

Und hier einige unregelmäßige Umstandswörter:

adjectives	irregular adverbs
good	He dances **well**.
hard	They work really **hard**.
fast	Do you drive **fast**?

G17 *Must* and *mustn't* ↩ U9B

a) question	b) positive	c) negative
Must you tell him?	**I must** tell him.	**I mustn't** tell him.
	d) short answers	
Must you tell him?	Yes, **I must**.	No, **I mustn't**.

Must ist für alle Personen gleich.
! *I mustn't* = ich **darf** nicht. (Nicht: muss nicht)

G18 Comparatives 1. Steigerungsstufe ↺ U10A

short adjectives	**+er**
My house is old / big.	My house is **older than / bigger than** my sister's house.
adjectives with y on the end	**y → ier**
My uncle is friendly.	My aunt is **friendlier than** my uncle.
long adjectives	**more ...**
The book is interesting.	The film is **more interesting than** the book.
irregular	**irregular comparatives**
This hotel is good / bad.	This hotel is **better than / worse than** the four-star hotel..

Ein Mitlaut am Ende wird verdoppelt, wenn davor ein Selbstlaut steht: *hot* → *ho**tt**er*.
Um etwas zu vergleichen, verwendet man *than*: *I'm taller than you.*
Eigenschaftswörter mit drei oder mehr Silben bilden die 1. Steigerungsstufe mit *more*:
com·fort·a·ble – My chair is more comfortable than your chair.

G19 Superlatives 2. Steigerungsstufe ↺ U10B

short adjectives	**+est**
My house is old / big.	My house is **the oldest / the biggest**.
adjectives with y on the end	**y → iest**
My uncle is friendly.	He's **the friendliest** man that I know.
long adjectives	**most ...**
The book is interesting.	It's **the most interesting book** that I've got.
irregular	**irregular comparatives**
This hotel is good / bad.	This hotel is **the best / the worst** in town.

Ein Mitlaut am Ende wird verdoppelt, wenn davor ein Selbstlaut steht: *hot* → *the ho**tt**est.*
Eigenschaftswörter mit drei oder mehr Silben bilden die 2. Steigerungsstufe mit *most*:
ex·pen·sive – Which is the most expensive car?

G20 Imperatives Befehlsform ↺ U11B

positive	**negative**
Park here.	**Don't park** here.

Die Befehlsform ist für alle Personen (du, Sie, ihr) gleich.

G21 Prepositions Verhältniswörter

time Zeit ↺ U4A	**at** 9.30, **on** Mondays, **on** June 7th, **in** the winter, **in** May, **in** 2004
place Ort ↺ U2A	**on** the table, **in** my bag, **under** my bed, **at** the station, **near** the church, **opposite** the bank, **next to** the school
movement Bewegung ↺ U11A	go **by** train, go **on** foot, go **to** the bus stop, go **past** the bank, go **along** the road

G22 *Going to* future Zukunft mit *going to* ↺ U12B

a) question	b) positive	c) negative
Am I going to meet him?	**I'm going to meet** him.	**I'm not going to meet** her.
Are you going to watch TV?	**You're going to watch** TV.	**You aren't going to watch** a film.
Is he going to be late?	**He's going to be** late	**He isn't going to be** early.
Is she going to phone him?	**She's going to phone** him.	**She isn't going to email** him.
Is it going to drink milk?	**It's going to drink** milk.	**It isn't going to drink** water.
Are we going to see her?	**We're going to see** her.	**We aren't going to see** him.
Are you going to buy one?	**You're going to buy** one.	**You aren't going to buy** two.
Are they going to eat it?	**They're going to eat** it.	**They aren't going to eat** it.
	d) short answers	
Are you going to visit her?	Yes, **I am**.	No, **I'm not**.
Is he going to text me?	Yes, **he is**.	No, **he isn't**.
Are they going to sing?	Yes, **they are**.	No, **they aren't**.

going to gebraucht man um zu sagen, was man in der Zukunft plant/vorhat.

G23 Irregular verbs Unregelmäßige Verben

Present	Past	German
to be	was	sein
to beat	beat	schlagen
to begin	began	anfangen
to break	broke	kaputt machen
to bring	brought	bringen
to buy	bought	kaufen
to choose	chose	(aus)wählen
to come	came	kommen
to do	did	tun, machen
to draw	drew	zeichnen
to drink	drank	trinken
to drive	drove	fahren
to eat	ate	essen
to feel	felt	fühlen
to find	found	finden
to get	got	bekommen
to give	gave	geben
to go	went	gehen
to have	had	haben
to know	knew	kennen, wissen
to learn	learned	lernen
to leave	left	(ver)lassen
to make	made	machen
to meet	met	treffen
to pay	paid	bezahlen
to put	put	setzen, legen, stellen
to read	read	lesen
to run	ran	laufen
to say	said	sagen
to see	saw	sehen
to send	sent	senden, schicken
to sing	sang	singen
to sit	sat	sitzen
to sleep	slept	schlafen
to speak	spoke	sprechen
to spend	spent	ausgeben
to stand	stood	stehen
to swim	swam	schwimmen
to take	took	nehmen
to tell	told	erzählen
to think	thought	denken
to understand	understood	verstehen
to wear	wore	tragen
to win	won	gewinnen
to write	wrote	schreiben

Unit 1 Part A (p. 12)

1a
K: Hello, **I'm** Karl.
L: **Hi, my** name's Laura.
K: Nice to **meet you**, Laura.
L: **Nice to** meet you, **too**.

1b
L: Karl, **this is** Astrid.
K: Hello Astrid, **nice to meet you**.
A: Hello Karl, **nice to meet you, too**.

1c
A: I'm Astrid. What's **your** name?
M: **My name's** Mark. Where **are you** from, Astrid?
A: **I'm from** Baden.
M: **Where's that**?
A: It's **in** Switzerland, **near** Zurich.

1d
K: Goodbye, Laura.
L: **Goodbye**, Karl. **See you next week.**

2a
(Australian), Austrian, Italian,
(Irish), English, Turkish
(French), German, Greek, Swiss, American

3.1a
1 He's from France / Paris.
2 She's from Ireland / Dublin.
3 Yes, he is.
4 It's from Turkey.

3.1b
2 She's from Ulm, she isn't from Berlin.
3 He isn't German, he's Austrian.
4 I'm not English, I'm Irish.

3.1c
1 (She's English.) **Is she** from London? – No, **she isn't**. **She's** from Liverpool.
2 He's Australian. **Is he** from Sydney? – No, **he isn't**. **He's** from Melbourne.

3.2a
His name's **Karl**. Her name's **Anna**.

3.2b
1 His, **2** Her, **3** My

3.3
1 an, **2** a, **3** an, **4** an, **5** a

4a
♀: (Donna) Jones, American, Chicago
♂: (Simon) Smith, Australian, Sydney

4b
Donna is **American**. **She's** from **Chicago**. **Her** surname **is Jones**.

4c
Simon is Australian. He's from Sydney. His surname is Smith.

4d
I'm ... / I'm from ... / My surname is ...

Unit 1 Part B (p. 18)

1a
1 Hello what's **your name**?
2 Can I **have** your name, **please**?
3 Can you **spell** your **first** name, please?
4 Can you spell your **surname** for **me**, please?
Correct order: 3, 1, 4, 2

1b
What's your **phone number**?
What's your **mobile number**?
What's your **address**?
What's your **email address**?

1c
a h j k
b c d e g p t v
f l m n s x z
i y o q u w r

2
nine, two, eight, one
seven, six, five
three, four
1 ✓, **2** ✗ eight, **3** ✗ four, **4** ✓, **5** ✗ seven, **6** ✗ two, **7** ✗ three

3.1a
■ Hello, **are** you John and Pat Smith from London?
◆ **We're** from London, but we **aren't** John and Pat Smith. This **is** Anna Smith, And **I'm** Jack Smith ... not John Smith.
■ Oh, sorry. **They're** in room 204 and you're in 304.

3.1b
1 Yes, they are. **2** No, they aren't.
3 Yes, he/she is. / No, he/she isn't.
4 No, we aren't.

3.2
Our surname's Smith. **My** name's Anna.
His name's Jack. **Her** name's Anna.
Their surname's Smith.

4a
Surname: Dwightman
First name: Lynda
Address: 9 Bank Street, London SE7 3DL
Phone number: 020 731 8456
Mobile number: –
Email address: ldwight@hotmail.com

Unit 2 Part A (p. 24)

1a
1 Is there a French or **an** Italian restaurant in your town?
2 Where is the French restaurant?

1b
A: **Excuse** me.
B: Yes, **can** I **help** you?
A: Is there a post office near here?
B: Yes, there is. It's opposite the station.
A: **Thank you**.
B: **You're welcome**.

1c
Where is it?
1 It's **in** George Street.
2 It's **on** the corner of George Street.
3 It's very **near** the station.
4 It's **next to** the station.
5 It's **opposite** the station.

2
1 post office, **2** bookshop, **3** cinema, **4** supermarket, **5** church, **6** bank, **7** art gallery, **8** museum, **9** swimming pool, **10** restaurant, **11** pub, **12** café, **13** school, **14** park, **15** train station, **16** department store

3a
1 Is there a park near your school?
2 Is there an Italian restaurant in your town?
3 Is there a café near your school?

3b
They're from a small town near Bristol. There's a big department store in their town and there's a good bookshop, too. There's a museum but there isn't an art gallery.

4a
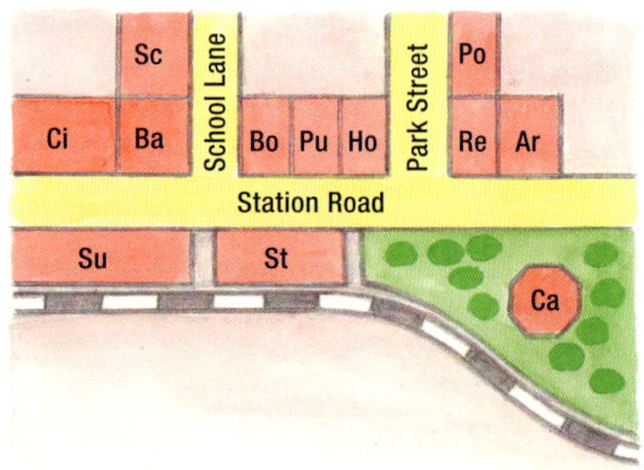

4b
1 Yes, it is.
2 No, there isn't.
3 Yes, there is.
4 No, it isn't.
5 It's on the corner of Station Road and Park Street. / It's in Station Road. / It's opposite the park and the restaurant. / It's next to the pub.
6 It's in School Lane. / It's next to the bank.
7 It's on the corner of Station Road and School Lane. / It's opposite the bank and the station. / It's next to the pub.

Unit 2 Part B (p. 30)

1a
1 Are there any parks in your town?
2 Is there a beach in your town?
3 Where is the park?

1b
1 There's a small river.
2 There isn't an international airport.
3 You can see a lot of churches.
4 There are some beautiful parks.
5 There aren't any famous old buildings.

1c
■ Hello. Where are you from?
◆ I'm from Bristol.
■ Where's that?
◆ It's about 100 miles from London.
■ Is there an airport near Bristol?
◆ Yes, there is – but it's very small.

2a
Essen und trinken: bar, café, pub, restaurant
Einkaufen: shop, department store, market, supermarket
Im Freien: beach, bridge, park, river
Geschichte/Kunst/Kultur: art gallery, church, museum, opera house

2b
big – small, busy – quiet, modern – old

2c
eleven, twelve, 14, fifteen, 20, twenty-four, 31, forty, fifty-five, 67, eighty-two, ninety

3.1a
1 ■ **Are there any parks** in your town?
◆ Yes, **there are some** very nice parks.
2 ■ **Are there any** Japanese restaurants in your town?
◆ No, **there aren't**. **There are some** Thai restaurants, but **there aren't any** Japanese restaurants.

3.1b
1 Are / any, **2** isn't / an, **3** are / some, **4** is / an / aren't / any

3.2
1 hotels, **2** babies, **3** matches, **4** bushes, **5** parties, **6** towns

4a
✓ next to: a famous street, a famous department store, a park, an opera house, a museum, a famous church, a famous bookshop
1 busy, **2** There aren't any, **3** There are 16

4b
There's a famous station in New York called Grand Central.
There's a famous art gallery in New York called The Met.

Unit 3 Part A (p. 36)

1a
1 Are you from a big family?
2 Have you **got a** brother or a sister?
3 Are you **an** only child?
4 Are you married?
5 Have you **got any** children?

1b
1 I'm **from** a big family. **I've got** four sisters.
2 I'm married but we **haven't got** any children.
3 My husband is from a very small family. **He's** an only child.

1c
1 I've got **a** son. **His** name's Tom.
2 I've got **two** daughters. **Their** names are Sophie and Kate. I haven't got **any** grandchildren.
3 I've got **a lot of** cousins in Australia.

2a
: aunt, daughter, mother, niece, sister, wife
: brother, father, husband, nephew, son, uncle
: child, cousin, grandchildren, parent

2b
1 son, **2** daughter, **3** parents, **4** wife, **5** aunt, **6** mother, **7** cousin, **8** uncle, **9** niece, **10** nephew, **11** husband

3.1a
1 No, she hasn't. **2** Yes, he has.
3 Yes, they have.

3.1b
1 She **hasn't got** a German car.
2 He**'s got** a big car.
3 They**'ve got** two daughters.
4 They **haven't got** a garden.

3.2
1 She's John's wife. **2** He's Sue's husband.
3 She's Jessica's sister. **4** She's Sue's daughter.

4
1 F, **2** F, **3** T, **4** T, **5** F, **6** T

Unit 3 Part B (p. 42)

1a
1 Can you describe him?
2 Can you describe him for me, please?
3 Is she tall or short?
4 Has he **got** long hair or short hair?

1b
1 He's got a long beard.
2 She's beautiful.
3 She's got beautiful red hair.
4 He's a very tall man.

2a
1 black, **2** blue, **3** brown, **4** green, **5** grey, **6** orange, **7** pink, **8** red, **9** white, **10** yellow

2b
1 His trousers, **2** Her skirt, **3** Her blouse, **4** His jacket, **5** Her shoes, **6** His shirt, **7** Her pullover

2c
on the face: beard, glasses, moustache
eyes: big, blue, green, small
hair: black, blonde, long, red, short, white
eyes and hair: beautiful, brown, grey

3a
1 Yes, I can. / No, I can't.
2 Yes he/she can. / No, he/she can't.
3 Yes, he/she can. / No, he/she can't.
4 Yes, we can. / No, we can't.
5 No, they can't.

3b
1 I can use a computer.
2 She can take good photos.
3 They can't speak Spanish.
4 We can do this exercise.

3c
1 can, **2** can, can't, **3** can't, **4** can, can't

4a
a person's appearance: 1, 4
what a person can do: 2, 3

Test yourself 1 (p. 45)

1
1a, **2**b, **3**b, **4**a, **5**b, **6**a, **7**b, **8**a, **9**a, **10**a, **11**b, **12**b, **13**b, **14**a, **15**b

2
16b, **17**a, **18**a, **19**b, **20**a

3 Part A
21b, **22**c, **23**a

3 Part B
24h, **25**e, **26**f

4
27a, **28**b, **29**b, **30**b

Unit 4 Part A (p. 50)

1a
1 What's **the time**?
2 Excuse me, what's the time?
3 Excuse me, **what's the time, please**?

1b
1 It's seven **o'clock**.
2 It's quarter **past** seven.
3 It's **half past** seven.
4 It's quarter **to** eight.

1c
1 at, **2** from / to, **3** in, **4** before / after, **5** at, **6** on

2a
1 Monday, **2** Tuesday, **3** Wednesday, **4** Thursday, **5** Friday, **6** Saturday, **7** Sunday

2b
2, 3, 1, 4
1, 3, 2

2c
3, 4, 6
2, 1, 5
It's half past one.

3a
2 get up at 5.30, **3** go to bed before midnight, **4** have breakfast in the morning, **5** like champagne, **6** work in an office

3b
2 Do you get up at 5.30?
3 Do you go to bed before midnight?
4 Do you have breakfast in the morning?
5 Do you like champagne?
6 Do you work in an office?

3c
1–6 Yes, I do. / No, I don't.

4a
1 Where do you live?
2 Do you work?
3 Do you like your boss?
4 What time do you get up?
5 Do you have breakfast in a café?
6 Do you go out for lunch?
7 What do you do after work?
8 When do you go to your yoga class?

4b
I: Do you go to a pub in Wantage?
J: Yes, I do.
I: And do you have dinner in the pub?
J: No, I have dinner at home.

Unit 4 Part B (p. 56)

1a
1 Where **do you** work?
2 I **work in** a shop.
3 I work **for** Lufthansa.
4 What do you do **at** work?
5 I'm **a** pilot.

1b
1 Susan? **She likes** her job but **she doesn't like** her boss.
2 Me? **I like** my boss but **I don't like** my office.

1c
1 What do you **think**?
2 I think it's a very **boring** job.
3 Yes, I think **so, too**.
4 Oh, I **don't** think **so**.

2a
1 teacher, **2** train driver, **3** police officer, **4** opera singer, **5** hotel doorman, **6** shop assistant, **7** nurse, **8** taxi driver, **9** television presenter

2b
1 boring, **2** dangerous, **3** interesting, **4** overpaid, **5** stressful, **6** underpaid, **7** useful

3a
1 Do, **2** Does, **3** Do, **4** Does

3b
1 She lives in Scotland.
2 He works in a school.
I live in ... / I work in / for ...

3c
1 No, she doesn't. **2** Yes, he does.
3 Yes, I do. / No, I don't.

3d
1 Anna doesn't live in London. **2** George works in a school. **3** I work / don't work in a school. **4** I live / don't live near an airport.

4a
2 She has dinner with her mum (at her mum's house). **3** She goes to a yoga class (at the sports centre). **4** She goes out with friends (to a restaurant or they go dancing).

4b
1 It starts at quarter past seven. **2** No, she doesn't. **3** She comes home at half past nine. **4** She goes to her yoga class on Thursdays. **5** Yes, she does.

Unit 5 Part A (p. 62)

1a
How often do you see your best friend?
– I see her **every day** – Monday to Friday – at work.
– I see him **twice a week** on Tuesdays and Thursdays.
– I see him **every weekend** – every Sunday.
– I see her about **four times** a year.

1b
■ **What day** do you have your English lesson?
◆ **On** Wednesdays.
■ **What time** does the lesson start?
◆ **At** 7.30.

1c
Yes, I do. I **enjoy playing** tennis but I **don't like watching** it on TV.

2a
I play basketball, table tennis, football.
I go swimming, walking, skiing.

2b
1 go: on holiday, swimming
2 have: a lesson, breakfast
3 meet: new people, my friends
4 play: chess, golf
5 talk: to a friend, about sport

2c
an hour, a day, the weekend, a week, a year

3a
1 Does – Yes, she does.
2 Do – Yes, they do.
3 Does – No, he doesn't.
4 Do – Yes, I do. / No, I don't.
5 Do – Yes, we do. / No, we don't.

3b
1 F, **2** T, **3** F, **4** T, **5** T
1 Paul doesn't live in Wantage.
3 He and his wife don't go walking every weekend.

4
Paul's daughter and her partner work in a school. They're teachers. They start work at 9 o'clock and they go home at 5 o'clock. They like their jobs but they don't like their boss. In their free time they read a lot and they like listening to music. They've got a friend called Tom in Oxford. They see him every weekend.

Unit 5 Part B (p. 68)

1a
I've got a problem and I don't know what to do.
1: **Why don't you** ask a friend?
2: **You could** ask a friend.

1b
■ Why don't you start boxing in your free time?
◆ I **don't think** that's a very **good idea**.
■ Well ... you could go running.
◆ Hmm – **maybe**.
■ Or, I know, you could buy a fitness DVD.
◆ Now **that's** an **excellent** idea!

1c
1 I **always** walk to work – every day.
2 I **usually** walk up the stairs – but not when I'm very tired.
3 I **often** go running – two or three times a week.
4 I **sometimes** go swimming – about once a month.
5 I **never** smoke.

2
1 fresh, **2** smoking, **3** interesting, **4** all, **5** drives, **6** lift, **7** tired, **8** stressful, **9** cocktails, **10** healthy, **11** alcohol, **12** never
His lifestyle is very unhealthy.

3a
1 She often walks to work.
2 He never works on Saturdays.
3 Her job is sometimes stressful.
4 They always go home at 6.
5 I usually go to bed early.

3b
2 She always goes to work at 8.
3 They often eat Chinese food.
4 He never comes to the lesson late.
5 They are sometimes tired on Fridays.

4a
✓ next to: healthy food, smoking, stressful job, walking, good friends, sport, free time

4b
1 Why don't you tell your boss that you can't work late every evening?
2 You could see some friends once or twice a week.
3 Why don't you buy some fresh food at the market once a week?
4 You could do some sport every day.
5 Why don't you stop smoking today?

Unit 6 Part A (p. 74)

1a
1 What is your favourite dessert?
2 Where is your favourite café?
3 Who is your favourite singer?

1b
A: Good evening, can I help you?
B: **Yes, could I have the menu, please?**
A: Yes, of course. Here it is.
B: **Thank you.**
A: Would you like to order now?
B: **Yes, I'd like the chicken, please.**
A: With chips or with salad?
B: **Can I have chips and salad?**
A: Yes, of course. And would you like to see the wine menu?
B: **No, thank you – I don't drink wine.**
A: What would you like to drink then?
B: **Mineral water, please.**
A: Thank you.

2a
1 tomato, **2** apple, **3** egg, **4** cake, **5** cheese, **6** orange juice, **7** tea, **8** wine, **9** fish, **10** ham, **11** chips, **12** bread, **13** vegetables, **14** pasta, **15** milk, **16** soup

2b
1 tomatoes, fish, ham, vegetables
2 tomatoes, apples, eggs, cheese, fish, ham, vegetables, pasta
3 orange juice, tea, wine, milk
4 tomatoes, eggs, cheese, fish, ham, bread

3a
1 Would you like a cup of tea?
2 Would you like to order now?
3 Would you like chips with your omelette?
4 What would you like?
5 What would you like to order?

3b
3, 1, 2, 1, 2, 3

4a
The Chinese Garden: atmosphere 3, food 3, service 5, prices 2, total 13
The Taj Mahal: atmosphere 4, food 3, service 2, prices 3, total 12
The Pizza Palace: atmosphere 2, food 5, service 3, prices 4, total 14

4b
1 The Taj Mahal. **2** The Pizza Palace.
3 The Pizza Palace.

Unit 6 Part B (p. 80)

1a
1 Would you like to come to dinner on Friday?
2 I'd like to **invite** you to my party on Saturday. **Can** you **come**?

1b
Would you like to come to dinner on Friday?
– I'm **sorry**, I **can't** come on Friday. But **thanks** for the invitation.
Well, can you come on Saturday?
– Oh yes, I'd **love** to. **Thank** you.

2a
3rd Feb: the third of February
15th June: the fifteenth of June
1st Nov: the first of November
10th Sept: the tenth of September
31st Jan: the thirty-first of January
22nd Mar: the twenty-second of March
12th Apr: the twelfth of April
4th July: the fourth of July
5th Oct: the fifth of October
20th Dec: the twentieth of December
19th May: the nineteenth of May

2b
24 hours = 1 day, 7 days = 1 week, 4 weeks = 1 month, 12 months = 1 year

2c
1 a cocktail party, **2** a birthday party, **3** a jazz evening, **4** a gallery opening, **5** an anniversary party, **6** a dinner party

3a
1 How many, **2** How much, **3** How many, **4** How much, **5** How many, **6** How much

3b
1 Not many. / A lot. **2** Not much. / A lot.
3 Not many. / A lot. **4** Not much./ A lot.
5 Not many. / A lot. **6** Not much. / A lot.

3c
1 many + lot, **2** lot + much, **3** many + lot, **4** much + lot

4a
1 F, **2** F, **3** T

4b
1 Where is the party?
2 What time does the party start?
3 Can I bring something?
4 Is there a small hotel near the club?
5 How much is a taxi from the station?

4d
1 It's at my tennis club.
2 Oh, I don't know ... 8 o'clock.
3 No, no, I've got everything – a lot of everything.
4 It's OK, you can stay at my place.
5 It's about £10, I think.

Test yourself 2 (p. 83)

1
1a, **2**b, **3**b, **4**b, **5**a, **6**a, **7**b, **8**a, **9**b, **10**b, **11**a, **12**b, **13**b, **14**b, **15**b

2
16 T, **17** F, **18** F, **19** T, **20** F

3 Part A
21b, **22**d, **23**a

3 Part B
24g, **25**f, **26**h

4
27b, **28**b, **29**a, **30**b

Unit 7 Part A (p. 88)

1a
1 How much is the guidebook?
2 How much are these postcards?
3 How much are the sunglasses?
4 How much is the suitcase?

1b
1 The guidebook **is nine pounds sixty**.
2 The postcards **are sixty pence**.
3 The sunglasses **are twenty pounds**.
4 The suitcase **is fifty pounds ninety pence**.

1c
He can speak French because his mother is French.
He never drinks wine because he doesn't like it.

2a
1 a towel, **2** a digital camera, **3** a book, **4** suncream, **5** a guidebook, **6** sunglasses

2b
I can stay in a **hotel** and eat in the **restaurant** there. I can swim in the **sea** and then sit on the **beach** and write some **postcards** to my friends or read my **book**. I can go to a **market** and buy some **presents** for people at home. I can eat good **food** and drink good **wine**.

2c
There are nine **people**: two **men**, three **women** and four **children**.

2d
cold – hot, bad – good, dirty – clean, friendly – unfriendly, awful – fantastic, cheap – expensive

3a
1 were, **2** was, **3** wasn't, **4** were, **5** was, **6** weren't

3b
1 Was - was – wasn't, **2** Were – weren't – was, **3** Were – were – was

3c
1 Yes, I was. / No, I wasn't. **2** Yes, there was. / No, there wasn't. **3** Yes, there were. / No, there weren't.

Unit 7 Part B (p. 94)

1a
I saw him **last night, last month, ten days ago, last year, two years ago**.

1c
1 We **went** to Paris.
2 We **stayed** in a small hotel.
3 We **bought** some presents and postcards.
4 We **were** very happy there.
5 We **saw** The Eiffel Tower.

2a
blue words: have lunch, hire a car, stay in a hotel, take photos, talk to a friend, watch a film
red words: have breakfast, stay at home, talk to my teacher, watch a football match

2b
three things in a national park: bears, mountains, waterfall
three things you can read: book, magazine, newspaper
three buildings you can visit: art gallery, lighthouse, museum
three things you can do: buy presents, take photos, visit buildings

3a
1 went, **2** flew, **3** drove, **4** parked, **5** was, **6** was, **7** hired, **8** lived, **9** talked, **10** saw, **11** was, **12** were, **13** was, **14** liked, **15** worked, **16** had, **17** went, **18** bought, **19** visited, **20** went, **21** took, **22** stayed

3b
past: 2, 4, 5, 7, 9
present: 1, 3, 6, 8, 10

4b
1 She went to Switzerland two months ago.
2 She drove from London to Interlaken.
3 It was very, very cold.
4 She saw a lot of mountains.
5 She had a very big room.
6 She had breakfast early.
7 She stayed there for three nights.

Unit 8 Part A (p. 100)

1a
1 I **was** born in 1968 in Hamburg.
2 I **went** to school in Hamburg.
3 After that I **started** work.
4 I **worked** in my first job for 6 years.
5 I **got married** in 1994.
6 Our first child **was born** in 1997.
7 I **was married** from 1994 to 2003.
8 Then we **got divorced**.
9 I **met** my new partner about six months ago.

1b
1 My cousin was born **in** 1971.
2 Her family lived **in** London.
3 She started school **in** 1976.
4 She went **to** school there **for** 13 years.
5 She worked **in** a hotel **from** 1999 **to** 2002.

2a
flamenco, polka, jive, tango, twist, ballet, salsa

2b
2 He's a singer. He sings in opera houses.
3 He's a writer. He writes at home

3.1
1 didn't dance, **2** didn't go, **3** didn't have, **4** didn't buy

3.2
1 Yes, I was. / No, I wasn't. **2** Yes, he was. / No, he wasn't. **3** No, they weren't. **4** Carlos Acosta was born in Havana.

4.2
1 Dublin, **2** 12 years, **3** 17, **4** work, **5** acting school, **6** on TV, **7** a film actor, **8** ten years ago, **9** two children

Unit 8 Part B (p. 106)

1a
1 Where did you go?
2 Which restaurant did you go to?
3 What did you eat?
4 Was the food good?
5 Did you have a good time?
6 Were the waiters friendly?

1b
1 I saw it on **television**.
2 I saw it at the **cinema**.
3 The **story** was very exciting.
4 But the end of the film was a bit **sad**.
5 The **actors** were fantastic.

1c
correct order: 6, 8, 3, 1, 4, 2, 5, 7

2a
1 read a book, **2** watch television, **3** listen to music, **4** play cards, **5** have dinner with friends, **6** spend time online, **7** phone friends, **8** write emails

2b
1 funny, **2** sad, **3** frightening, **4** boring, **5** exciting, **6** romantic

2c
1 the headline, **2** paragraph 1, **3** paragraph 2, **4** the page number, **5** a picture

3a
1 Which film did you see yesterday?
2 What time did the film start?
3 Was the film good?
4 Where did you see the film?

3b
1 Where did they go?
2 Where did they have lunch?
3 How many postcards did they send?
4 What did they see in the evening?

4
Topic 1: an opera, 3, Three of the singers gave interviews.
Topic 2: a football match, 3–1, The players won the match 3–1.
Topic 3: something that happened in a restaurant, 2, Two men came into the restaurant and took all the money that was there.

Unit 9 Part A (p. 112)

1a
1 I'm **sorry I'm** late.
2 I'm **sorry I didn't** phone you yesterday.
3 I'm **sorry I can't** meet you this afternoon.

1b
1 I **had** a problem with my daughter at breakfast **this morning**.
2 I'm **busy** all **day** today.
3 I **was** very tired **yesterday evening**.

1c
1 No **problem**. Can you call me this evening?
2 Don't **worry**, you're here now.
3 That's **alright**, but I'd like to see you soon.
dialogue 1: a1, b1, c2
dialogue 2: a2, b3, c1
dialogue 3: a3, b2, c3

2a
well – badly, slow(ly) – fast, always – never, late – early, come – go

2b
Why, How, Who, What, Where, Which, When

2c
1 Who did you have dinner with yesterday?
2 Which sport do you like watching on TV?
3 Why do you always walk to work?
4 How does your teacher speak?
5 When do you do sport?
6 What is your favourite food?
7 Where do you live?

3.1
1 We saw a good marathon last year.
2 The African runners ran very fast.
3 It was very exciting.

3.2a
1 He writes slowly. **2** She cooks well.
3 He drives fast.

3.2b
1 No, they dance very well. **2** No, she works very fast. **3** Yes, he speaks very clearly.

Unit 9 Part B (p. 118)

1
1 Merry Christmas. (D), **2** Good luck. (B), **3** Thanks very much. (F), **4** Happy birthday. (A), **5** Have a good trip. (C), **6** Oh, that's a pity. (E), **7** Happy New Year. (G)

2a
1 Christmas (Day), **2** birthday, **3** Valentine's Day, **4** Easter, **5** New Year (New Year's Day), **6** wedding anniversary

2b
1 capital, **2** garden, **3** card, **4** present, **5** punctual, **6** news, **7** interview, **8** leave

3a
on the left: 8, 1, 5, 6
on the right: 7, 3, 2, 4

3b
1 must, **2** mustn't, **3** mustn't, **4** must, **5** mustn't, **6** must, **7** must, **8** must

4a
1 picture on the right, **2** picture on the left

4b
The woman mustn't smoke in here (in the hospital). She must go outside.
The man mustn't park here. He must (drive around the corner and) park in the next street.

Test yourself 3 (p. 121)

1
1b, **2**b, **3**b, **4**b, **5**a, **6**b, **7**a, **8**a, **9**b, **10**b, **11**b, **12**a, **13**b, **14**b, **15**a

2
16b, **17**b, **18**a, **19**b, **20**b

3 Part A
21c, **22**d, **23**a

3 Part B
24f, **25**h, **26**g

4
27e, **28**b, **29**d, **30**a

Unit 10 Part A (p. 126)

1a
1 Do you **live** in a house or **a flat**?
2 Where is your flat?
3 How many floors are there in the **building**?
4 Is your flat **near** the station?
5 Is it old or **modern**?
6 What's **the name** of your **street**?

1b
1 I **live** in a flat.
2 My friends live in a **big house**.
3 My flat is very **old**.
4 It's on the **ground floor**.
5 There is one **bathroom** in my flat.
6 There are two **bedrooms** in my flat.

1c
John: Yes, I think so, too. / John: Oh, I don't think so.

2a
from the top: the fifth floor, the fourth floor, the third floor, the second floor, the first floor, the ground floor

2b
1 office, **2** bathroom, **3** kitchen, **4** bedroom, **5** living room, **6** toilet

2c
chair, television, bed, sofa, bath, fridge, cooker, computer, table, toilet, lamp

3.1a
1 bigger than, **2** better than, **3** healthier than, **4** more popular than, **5** worse than

3.1b
1 Paul is shorter than Mark.
2 Mark is fitter than Paul.
3 Paul is heavier than Mark.
4 Mark is taller than Paul.

3.2
1 It's Sue's car. / It's Sue's.
2 It's John's car. / It's John's.

4a
oben: balcony, kitchen, bathroom
unten: living room, bedroom

4b
the new flat: 2 bedrooms, 5th floor, 20 years old, £210/week, with balcony, no garage
the old flat: 1 bedroom, ground floor, 15 years old, £910/month, no balcony, with garage

4c
The new flat has one more bedroom and a balcony. It is cheaper and on a higher floor.

Unit 10 Part B (p. 132)

1a
1 It's near the airport.
2 There's a swimming pool.
3 There are 168 rooms on eight floors.
4 It's a 5-star hotel.
5 You can see the sea from all the rooms.

1b
1 I'd like to book a double room, please.
2 I'd like to have a room with a shower.
3 Have you got a room for 3 nights, please?
4 How much is the room per night?
5 Is breakfast included in the room price?
6 Is there a lift in your hotel?

1c
1 We'd like to **check out**, please.
2 We **were** in room 306.
3 The room **was** very comfortable.
4 We **didn't have** anything from the minibar.
5 Can I **pay** with this credit card?

2a
1 bath, **2** service, **3** per, **4** conference, **5** baby, **6** single, **7** minibar, **8** access, **9** reception, **10** area, **11** shower, **12** double, **13** family
2b
map, passport, hotel reservation, ticket
3a
1 Paul is the oldest.
2 Tom is the shortest.
3 Mark is the youngest.
4 Mark is the fittest.
5 Tom is the heaviest.
6 Mark is the tallest.
3b
2 Where is the best restaurant in London?
3 most interesting museum
4 biggest market
5 worst modern building
6 highest building
4a
1 B, **2** C, **3** B, **4** A, **5** A, **6** C
4c
underlined: **1** small and old, **2** near the beach, **3** for older people, **4** no sports activities, **5** breakfast only is possible

Unit 11 Part A (p. 138)

1a
1 How do you **go** to work? – I go **by** bus.
2 **How** do you usually go **on holiday**?
3 **Do** you go to the supermarket by car? – No, I don't. I go **on** foot.
4 **How often** do you travel by train? – Not **very** often.
1b
1 The 19.10 goes **to** Heathrow.
2 It leaves **from** platform 6.
3 It arrives **at** 19.33.
4 It is **on** time.
5 The train to Newbury is more than an hour **late**.
1c
1 **When** is the next train to Newbury?
2 **What time** is the fast train to Newbury?
3 Which **platform** does it leave from?
4 **Which** platform does it arrive at?
5 **How long** does it take?
2a
first row: bus, plane, taxi
second row: train, tram, underground
2b
1 platform, **2** help, **3** timetable, **4** passenger, **5** return, **6** fast, **7** late, **8** ticket, **9** board, **10** single
3.1a
on the left: 2, 5, 1 / *on the right:* 3, 6, 4
3.1b
1 He bought them in Italy.
2 She last saw her yesterday evening.
3 They parked it in the street.
4 They gave him some socks.
5 She asked us a lot of questions.
3.2
1 He went by plane. **2** She went by car.
3 They went on foot.
4a
the airport: 2, 5 / *the station:* 1, 6 / *the bus stop:* 3, 4
4b
1 24th May 2008, **2** Gatwick Airport, **3** Brighton, **4** No, it wasn't. **5** £8.30

Unit 11 Part B (p. 144)

1a
1 Excuse me, **can you** tell me **the way** to the station, please?
2 Excuse me, do you **know** where **the nearest** bus stop is?
3 Excuse me, **is there** a post office **near** here?
1b
1 Go **right**.
2 Go **left**.
3 Go **along** Park Road.
4 Go **past** the bank. The Post Office is **on** the left.
5 **Go** right **into** Station Road.
6 **Take** the third street on the right.
2
1 post office, **2** theatre, **3** tourist information office, **4** pub, **5** hotel, **6** hospital, **7** football stadium, **8** church, **9** restaurant, **10** cinema, **11** car park, **12** zoo, **13** flower shop, **14** station, **15** market, **16** park, **17** bank, **18** taxi stand, **19** bookshop, **20** supermarket, **21** leisure centre, **22** bus stop
3.1a
1 Read, **2** Speak, **3** Watch, **4** Do, **5** Come, **6** Buy, **7** Ask
3.1b
1 Don't worry about mistakes. **2** Don't be nervous in class. **3** Don't speak German in the lesson.
3.2
1 At, **2** On, **3** To, **4** Opposite, **5** In
4a
1 It's in Post Office Lane. **2** In / He lives in Willow Lane. **3** No, she doesn't.
4b
The woman wants to go to the school.
The man wants to go to the Chinese restaurant.
directions: Go out of the museum and go right. Walk to Newbury Street. The go right into Post Office Lane. Walk past the school. Wantage Electronics is on the right.

Unit 12 Part A (p. 150)

1a
1 What's the **weather** usually **like** there?
2 It's often **cold**.
3 It usually **snows** a lot in winter.
4 What's the weather like there **today**?
5 What was the weather like there **yesterday**?
1b
We're going to visit them …
after the class tonight.
tomorrow evening.
on Friday the 22nd.
at the weekend.
next winter.
1c
1 It's a **great** conference. – Yes, it's really interesting.
2 The speakers are **very good**. – Yes, they are.
3 I think you **know** my colleague, Ben. – Oh yes, I know him very well.
4 Is this your **first** conference here? – No, it's my third or fourth, I think.
5 Where **are you from**? – A very small place near Manchester.
correct order: 2, 4, 5, 1, 3
2a
on the left: cloudy, cold, hot, rain
on the right: snow, sunny, warm, windy
1 hot / warm / sunny, **2** cloudy, **3** windy, **4** cold, **5** snow, **6** rain
2b
Dec – Feb: winter (England) / summer (NZ)
March – May: spring (England) / autumn (NZ)
June – Aug: summer (England / winter (NZ)
Sept – Nov: autumn (England / spring (NZ)
1 summer in New Zealand, **2** autumn in England (only October has 31 days), **3** winter in England (February is the shortest month), **4** winter in NZ (June, July)

3.1

1 + 2: She's going to cook a special dinner. She's going to read a book in the garden.
3 + 4: She's going to buy some shoes. She's going to meet her friends.
5 + 6: She's going to have a meeting with her boss. She's going to send some emails.

3.2

1 He's going to the pub on Friday evening. He's going to meet some friends.
2 We're going to the lesson (*or* We're going to have a lesson) next *(___day)*. We're going to speak English.

4a

1a, **2**b, **3**c, **4**c, **5**c

Unit 12 Part B (p. 156)

1a

1 We're **going** to Liverpool **next weekend**.
2 We're going **to stay** in a spa hotel.
3 We're going to celebrate our wedding anniversary.
4 Are you going **away** next weekend?

1b

Sue: Hello.
Kath: Hello, **it's Kath here**.
Sue: Hello Kath, **how** are you?
Kath: I'm **fine** thanks, and **you**?
Sue: I'm fine, too.
Kath: Sue, **is John there**, please?
Sue: Yes he is, just a **minute**.
...
John: Hello, Kath.
Kath: Hi, John.
John: Is there a problem with tomorrow?
Kath: No, but we're going to leave an hour later, at ten.
John: Oh that's good. Thanks **for calling**.
Kath: You're **welcome**. **See you** tomorrow. Bye.
John: **Bye**.

2

1 play golf, **2** watch television, **3** a head massage, **4** have a manicure, **5** a wedding anniversary, **6** a beauty salon, **7** a cocktail bar, **8** a free bottle of champagne

3

1 She isn't going to come to the lesson next week.
2 Is she going to phone us?
3 She's going to phone next Friday.
4 Are they going to drive here?
5 They aren't going to drive here.
6 They're going to walk.

Test yourself 4 (p. 159)

1

1b, **2**a, **3**b, **4**b, **5**a, **6**a, **7**b, **8**b, **9**a, **10**b, **11**b, **12**b, **13**a, **14**b, **15**b

2

16 T, **17** F, **18** F, **19** F, **20** F

3 Part A

21b, **22**c, **23**d

3 Part B

24g, **25**h, **26**e

4

27 T, **28** F, **29** F, **30** F

Unit 8 Part A Exercise 3 (Page 98)

1 The Rolling Stones sang *Jumpin' Jack Flash*. 2 Films can't win a Nobel Prize. 3 Goethe wrote *Faust*.
4 Richard Gere and Julia Roberts starred in *Pretty Woman*. 5 Boney M sang *Rivers of Babylon*.

Unit 8 Part A Exercise 5 (Page 99)

Job: actor Born: (country) USA, (year) 1899 Died: (year) 1957 Married: four times.
Most famous film: Casablanca Initials: HB Name: Humphrey Bogart

Unit 8 Part B Biography game (Page 105)

John Lennon of the Beatles wrote and sang hit songs *(She loves you / Help)* with Paul McCartney. Swedish-born Greta Garbo was a Hollywood actress in the 1920s and 1930s. Polish-born John Paul II was pope for 27 years. British-born Charlie Chaplin made and starred in films from 1914 to 1967. German-born Albert Einstein won the Nobel Prize for physics in 1921. Queen Victoria was the Queen of England from 1837 to 1901. Austrian-born Wolfgang Amadeus Mozart went on his first concert tour when he was six years old. John Fitzgerald Kennedy was the youngest American president – from 1961 to 1963. William Shakespeare wrote plays *(Hamlet* and *Othello)*. Sisi was born in Bavaria and married Franz-Josef I, the Emperor of Austria in 1854. Marlene Dietrich was a singer *(Lili Marleen)* and film star – her last tour was when she was 75 years old. Diana, Princess of Wales died in a car crash in Paris. Fred Astaire was a dancer who starred in Hollywood films. Albanian-born Mother Teresa won the Nobel Peace Prize in 1979 for her work with poor people in India. Marilyn Monroe was a Hollywood actress, singer and sex-symbol. Rudolf Moshammer had a fashion shop in Munich and was a Munich celebrity. Roy Black was a German singer and actor. Elvis Presley was 'the king of rock'n'roll'. Bavarian Franz Josef Strauß was a CSU politician. Black American Martin Luther King was a civil rights activist.

Unit 1 Part A: 4a (p. 13)

Donna: Hi, my name's Donna.
Simon: Ah, hello Donna, nice to meet you.
Donna: Nice to meet you, too – erm – er … what's your name?
Simon: Oh, sorry – it's Simon, Simon Smith. Cheers.
Donna: Cheers.
Donna: That's funny – you're Simon Smith and I'm Donna Jones. There's something on television called *Smith and Jones*, I think.
Simon: Yes, I think you're right. *Smith and Jones* – two detectives. Erm – where are you from Donna? Now … I think you're from America – is that right?
Donna: Yes, that's right. I'm American – from Chicago.
Simon: Ah, Chicago – a great place.
Donna: Yes, and you – where are you from?
Simon: Oh, I'm from down under … from Sydney, Australia … that's my city!
Donna: Oh, tell me about Australia … is it always warm and sunny or …

Unit 1 Part B: 4a (p. 19)

(R = receptionist, W = woman)
R: So that's fine then. Can I have your name, please?
F: Yes, it's Lynda …
R: Sorry, can I have your surname first, please?
F: Oh, yes, of course. It's Dwightman.
R: Oh can you spell that, please?
F: Yes, it's D W I G H T M A N.
R: D W I G H T M A N – is that right?
F: Yes, that's right … and my first name is Lynda with a Y.
R: And your address?
F: It's 9 Bank Street, in London. That's London SE7 3DL.
R: Let me read that back to you: 9 Bank Street, London FE
F: No – no SE … S for Sandra ..
R: Oh, thank you … SE7 3DL. And your phone number?
F: 020 – 731 8456.
R: Thank you … and your mobile number
F: No – no mobile.
R: Oh? No mobile?
F: No.
R: Well, can I have an email address – for if we want to contact you?
F: Yes, it's Ldwight – that's L D W I G H T at hotmail.com.
R: That's okay then – thank you. Oh, one last thing … what nationality are you?
F: Why do you need to know that?
R: It's for the statistics – the tourist statistics.
F: Oh, Ok – I'm Canadian.
R: Canadian. Thank you. Well, that's all. See you soon …

Unit 2 Part A: 4a (p. 25)

Right, so I want to tell you about my town and where you can find the buildings and places in it. First, the school – the school is in School Lane, of course. Next to the school, on the corner of School Lane and Station Road, there's a bank. And next to the bank there's a very big cinema. That's very nice. Opposite the bank, on the other corner of Station Road and School Lane, there's a bookshop, and next to the bookshop there's a pub … it's an Irish pub called The Dubliner. The station is opposite the bookshop and the pub. Next to the station there's a park, and in the park there's a small café – very nice. There's a very big supermarket next to the station, too … on the other side. Erm … next to the pub there's a hotel and opposite the hotel, on the corner of Park Street and Station Road, you can find a restaurant. It's new, it's Italian, I think. There's a Post Office in Park Street next to the restaurant and next to the restaurant in Station Road, there's an art gallery. It's a very nice town – my town.

Unit 2 Part A: 4b (p. 25)

1 Is the pub in Station Road?
2 Is there a leisure centre in Station Road?
3 Is there a station in this town?
4 Is the hotel next to the station?
5 Where's the hotel?
6 Where's the school?
7 Where's the bookshop?

Unit 2 Part B: 4a (p. 31)

Hi, I'm Dan and I'm your guide for today. Here's our station – the Grand Central. It's a beautiful station. This part of New York is very busy – 24 hours a day.
Here you can see MoMA, that's the Museum of Modern Art – fantastic art museum.
Here you can see one of our famous Barnes and Noble bookshops. There are 16 Barnes and Noble shops in New York. And here you can see our very special department store called Macy's. Shopping there is great.
Here we are at Central Park – every New Yorker loves it.
Now we're on Fifth Avenue – a very famous and exclusive shopping street – there are a lot of millionaires here. There aren't any small bars near here – only classy restaurants … for millionaires … not for you and me.
This building is our very famous opera house – the Met. Do you have any famous opera houses back home?
Oh my, you're from Australia. Well yes, there's a famous opera house there, too.
So, now we can go straight …

Unit 3 Part A: 4 (p. 37)

My name's Danielle. I'm thirteen years old and I live in a place called Ipswich – that isn't very far from London. We've got a small house but my family's small, so that's okay. I've got a brother, he's twelve years old but I haven't got any sisters.
My mum and dad are fantastic. My mum is like a sister to me – we go to the shops and sometimes to the cinema together. I've got two grandmas but I haven't got any grand-fathers. My mum's father is dead, and my dad's father – well, I don't know really.

Hi, I'm Becky … oh, *(little giggle)* sorry, that's Rebecca. I'm fourteen and I live near Ipswich. I haven't got any brothers or sisters … but I've got a lot of friends. I'm happy to say that some of my friends have got big families. At home, there's only my mum and me. My dad isn't here in Ipswich with us. He's in Scotland, in Glasgow … I think. But my mum's mum and dad live in the house next to us. My grandma is great – they've got hundreds of books and films in their house. We've got a small house with a small garden. The best thing about our house is that it's next to my grandma's house!

Unit 3 Part B: 4 (p. 43)

1 A: Oh, look at Anita. She looks great, doesn't she?
B: Yes, that's fantastic on her.
A: Yeah, the colour is perfect with her hair …
B: And, of course … it looks really good on her because she's tall and …

2 A: We can ask Alicia.
B: Do you think she can do that?
A: Alicia? Yes, of course. She can do everything.
B: Huh?
A: Well … not everything … but Alicia is very clever and I'm sure she can …

3 A: And Tom? Do you think he can help?
B: Tom? Oh, no – I don't think so.
A: Why not?
B: Well he *is* a good cook … but for twenty people. I think that's a bit too much.
A: Hmm …

4 A: But there are always millions of people at the airport.
B: Yes … but look … here's a photo …
A: What? That photo must be ten years old.
B: Yes, you're right … she hasn't got brown hair now – I think it's red … or maybe blonde …
A: An …

Test yourself 1 (p. 45–46)

Listening comprehension

Hi, my name's Jack Clements and my wife, Sabine, and I have got a house in a small town near London. Our house is in Wyndham Road – erm that's Wyndham – _W Y N D H A M … Our house is on a corner, it's number 18, 18 Wyndham Road. Wyndham Road is very nice. There's a French restaurant in our road and there's a small park opposite our house and in the park there's a very nice small café. Now, our town is a small town, there aren't any very big shops here. There's a supermarket near the station, but it isn't very big – the supermarket I mean, not the station. Hey, you can come here and see our town. Phone me – my phone number is 01923 739886 … have you got it? 01923 739886.

Situational responses Part A

21 Hello again, nice to see you again. How are you?
22 Oh, hello – I'm Diana, Diana Steele from Paris.
23 Oh, really. I'm from Germany, too. I'm from Munich – are you from there, too?

Situational responses Part B

24 Excuse me.
25 Excuse me, can you help me? Erm, is there a post office near here?
26 Thank you.

Unit 4 Part A: 4b (p. 51)

(I = interviewer, J = Jill)
I: Where do you live?
J: I live in Wantage.
I: Do you work?
J: Yes, I do. I'm a PA.
I: Do you like your boss?
J: My boss? Oh, yes – David is very nice.
I: What time do you get up?
J: At about 7 o'clock in the morning.
I: Do you have breakfast in a café?
J: In a café? Oh, no. I have breakfast at home.
I: Do you go out for lunch?
J: Out for lunch? No, I don't, I have lunch in my office.
I: What do you do after work?
J: After work I go home, or I go to the pub or to my yoga class.
I: When do you go to your yoga class?
J: The class is on Mondays. At 6.30.
I: Do you go to a pub in Wantage?
J: Yes, I do.
I: And do you have dinner in the pub?
J: No, I have dinner at home.

Unit 4 Part B: 4a (p. 57)

(J = Jill, S = Susie)
J: I know you like your new job Susie, but what do you do in the evenings?
S: Well, on Monday evenings I go to my Italian course – I like that a lot. The people there are very nice. And then I go to bed at about half past ten. In fact, I go to bed at about 10.30 on Mondays, Wednesdays and Thursdays.
J: And on Tuesdays. Do you go out on Tuesdays, too?
S: No, I don't. I stay at home all evening on Tuesdays.
J: And what time do you go to bed?
S: Oh, I don't know. And then on Wednesdays I have dinner with my mum at her house. That's good, She's a very good cook.
J: Oh, that's nice. And what do you do on Thursdays then?
S: I go to a yoga class at the sports centre.
J: Oh? Yoga – is it interesting?
S: Yes, it is. I like it. And then on Fridays I go out with friends to a restaurant or we go dancing.
J: And what time do you come home on Fridays?
S: Oh, about half past eleven … or sometimes a bit later.

Unit 4 Part B: 4b (p. 57)

1 What time does Susie's Italian class start?
2 Does Susie go out on Tuesdays?
3 What time does Susie come home from her mother's house on Wednesdays?
4 Does Susie go to her yoga class on Tuesdays or Thursdays?
5 Does Susie go out on Friday evenings?

Unit 5 Part A: 3b (p. 63)

(J = Jill, D = David)
J: Have you got any brothers or sisters, David?
D: No, I haven't. But I've got some good friends. My best friend is an old school friend called Paul.
J: Does he live here in Wantage, too?
D: No, he doesn't like Wantage at all. No, he lives in the centre of London. He likes the big city. It's important that he lives near his work.
J: What does he do?
D: He works in a very big hospital in London. His wife works there, too. They live very near the hospital.
J: What do they do at the weekends? Do they stay in London or go to the countryside?
D: They stay in London because they work at the weekends … not every weekend but two or three times a month.

J: What do they do in their free time?
D: Well, they don't have a lot of free time. But I know that they play chess when they can.
J: Do they play in a chess club?
D: Yes, they do and Paul is very good. He wins every time they play, but his wife doesn't give up. Oh no – she wants to win one day!
J: Yes, well – I can understand that.

Unit 5 Part B: 4a + b
(p. 69)

(RP = radio presenter, J = Janey, a fitness expert)

RP: Today we've asked a fitness expert to give us some tips about what we can do to be healthier. Janey?
J: Well, thank you. There are a lot of things that we can do to be healthier. What about that stressful job? Why don't you tell your boss that you can't work late every evening? This would give you more free time. And then you can enjoy that free time more and more. You could see some friends once or twice a week. What do you think of that suggestion? Not the same friends all the time – different friends with different interests ... but good friends, really good friends.
To be healthy you must eat healthy food as often as you can. So why don't you buy fresh food at the market once a week? But, of course you can't sit at home all the time. You can't just sit there and watch television all day. You could do some sport every day. Go swimming, walk to work ... even do a fitness programme. And my last suggestion for today is for the smokers out there. Why don't you stop smoking *today*? Smoking really is bad for you – we all know that.
RP: Thanks a lot Janey. Maybe the people out there can try to be a little healthier. Thanks for the tips. And now we have the sports news for you.

Unit 6 Part A: 4a (p. 75)

(RP = radio presenter, 1, 2, 3 = reporters)

RP: This evening we've got three of our reporters in the studio. We want to hear what they think about our local restaurants. Sally, you first.
1: Well, my report is about The Chinese Garden. It gets 3 points for atmosphere – it's good but a bit TOO Chinese for me ... too much Chinese music all the time. The food there is good, but not VERY good – so it gets 3 points for food, too. And then we've got the question of service. And I must say, the service there is fantastic, really great – so that's 5 points for service. And the last thing ... the prices. It is very, very expensive ... so, I'm sorry – but it only gets 2 points – it's too expensive.
RP: OK, thanks Sally. Now you Tony.
2: Right, well, thanks. I've got the points for the Taj Mahal. I like this restaurant and the food is good but not VERY good – so it's a 3 for the food. And the prices are okay for the food – it isn't too expensive so it gets a 3 for prices. I'm sorry to say that the service really isn't very good there. I think all the waiters are new at the restaurant or something. But I would like to have better service. So it's only 2 points for service. Sorry about that because the atmosphere is great. There's some nice and interesting Indian art there and the music is good too – so it gets 4 from me for atmosphere.
RP: Thanks Tony. And now you Rob.
3: So, I'd like to talk about the Pizza Palace. The service is okay there – good waiters – yeah, they get 3 points for service. And their prices? Fantastic. Good pizzas for good prices – what more do you want? I give them 4 points for their prices. The atmosphere isn't really very good. In fact, there's no atmosphere there. Only 2 points for atmosphere. And the food – well I said that the prices and the food are good – but the food is really excellent – the best pizzas you can get. Top marks – they get 5 for the food.
RP: Mmm, sounds good. OK, well thanks a lot – and ... now would you like to go to your restaurants again?

Unit 6 Part B: 4a + c
(p. 81)

(H = Hilary, P = Pete)

H: Hello.
P: Hi Hilary, it's Pete.
H: Oh, hi Pete, how are you?
P: I'm fine thanks, and you?
H: Great thanks.
P: Listen Hilary, I'd like to invite you to a party, next week – on Friday evening.
H: A party – well that's very nice, thank you. It isn't your birthday, is it?
P: No, you know when my birthday is. No, it's just a party because I'd like to have a party, that's all.
H: Oh great. Where is the party?
P: It's at my tennis club.
H: OK and next Friday, you said ... good. What time does the party start?
P: Oh, I don't know ... er ... 8 o'clock.
H: OK, that's fine. Can I bring something?
P: No, no I've got everything – a lot of everything!
H: OK ... and tell me, is there a small hotel near the club? I don't want to go home late.
P: It's OK, you can stay at my place. That's fine.
H: Oh great, thanks very much. And one last question ... how much is a taxi from the station? I don't want to come in my car.
P: It's about £10, I think.

Test yourself 2 (p. 83–84)

Listening comprehension

16 You want a table for six on Friday. Just a moment, please. Hmm – sorry ... we can do a table for four on Friday, but not six. We've got a table for six for Saturday.
17 Ok, that's fine then. Your birthday dinner from me at the China Garden. Great. See you next Wednesday then.
18 That's fine. So, you'd like chicken soup to start. And then you'd like a Greek salad ... oh ... I'm sorry, we haven't got a Greek salad today. We've got a green salad or tomato and mozzarella – but not a Greek salad, sorry.
19 First we have the sports round up and then, in quarter of an hour ... there's the Sunday night film.
20 Ladies and gentlemen – it's 5.30 and as you know it's Sunday today and on Sundays we close at 6 p.m. So I'd like to say goodbye – and have a nice evening.

Situational responses Part A

21 Would you like to come to our party on Friday?
22 Would you like a cup of coffee?
23 What would you like?

Situational responses Part B

24 How often do you go to the cinema?
25 When do you see your friends?
26 What time does the film start?

Unit 7 Part A: 3c (p. 89)

1 Were you at the last English lesson?
2 Was there a festival in your town last month?
3 Were there any new students in your class last week?

Unit 7 Part B: 3b (p. 95)

1 The weather's very nice.
2 We all worked hard in the lesson.
3 They're good students.
4 The people were very friendly.
5 The food was good.
6 The food there is always good.
7 We flew.
8 We live near the airport.
9 He took a lot of photos.
10 He likes taking photos.

Unit 7 Part B: 4b (p. 95)

(RP = radio presenter, R = reporter)

RP: And this week we have a report coming to you from our travel reporter, Anna.

R: Thank you. Hello everybody, I'd just like to tell you about my trip to Switzerland. I went to Switzerland two months ago for the first time in my life.
I drove from London to Interlaken – that was a long way. I drove because I wanted to take my skis with me. It was very, very cold in Switzerland – I can tell you. But that was very good for the skiing. On the way to the hotel, I saw a lot of mountains … mountains, mountains and more mountains – it was wonderful. My hotel was good. I had a very big room – for four people and I was alone!
It was a nice room. I had breakfast early when I was there – when the weather's good for skiing, it's good to go up into the mountains early in the day. I stayed there for three nights and then I came back home again. I'd like to go there again!

RP: Well, thanks for that Anna. Perhaps you can go there again next year …

Unit 8 part A: 4a (p. 101)

(I = interviewer, J = Jason, an actor)

I: Welcome to the show, Jason.

J: Thank you.

I: We'd just like to know about your past and how you started your career as an actor. Well to start – I know that you live in London now, but were you born in London?

J: No, I wasn't. I was born in Dublin but I came to London with my parents when I was three years old. I went to school here in London from the age of 5 to the age of 17. I wasn't very good at school, I didn't want to learn … I don't know why.

I: And after school?

J: After school I started work. I worked in a bookshop – that was a great job. I was happy there. But at that time I went to the theatre a lot and I loved it – I loved everything about it. So, after two years I started at acting school. It was difficult for me to go back to school – but I was a bit older then and I really, really wanted to do it.

I: And then, after acting school, what happened then?

J: Then my first job as an actor came along. It wasn't in the theatre but in television. I was in a children's show for about three years, I think.

I: And are you in television now?

J: No, I'm not. I work in films now. Film studios are fantastic places, I love the work. And it was in a film studio that I met my wonderful wife, Sasha – about ten years ago.

I: Is Sasha a film actor, too?

J: No – no she isn't. She's a singer – but she's a stay-at-home mother at the moment … we've got two small children.

I: Singers or actors?

J: Ah … now that's a very good question.

Unit 8 Part B: 4a–c (p. 107)

Good evening. It's Monday again and here is the news from our town this weekend.
On Saturday we had the opening night of La Traviata at the school theatre. It was a fantastic first night and after it there was a late night party for all the singers. Three of the singers gave interviews. You can hear the interviews on Tuesday evening.
On Sunday afternoon, the school football team was in the final. They were in the final last year, too. Last year they didn't win, but this year was better. The players won the match 3-1. Well done, boys.

On Sunday evening the Pizzeria Milano was a frightening place to be. Two men came into the restaurant and took all the money that was there. The waiter wanted to stop them but it just wasn't possible. They were very fast and ran out with the money to a car in the street. If you have any information, please call the police.

Well that's all for this weekend. Bye, and have a good week.

Unit 9 Part A: 2c (p. 112)

1 With some friends from the office.
2 Tennis.
3 Because it's good for me.
4 Very clearly, of course.
5 On Friday evenings.
6 Pizza.
7 In Oberhelfenschwil.

Unit 9 Part B: 4a+b (p. 119)

1 I'm very sorry madam, but you mustn't smoke in here. This is a place where people come to get healthy and you see that notice over there. Now please … you must go outside if you want to smoke. Thank you.

2 *(A = policeman, B = man)*
A: Excuse me, sir – you mustn't park here.
B: Oh, but I only want to leave it for 5 minutes, at the most.
A: Sorry sir, please drive around the corner and park it in the next street.
B: Why?
A: Because, sir, there is no parking in this street. Understand?
B: Oh, okay.

Test yourself 3 (p. 121–122)

Listening comprehension

I work for a computer company and my wife works in a bookshop. Before we go to work we have breakfast at home. Some of the people who work with me have breakfast in a café … but we don't want to do that.

I leave the house at 8 o'clock every morning, and Sabine leaves about half an hour after me. That's nice for her … she has half an hour longer at home.

I like my job. I work from 9 to 5 every day from Monday to Friday … and sometimes I work on a Saturday morning, too. But that's OK – it's only one Saturday a month … so there are three Saturdays a month when I don't work.

Sabine works every morning from Monday to Friday and all day Saturday, too – morning and afternoon. She always says that Saturday is a very long day for her.

I do the shopping on Saturday when Sabine is at work. And I like cooking, so I usually cook something nice for her when she comes home from the bookshop. She usually arrives home at about 6 o'clock. She's sometimes very tired then.

Situational responses Part A

21 Do you want to buy this book?
22 How much is this map?
23 These big postcards are really nice.

Situational responses Part B

24 I've got my driving test tomorrow.
25 I'm sorry, I'm busy all day today.
26 I'm sorry I'm late.

Unit 10 Part A: 4b (p. 127)

(M = man, W = woman)

M: … well, was it good ... was it great? Tell me about it.
W: It was OK but it wasn't perfect. I'll compare it with the flat that I've got now and then perhaps I can decide about it.
M: Good.
W: Well, it's got two bedrooms and my flat has only got one bedroom. Erm … it's on the 5th floor – that's nice. Much higher than my ground floor flat. I never liked the ground floor. It's a bit older than my flat – my flat's about 15 years old and this one is … erm let me see … yes it's 20 years old. Erm … now, what else …
M: And the price? What about the price?
W: Oh yes, the price. It's 210 pounds per week – yes, 210 and my flat is 910 pounds per month. Is that cheaper or more expensive? … oh, I'm no good at numbers
M: I think that's a bit cheaper then – so that's good.
W: Oh yes, that is good. Oh, something else – there's a balcony, a nice balcony … hmm … but there isn't a garage. Not to worry … I think I can park on the street there. So that's OK. Oh, and there's a kitchen and bathroom, of course.
M: So all you have to do now is decide if you want to take this one. It's got a lot of positive things about it.

Unit 10 Part A: 4d (p. 127)

(M = man, W = woman)

M: … all you have to do is decide if you want to take this one. It's got a lot of positive things about it.
W: Yes, it has. In fact, it's got nearly everything I wanted.
M: Well, what isn't good about it then?
W: Well, I really wanted a more modern flat and this one is older. And I wanted a garage, too. Oh, but that isn't important, I can park on the street – that's OK for my old car.
M: Yes, that's true.
W: But the rooms and the balcony are super. OK …
M: OK what?
W: OK – I want it.
M: Good. Well done. When can I come and have a look …

Unit 10 Part B: 4c (p. 133)

Friend: Mmm, these photos look wonderful. Tell me, why do you like the hotel there so much? You went there last year, too, I think.
Sue: Yes, I'd like to go there every year.
Friend: Why? What's so special about it?
Sue: Well, it's a really nice hotel. It's small and it's old, very traditional, very *Greek* if you know what I mean.
Friend: Yes, I think I know.
Sue: And it's right opposite the beach – one minute from bed to sea. Wonderful. It's also very quiet there. I think families go to a holiday centre on the other side of the town – so there are never any children there. I *like* children, but sometimes it's just nice to be quiet. I suppose you could say that the guests *aren't* the youngest.
Friend: Oh Sue …
Sue: Well, yes … and there isn't a swimming pool at the hotel so that's good – it's so near the sea – and there aren't any sports activities there but a lot of people go for nice long walks.
Friend: And in the evenings?
Sue: In the evenings, there's a piano player in the bar. The bar isn't very big and it's lovely to sit there and have a drink and listen to him. He's very good.
Friend: Do you have dinner there every evening?
Sue: No, not every evening. I book a room with breakfast only, then I can go out in the evening – there are *thousands* of restaurants nearby – or I can order something in the hotel if I want.
Friend: Mm – it sounds perfect.
Sue: Yes, why don't you come with me next year?

Unit 11 Part A: 4a (p. 139)

1 If you want to travel on the 9.47 to Birmingham, could you please go to platform 7. Platform 7 for Birmingham, thank you.
2 We would like to remind passengers that only one bag is allowed. Please check in with one bag only. Thank you.
3 A: Well, I don't know where it is. I was here yesterday, too and it didn't come.
B: It didn't come?
A: No, I was here for an hour and it didn't come, so I went home again.
B: Oh.
4 A: Excuse me, do you go to the station?
B: No, sorry. We go into the town centre from here and then we go out to the shopping centre. We don't go to the station. You want the number 5. That goes to the station.
A: Oh, thank you.

5 This is the last call for all passengers on British Airways flight 0952 to Munich, please go to departure gate number 62 immediately. Thank you.

6 We are sorry to announce that the Intercity Express from Manchester is running 30 minutes late. Expected arrival time is now 14.47.

Unit 11 Part B: 4b (p. 145)

(J = Jill, W = woman)

J: Yes, I can help you with that.

W: Oh, good.

J: OK, this is Grove Street – where we are now. So … walk along Grove Street and then go left into Mill Street. Go along Mill Street to the market place.

W: Market place – good I've got that.

J: Then go right into Newbury Street. Walk along Newbury Street and take the second street on the right.

W: Second on the right … yes …

J: Walk past the Civic Hall on your right and then you come to the place you want on the right.

W: Good, thanks very much for your help.

J: You're welcome.

(J = Jill, M = man)

J: Oh, yes, I know it – I often go there.

M: Oh, good.

J: Walk along Grove Street – here in this direction – to Grove Road.

M: So we're in Grove Street now.

J: Yes, that's right. Walk to Grove Road and go left into Grove Road, and then go right immediately … after a minute, that's all … into Garston Lane.

M: Immediately right.

J: Then take the second road on the left and it's the second or third building on the right.

M: Good, thanks … that's not too difficult then.

J: No, it isn't. I hope you like it there.

M: Thanks. Bye.

J: Bye.

Unit 12 Part A: 2a (p. 150)

1 Oh, phew, oh, phew – not the weather for working in the garden – phew – give me some water, please – now!

2 Oh dear! Look over there – it's very grey over there – but it isn't going to rain – it's just a bit grey up there.

3 *the sound of wind*

4 *someone shivering, teeth chattering, they're cold*

5 Ok, yes … you can go out and play. You can make a man if you like – or a woman – here where I can see him – or her – from the kitchen. Go on – off you go … have fun.

6 *the sound of rain*

Unit 12 Part A: 4a (p. 151)

(J = John, S = Sue)

J: So that's really nice … that we're going to see Henry and Christine at the weekend.

S: John, they're French. It's *Henri* and *Christiane*.

J: Oh, OK. But they're here now … well, in Wales … so why can't I say Henry and Christine?

S: Because that's not what their names are, that's why.

J: Well anyway, I'm going to walk into town tomorrow morning and buy the tickets.

S: Tickets? What for?

J: For the train, of course.

S: Oh, no. I'm not going to travel all that way by train. We've only got two days.

J: Oh, so that means we're going by car … yes?

S: Yes, we are.

J: And I'm going to drive all the way there in the rain.

S: John, what's the matter with you this evening?

J: Oh, I don't know. I'm tired.

S: It isn't going to rain.

J: No?

S: No, it's going to be grey … very grey all weekend … but …

J: Oh great, a grey weekend in Wales.

S: Oh John, come on. You know they're going back to France soon.

J: Oh, yes. Before Christmas?

S: No, they're going to come here at Christmas – and they're going back to live in France in April, I think.

J: Oh dear – no more trips to Wales then.

S: No, but we can go to France by train … on the Eurostar.

J: *(groans)*

S: I'm going to do that every summer.

J: What? We can't do that.

S: I said I not we!

J: Oh.

Test yourself 4 (p. 159–160)

Listening comprehension

16 Oh yes, here's my credit card. Thank you very much. This was a very nice place to stay. I'm sorry I have to leave really. And tomorrow, it's back to work again.

17 We are very sorry to announce that the 10.40 from London Paddington is 30 minutes late. Expected arrival time is now 11.10.

18 Yes, we have a very nice flat in Willow Lane. There are three bedrooms and a very big living room with a balcony. It's got a modern kitchen and bathroom … Yes, I saw it yesterday – I think it's perfect for you. It's £800 a month. Would you like to go and see it?

19 The hotel was really good – the food was great and the service was excellent. But, you know, I had a real problem. I don't know – perhaps I ate something bad … some fish perhaps … and out of the seven days holiday, I was in hospital for three days. Not my best holiday!

20 The bus to the airport … erm, now this bus stop here … it's for the bus to Marble Arch and Oxford Street. Hhm, that's no good. Erm … you see, I always go to the airport by train. Perhaps this lady can help you … excuse me, do you know where the bus to Heathrow Airport …

Situational responses Part A

21 I think this is a very nice hotel.

22 Where's the manager?

23 Hello, how are you?

Situational responses Part B

24 How long are you going to stay?

25 I'd like to book a room, please.

26 Where's the lift?

Unit 1 Part A

Nice to meet you.

Nett dich / Sie kennen zu lernen.

Hello. How are you?

Hallo. Wie geht es dir / Ihnen?

and	und
English speaker	Sprecher(in) des Englischen
I'm (I am)	ich bin
first	erste(r, -s)
how	wie
make contact	Kontakt herstellen
meet	treffen
my	mein(e)
name	Name
nice	nett
normally	normalerweise
thank you / thanks	danke
too	auch
use	verwenden
very	sehr
what's (what is)	was ist
you	du
your	dein(e)

How to say hello Jemanden begrüßen

Hello. I'm Jill. Hallo. Ich bin Jill.	Hi. My name's Richard. Hallo. Mein Name ist Richard.
How are you? Wie geht es dir / Ihnen?	I'm very well, thank you. Mir geht es gut, danke. Fine, thanks. And you? Gut, danke. Und dir / Ihnen?

How to introduce someone

Wie Sie jemanden vorstellen

This is Emma. Das ist Emma.	Nice to meet you. Nett dich / Sie kennen zu lernen.	Nice to meet you, too. Nett auch dich / Sie kennen zu lernen.

Where are you from?

Woher kommst du / kommen Sie?

a / an	ein(e)
always	immer
American	amerikanisch
capital letter	Großbuchstabe
from	von, aus
her	ihr(e)
his	sein(e)
I think ...	ich denke, ...
in	in
near	nahe
stamp	Briefmarke
teacher	Lehrer
the	der, die, das
where's (where is)	wo ist

be	**sein**
I'm (I am) / I'm not ...	Ich bin / Ich bin nicht ...
He's (He is) / He isn't ...	Er ist / Er ist nicht ...
She's (She is) / She isn't ...	Sie ist / Sie ist nicht ...
It's (It is) / It isn't (Is not) ...	Es ist / Es ist nicht ...
Are you ...?	Bist du / Sind Sie ...?
Is he / she / it ...?	Ist er / sie / es ...?
Yes / No	Ja / Nein

Word focus Countries and nationalities

Länder und Nationalitäten

Where is it from?
Woher kommt es?
It's from England. It's English.
Es kommt aus England. Es ist englisch.

Australia / Australian	Australien / australisch
Austria / Austrian	Östereich / österreichisch
England / English	England / englisch
Greece / Greek	Griechenland / griechisch
Turkey / Turkish	Türkei / türkisch
France / French	Frankreich / französisch
Germany / German	Deutschland / deutsch
Ireland / Irish	Irland / irisch
Italy / Italian	Italien / italienisch
Switzerland / Swiss	Schweiz / schweizer

* Ländernamen und Nationalitätenbezeichnungen beginnen mit Großbuchstaben.

Goodbye Auf Wiedersehen

Goodbye. Auf Wiedersehen.	Bye. See you next week. Tschüss. Bis nächste Woche.

Unit 1 Part B

More about you. Mehr zu dir / Ihnen.

Contact details Kontaktdaten

How to give your name Den Namen sagen

What's your name? Wie heißt du / heißen Sie?	It's Louise. Louise.

Can I have your surname, please? Kannst du mir bitte deinen / Können Sie mir bitte Ihren Namen sagen?	It's Hanley. Hanley.
Can you spell your first name for me, please? Kannst du mir bitte deinen / Können Sie mir bitte Ihren Namen buchstabieren.	Yes, it's L-O-U-I-S-E. Ja, das ist L-O-U-I-S-E.

Word focus Numbers Zahlen

one	eins	four	vier	seven	sieben
two	zwei	five	fünf	eight	acht
three	drei	six	sechs	nine	neun

How to say a phone number
Eine Telefonnummer sagen

- ■ What's your phone number?
  Wie ist deine / Ihre Telefonnummer?
- ■ Can I have your mobile number, please?
  Kannst du mir bitte deine / Können Sie mir bitte Ihre Handynummer sagen?
- ◆ It's oh six four three two nine one.
  Das ist null sechs vier drei zwei neun eins.
- ■ Can you repeat that, please?
  Kannst du / Können Sie das bitte wiederholen?

* 0 = oh (GB), zero (US)
Handy = mobile phone (GB), cell phone (US)

How to say an email address
Eine E-Mail-Adresse sagen

- ■ What's your email address?
  Wie ist deine / Ihre E-Mail-Adresse?
- ■ Can I have your email address, please?
  Kannst du mir bitte deine / Können Sie mir bitte Ihre E-Mail-Adresse sagen?
- ◆ It's JennyCohen@bookworld.com
  Es ist JennyCohen@bookworld.com
- ■ Can you spell that for me, please?
  Kannst du mir / Können Sie mir das bitte buchstabieren?
- ◆ It's Jenny Cohen at book world dot com
  Das ist Jenny Cohen at book world Punkt com

Welcome Willkommen

language school	Sprachschule
our	unser(e)
their	ihr(e)
room	Raum, Zimmer
Vienna	Wien

Are they ...?	Sind sie ...?
They're (they are)	Sie sind
They aren't	Sie sind nicht
We're (we are)	Wir sind
We aren't (are not)	Wir sind nicht

Unit 2 Part A
In town In der Stadt

What's in your town?
Was gibt es in deiner / Ihrer Stadt?

art gallery	Kunstgalerie
bank	Bank
bookshop	Buchhandlung
café	Cafe
car park	Parkplatz
swimming pool	Swimmingpool
Chinese restaurant	chinesisches Restaurant
church	Kirche
cinema	Kino
department store	Kaufhaus
hotel	Hotel
ice-cream shop	Eisdiele
Irish pub	Irisches Pub
leisure centre	Freizeitzentrum
market place	Marktplatz
museum	Museum
park	Park
post office	Postamt
sandwich shop	Imbissrestaurant
school	Schule
supermarket	Supermarkt
Thai restaurant	thailändisches Restaurant
train station	Bahnhof

Is there a / an ...?	Gibt es ein(e) ...?
There's a / an ...	Es gibt ein(e) ...
There isn't a / an ...	Es gibt kein(e) ...
beer	Bier
before	vor, bevor
big	groß
house	Haus
good	gut
in your part of town	in Ihrem / deinem Teil der Stadt
It's called ...	Es heißt ...
lane	kleine Straße
people	Leute
small	klein
street plan	Stadtplan

Is there a bank near here?
Gibt es eine Bank in der Nähe?

How to ask and say where things are in a town
Danach fragen und sagen, wo Dinge in einer Stadt sind

■ Excuse me. Is there a bank near here?
Entschuldigung. Gibt es hier in der Nähe eine Bank?
◆ Yes, there's a bank in West Street.
Ja, es gibt eine Bank in der West Street.
■ Where in West Street?
Wo in der West Street?
◆ It's near / next to / opposite the bank.
Es ist nahe / neben / gegenüber der Bank.

road	Straße
on the corner	an der Ecke
Excuse me.	Entschuldigung.
You're welcome.	Gern geschehen.
help	Hilfe, helfen

Unit 2 Part B
City break Kurzurlaub in der Stadt

Cities of the world Städte der Welt

airport	Flughafen
beach	Strand
bridge	Brücke
building	Gebäude
city centre	Stadtzentrum
fast food restaurant	Schnellrestaurant
opera house	Opernhaus
ask	fragen
famous	berühmt
know	kennen, wissen
river	Fluss
tourist	Tourist(in)
want	wollen
when	wann, wenn

How to talk about a town or city
Über eine Stadt sprechen

It's international / romantic / quiet / busy.
Es ist international / romantisch / ruhig / belebt.
You can see modern buildings.
Sie können / du kannst moderne Gebäude sehen.

There's a big river.
Es gibt einen großen Fluss.
There are some beautiful old churches.
Es gibt schöne alte Kirchen.
There are a lot of tourists.
Es gibt viele Touristen.
Are there any ...?
Gibt es ...?
There aren't any ...
Es gibt keine ...

Numbers Zahlen

Word focus Numbers 10–99 Zahlen 10–99

ten	zehn	thirty	dreißig
eleven	elf	forty	vierzig
twelve	zwölf	fifty	fünfzig
thirteen	dreizehn	sixty	sechzig
fourteen	vierzehn	seventy	siebzig
fifteen	fünfzehn	eighty	achtzig
sixteen	sechzehn	ninety	neunzig
seventeen	siebzehn	twenty-one	einundzwanzig
eighteen	achtzehn	thirty-two	zweiunddreißig
nineteen	neunzehn	forty-three	dreiundvierzig
twenty	zwanzig		

* four fourteen forty

Britain	Großbritannien
college	*Teil einer Universität*
distance	Entfernung
facts and figures	Daten und Zahlen
holiday	Ferien
including	einschließlich
mile	Meile
oldest	älteste(r, -s)
open	offen
over	über
public	Öffentlichkeit, öffentlich
theatre	Theater
twin town	Partnerstadt
university	Universität

Unit 3 Part A
The family Die Familie

Family Familie

Word focus Family members
Familienmitglieder

father	Vater
mother	Mutter
brother	Bruder
sister	Schwester

son	Sohn
daughter	Tochter
grandfather	Großvater
grandmother	Großmutter
grandson	Enkel
granddaughter	Enkelin
grandchildren	Enkelkinder
husband	Ehemann
wife	Ehefrau
uncle	Onkel
aunt	Tante
niece	Nichte
nephew	Neffe
cousin	Cousin
parent	Elternteil
married	verheiratet
divorced	geschieden
an only child	Einzelkind

* grandchild: Enkelkind   grandchildren: Enkelkinder

another	noch ein(e, -s)
best	beste(r, -s)
both	beide
but	aber
can	kann, können
can't	kann / können nicht
choose	aussuchen
David's parents	Davids Eltern
dead	tot
friend	Freund
loving	liebevoll
member	Mitglied
or	oder
a sort of	eine Art von
test	Test, Prüfung
time	Zeit
warm	warm
have got	
I've got … (have got)	Ich habe …
He's got … (has got)	Er hat …
Have you got …?	Haben Sie / hast du …?
Has she got …?	Hat sie …?
They haven't got (have not got) …	Sie haben nicht …
It hasn't got (has not got) …	Es hat nicht …

A new member of the family
Ein neues Familienmitglied

adopt	adoptieren
adopted	adoptiert
all	alle
boy	Junge
bring	bringen
energy	Energie
fit	fit, in Form
grandma	Oma
grandparent	Großelternteil
great	groß
happy	glücklich
house	Haus
interested	interessiert
little	klein
now	jetzt
problem	Problem
real	echt
really	wirklich
scheme	Plan, Projekt

Unit 3 Part B
Describing people
Menschen beschreiben

What can you do? Was können Sie?

Can you …?	Können Sie / kannst du …?
I can …	Ich kann …
I can't (can not) …	Ich kann nicht …

answer	Antwort, antworten
cake	Kuchen
car	Auto
career	Karriere
class clown	Klassenclown
computer expert	Computerexperte, -expertin
cook spaghetti	Spaghetti kochen
course	Kurs
creative	kreativ
dance	Tanz, tanzen
decorate a cake	Kuchen verzieren
do	tun, machen
feminist	Feminist(in)
find	finden
go	gehen
hobby	Hobby
macho man	Macho
number	Zahl, Nummer
optimist	Optimist(in)
party person	Partymensch

pessimist	Pessimist(in)
play tennis	Tennis spielen
practical	praktisch
repair	reparieren
run	rennen, laufen
sing	singen
speak	sprechen
sports fan	Sportsfan
sporty	sportlich
superdad	Superpapa
supermum	Supermama
swim	schwimmen
take a photo	fotografieren
use	verwenden
walk	gehen
washing machine	Waschmaschine

Colours Farben

Word focus Colours Farben

black	blue	brown	green	orange
schwarz	blau	braun	grün	orange
red	white	yellow	grey	pink
rot	weiß	gelb	grau	rosa

What colour is it? – It's blue.
Welche Farbe hat es? – Es ist blau.
What colour are they? – They're black.
Welche Farbe haben sie? – Sie sind schwarz.

Clothes Kleidung

Word focus Clothes Kleidung

blouse	Bluse	shirt	Hemd
dress	Kleid	shoes	Schuhe
jacket	Jacke	shorts	kurze Hose
jeans	Jeans	skirt	Rock
pullover	Pullover	trousers	Hosen

* My trousers / jeans / shorts <u>are</u> blue.

Appearance Aussehen

buy	kaufen
extra information	Zusatzinformation
flight number	Flugnummer
go	gehen
must	müssen
Russian	Russe, Russin, russisch
ticket	Flugschein, Fahrkarte

How to describe someone's appearance
Das Aussehen von jemanden beschreiben

■ Can you describe him / her?
Können Sie / kannst du ihn / sie beschreiben?
◆ She's black / white / Asian.
Sie ist schwarz / weiß / asiatisch.
◆ He's tall / short.
Er ist groß / klein.
◆ She's got blonde / short / long hair.
Sie hat blonde / kurze / lange Haare.
◆ She's got big / blue / nice eyes.
Sie hat große / blaue / schöne Augen.
◆ He's got a beard / a moustache / sunglasses.
Er hat einen Bart / einen Schnurrbart / eine Sonnenbrille.
◆ She's beautiful. He's good-looking.
She ist schön. Er sieht gut aus.

* My glasses / sunglasses <u>are</u> new.

Unit 4 Part A

Routines Gewohnheiten

What's the time? Wie spät ist es?

How to tell the time Sagen, wie spät es ist

It's (one) o'clock.
Es ist (ein) Uhr.
It's five / ten / quarter past nine.
Es ist fünf / zehn / Viertel nach neun.
It's twenty-five / twenty / quarter to ten.
Es ist fünfundzwanzig / zwanzig / Viertel vor zehn.

* **9**.30 = half past **nine**

clock	Uhr	today	heute
punctual	pünktlich	watch	(Armband)Uhr

* We don't use the 24-hour clock in everyday speech.
Wir verwenden die 24-Stunden-Zählung nicht im Alltag.

Daily routines Tägliche Gewohnheiten

What time do you ...	Zu welcher Zeit ...
When do you ..	Wann ...
come home?	kommen Sie / kommst du nach Hause?
do the housework?	machen Sie / machst du die Hausarbeit?
finish work?	hören Sie / hörst du mit der Arbeit auf?
get up?	stehen Sie / stehst du auf?
go to bed?	gehen Sie / gehst du zu Bett?

have breakfast / lunch / dinner?	essen Sie / isst du Frühstück / Mittagessen / Abendessen?
relax?	ruhen Sie sich / ruhst du dich aus?
start work?	beginnen Sie / beginnst du zu arbeiten?

I stay at home.	Ich bleibe zu Hause.
I don't (do not) stay at home.	Ich bleibe nicht zu Hause.
When do you stay at home?	Wann bleiben Sie / bleibst du zu Hause?

daily life	Alltag
in the morning	am Morgen / Vormittag
in the afternoon	am Nachmittag
in the evening	am Abend
midday	Mittag
midnight	Mitternacht
Sorry, I don't understand.	Tut mir leid, ich verstehe das nicht.

File activity

after	nach	on television	im Fernsehen
feel	fühlen	owl	Eule
film	Film	strong	stark
lark	Lerche	tired	müde
late	spät	watch	anschauen
night	Nacht	weekday	Wochentag

Word focus Days of the week Wochentage

Monday	Tuesday	Wednesday	Thursday
Montag	Dienstag	Mittwoch	Donnerstag
Friday	Saturday	Sunday	
Freitag	Samstag	Sonntag	

* My course is **on** Tuesdays. Mein Kurs ist **am** Dienstag.

When's it open? Wann ist es geöffnet?

at six o' clock	um sechs Uhr
from six o'clock to half past six	von sechs bis halb sieben
in the morning	am Vormittag, morgens
at night	in der Nacht, nachts
on Mondays	montags
at dinnertime	zur Abendessenszeit
before lunch	vor dem Mittagessen
after breakfast	nach dem Frühstück
am	morgens, vormittags (0–12 Uhr)
pm	nachmittags, abends (12–24 Uhr)

Unit 4 Part B

Work Arbeit

What's his / her job?

Was ist sein / ihr Beruf?

Word focus Jobs Berufe

astronaut	Astronaut(in)
builder	Bauarbeiter(in)
doctor	Arzt, Ärztin
film star	Filmstar
footballer	Fußballer(in)
formula one driver	Formel-Eins-Fahrer(in)
hotel doorman	Portier
househusband/-wife	Hausmann/-frau
IT technician	IT-Techniker(in)
lorry driver	Lastwagenfahrer(in)
nurse	Krankenschwester
PA (personal assistant)	persönliche(r) Assistent(in)
pilot	Pilot(in)
police officer	Polizist(in)
sales manager	Verkaufsleiter(in)
shop assistant	Verkäufer(in)
train driver	Zugführer(in)
TV presenter	Fernsehmoderator(in)

What's your dream job? – I want to be a pop star.
Was ist Ihr / dein Traumberuf? – Ich möchte ein Popstar werden.

What does he / she do at work?

Was macht er / sie bei der Arbeit?

Does he work?	Arbeitet er?
Yes, he does.	Ja, er arbeitet.
No, he doesn't (does not).	Nein, er arbeitet nicht.
He works.	Er arbeitet.
She doesn't work.	Sie arbeitet nicht.

arrive	ankommen
coat	Mantel
earn money	Geld verdienen
I don't know.	Ich weiß nicht.
if	falls
like	wie
look after	kümmern um
meeting	Treffen
office	Büro
outside	draußen
sort out	lösen
wear a uniform	Uniform tragen
who	wer
work for a company	für eine Firma arbeiten

A job at a hotel Ein Beruf in einem Hotel

live	leben
door	Tür
doorman	Portier
end of the day	am Ende des Tages
five-star hotel	Fünf-Sterne-Hotel
get a tip	Trinkgeld bekommen
good service	guter Service
hat	Hut
leave	verlassen
love	lieben, Liebe
often	oft
out here	hier draußen
perfect job	perfekter Beruf
rain and snow	Regen und Schnee
smart	schick
stand	stehen
summer	Sommer
taxi	Taxi
them	sie, ihnen
traditional	traditionell
warm	warm
welcome guests	Gäste willkommen heißen
winter	Winter
worst	schlimmste(r, -s)

I think it's a useful job
Ich denke, es ist ein nützlicher Beruf.

How to express opinions, agree and disagree
Meinungen ausdrücken, zustimmen und widersprechen

- ■ What about an opera singer?
  Was ist mit einem Opersänger?
- ■ What do you think?
  Was denken Sie / denkst du?
- ◆ I think it's a stressful job.
  Ich denke, es ist ein stressiger Beruf.
- ● Yes, I think so, too.
  Ja, das denke ich auch.
- ▲ I don't think so.
  Das denke ich nicht.

boring	langweilig	overpaid	überbezahlt
dangerous	gefährlich	underpaid	unterbezahlt
interesting	interessant	useful	nützlich

What does that mean?	Was bedeutet das?

Unit 5 Part A
Keeping active Aktiv bleiben

Free time activities Freizeitaktivitäten

Word focus Free time activities
Freizeitaktivitäten

I play ...	Ich spiele...
basketball	Basketball
chess	Schach
table tennis	Tischtennis
I go ...	Ich gehe ...
skiing	skifahren
swimming	schwimmen
walking	wandern

Do they play ...?	Spielen sie ...?
Yes, they do.	Ja, sie spielen.
No, they don't.	Nein, sie spielen nicht.
They play ...	Sie spielen ...
They don't play ...	Sie spielen nicht ...

basketball player	Basketballspieler(in)
boxer	Boxer(in)
player	Spieler(in)
walker	Wanderer(in)
swimmer	Schwimmer(in)
footballer	Fusballer(in)
runner	Läufer(in)

buy	kaufen
cheese rolling	Käserollen
church hall	Gemeindesaal
countryside	Landschaft
fun	Spaß, lustig
good idea	gute Idee
go on holiday	in Urlaub fahren
match	Spiel (*Sport*)
neighbours	Nachbarn
newspaper	Zeitung
phone	Telefon, telefonieren
play cards	Karten spielen
pullover	Pullover
silly	albern
T-shirt	T-Shirt
together	zusammen
underwater hockey	Unterwasser-Hockey
What day ...?	An welchem Tag ...?
wife carrying	Ehefrauen-Tragen

How to say how often you do things
Sagen, wie oft man etwas tut

- ■ How often do you do sport?
  Wie oft treiben Sie Sport?
- ◆ Once a week.
  Einmal in der Woche.
- ◆ Twice a month.
  Zweimal im Monat.
- ◆ Three / Four / Five times a year.
  Drei / Vier / Fünf Mal im Jahr.
- ◆ Every day / week / weekend / Tuesday.
  Jeden Tag / Jede Woche / Jedes Wochenende / Jeden Dienstag.
- ◆ Never.
  Nie.

Likes and dislikes
Vorlieben und Abneigungen

How to express likes and dislikes
Vorlieben und Abneigungen ausdrücken.

I love Scrabble / playing Scrabble.
Ich liebe Scrabble. / Ich liebe es, Scrabble zu spielen.
I like tennis / watching tennis.
Ich mag Tennis. / Ich schaue gerne Tennis an.
I don't like chocolate / eating chocolate.
Ich mag keine Schokolade. / Ich esse nicht gerne Schokolade.

beer garden	Biergarten
calorie	Kalorie
classical music	klassische Musik
dancing	Tanzen
early	früh
favourite	liebste(r, -s)
Iceland / Icelandic	Island / isländisch
in that order	in dieser Reihenfolge
learning English	Englisch lernen
meeting people	Leute treffen
negative	negativ
new	neu
outdoor swimming pool	Freibad
sour milk	Sauermilch
training	trainieren
winning medals	Medaillen gewinnen

Unit 5 Part B
Keeping healthy Gesund bleiben

Healthy or unhealthy?
Gesund oder ungesund?

How often?	Always.	Usually.	Often.	Sometimes.	Never.
Wie oft?	Immer.	Meistens.	Oft.	Manchmal.	Nie.

alcohol	Alkohol	for us	für uns
all day	den ganzen Tag	fresh	frisch
an active life	ein aktives Leben	genes	Gene
		go out	ausgehen
at home	zu Hause	ill	krank
buffet	Büfett	late	spät
cocktails	Cocktails	lifestyle	Lebensstil
coffee	Kaffee	lift	Aufzug
cook	kochen	loud	laut
could	könnte, könnten	other	andere(r, -s)
		salad	Salat
doctor	Arzt, Ärztin	sit	sitzen
drink	trinken	smoke	rauchen
drive	fahren	something	etwas
eat	essen	tired	müde
escalators	Rolltreppe	upstairs	oben
food	Essen	walk	gehen

Making suggestions Vorschläge machen

How to make suggestions and respond
Vorschläge machen und darauf reagieren

- ■ Why don't you ...?
  Warum machen Sie / machst du nicht ...?
- ■ You could ....
  Sie könnten / Du könntest ... .
- ◆ That's a good idea.
  Das ist eine gute Idee.
- ◆ Maybe.
  Vielleicht.
- ◆ I don't think that's a very good idea.
  Ich halte das für keine gute Idee.

finish with	abschließen mit	too much	zu viel
		why	warum
sleep	schlafen	want	wollen

Unit 6 Part A

Eating out Auswärts essen

Food and drink Essen und Trinken

Word focus Food and drink
Essen und Trinken

bread	Brot	ham	Schinken
cake	Kuchen	milk	Milch
champagne	Champagner	orange juice	Orangensaft
cheese	Käse	pasta	Nudeln
chicken	Hühnchen	vegetable	Gemüse
egg	Ei	wine	Wein
fish	Fisch		

atmosphere	Atmosphäre
price	Preis
It's a sort of ...	Es ist eine Art ...

In a café In einem Cafe

apple	Apfel
chips	Pommes frites
dessert	Dessert
drink	Getränk
fruit juice	Fruchtsaft
mineral water	Mineralwasser
omelette	Omelett
salad	Salat
soup	Suppe
tea	Tee
tomato	Tomate
tuna	Thunfisch

bill	Rechnung
British	britisch
customer	Kunde
eat out	auswärts essen
hot	heiß, warm
cold	kalt
made with	gemacht mit
meal	Essen
menu	Speisekarte
polite	höflich
tonight	heute Abend
typical	typisch
manager	Geschäftführer(in)

How to order in a café or restaurant
In einem Cafe oder Restaurant bestellen

Would you like to order now? – Yes, please. / No, thank you.
Würden Sie jetzt gerne bestellen? – Ja, bitte. / Nein, danke.
I'd (I would) like a (tuna salad), please.
Ich hätte gerne einen (Thunfischsalat), bitte.

Could / Can I have a (ham sandwich), please?
Könnte ich / Kann ich ein (Schinkenbrötchen) haben, bitte?
Would you like a (salad)?
Möchten Sie einen Salat?
What can I get you?
Was kann ich Ihnen bringen?
We've got (ham and cheese sandwiches).
Wir haben (Schinken- und Käsebrötchen).

Unusual places to eat
Ungewöhnliche Orte zu essen

steak	Steak	underwater	unter Wasser
under	unter	unusual	ungewöhnlich

File activity

ask for	bitten um, fragen nach
bar	Bar
barman	Barkeeper
bedroom	Schlafzimmer
conference	Konferenz
facilities	Einrichtungen
contact	Kontakt
control	kontrollieren
coolest	coolste(r, -s)
Down's syndrome	Down-Syndrom
each	jede(r, -s)
even	sogar
flirt	flirten
friendly	freundlich
guest	Gast
hear	hören
historic	historisch
initiative	Initiative
lounge	Lounge
meat	Fleisch
minus	minus
normal	normal
quality	Qualität
remote	Fernsteuerung
screen	Bildschirm
seat	Sitz
sleeper car	Schlafwagen
temperature	Temperatur

video camera	Videokamera
waiter	Kellner
watch	beobachten

Unit 6 Part B

A party Eine Party

Dates Datum

Word focus Months of the year Monate

January	Januar	July	Juli
February	Februar	August	August
March	März	September	September
April	April	October	Oktober
May	Mai	November	November
June	Juni	December	Dezember

* My birthday's **on** the twenty-third **of** January.
Mein Geburtstag ist **am** dreiundzwanzigsten Januar.

Advent	Advent	Easter	Ostern
St Valentine's Day	Valentinstag	Easter egg	Osterei

Word focus Ordinal numbers
Ordnungszahlen

first	erste(r, -s)
second	zweite(r, -s)
third	dritte(r, -s)
fourth	vierte(r, -s)
fifth	fünfte(r, -s)
sixth	sechste(r, -s)
seventh	siebte(r, -s)
eighth	achte(r, -s)
ninth	neunte(r, -s)
tenth	zehnte(r, -s)
eleventh	elfte(r, -s)
twelfth	zwölfte(r, -s)
thirteenth	dreizehnte(r, -s)
twentieth	zwanzigste(r, -s)
twenty-first	einundzwanzigste(r, -s)
twenty-second	zweiundzwanzigste(r, -s)
twenty-third	dreiundzwanzigste(r, -s)
thirtieth	dreißigste(r, -s)

Organising an event
Eine Veranstaltung organisieren

bottle	Flasche
budget	Budget
formal	formell
glass of wine	Glas Wein
hamburger	Hamburger
informal	informell
How many do we need?	Wie viele brauchen wir?
Not many.	Nicht viele.
How much do we need?	Wie viel brauchen wir?
Not much.	Nicht viel.

Invitations Einladungen

anniversary	Jahrestag
Best wishes	Alles Gute
company	Firma
Dear	Liebe(r, -s) *Briefanrede*
film	Film
gallery opening	Ausstellungseröffnung
glass	Glas
jazz	Jazz

How to invite someone and respond to invitations
Einladungen aussprechen und annehmen

■ Would you like to come to my party next Saturday?
Möchten Sie / Möchtest du zu meiner Party nächsten Samstag kommen?

◆ Yes, I'd love to. / Yes, that would be very nice.
Ja, gerne. / Ja, das wäre sehr schön.

◆ I'm sorry I can't come. But thanks for the invitation.
Es tut mir leid, ich kann nicht kommen. Aber danke für die Einladung.

Unit 7 Part A

Summer holidays Sommerurlaub

Holiday shopping Urlaubseinkäufe

Word focus Holiday items
Urlaubsgegenstände

bag	Tasche	suitcase	Koffer
camera	Kamera	suncream	Sonnencreme
guidebook	Reiseführer	sunglasses*	Sonnenbrille
postcard	Postkarte	towel	Handtuch

* My sunglasses / glasses <u>are</u> new.

How to ask for and say prices
Nach Preisen fragen und Preise sagen

- ■ How much is the (book)?
  Wie viel kostet das (Buch)?
- ◆ It's ten pounds fifty.
  Es kostet zehn Pfund fünzig.
- ■ How much are the (postcards)?
  Wie viel kosten die (Postkarten)?
- ◆ They're seventy-five pence / forty p.
  Sie kosten fünfundsiebzig Pence / vierzig Pence.
- ■ That's cheap / OK / a bit expensive.
  Das ist billig / in Ordnung / etwas teuer.

A holiday postcard Eine Urlaubskarte

Word focus Adjective pairs
Eigenschaftspaare

cheap / expensive	billig / teuer
clean / dirty	sauber / schmutzig
fantastic / awful	fantastisch / schrecklich
friendly / unfriendly	freundlich / unfreundlich
good / bad	gut / schlecht
warm (or hot) / cold	heiß (oder warm) / kalt

Was it nice?	War es nett?
It was really nice.	Es war wirklich nett.
Were they nice?	Waren sie nett?
They were OK.	Sie waren in Ordnung.
bit	bisschen
because	weil
everything	alles
festival	Festival
present	Geschenk
sea	Meer
sunny	sonnig
weather	Wetter

Two festivals Zwei Festivals

carnival	Fasching, Karneval
costume	Kostüm
dancer	Tänzer(in)
fireworks	Feuerwerk
flower	Blume
last	letzte(r, -s)
more	mehr
orchestra	Orchester
See you soon	Bis bald
show	Aufführung
sports event	Sportereignis
woman, women	Frau, Frauen

Unit 7 Part B
Around the world Rund um die Welt

Famous tourist attractions
Berühmte Touristenattraktionen

Canada	Kanada
canyon	Canyon, Schlucht
capital	Hauptstadt
China	China
European	Europäer(in), europäisch
India	Indien
mountain	Berg
rock	Fels
rucksack	Rucksack
safari	Safari
see (saw)	sehen (sah)
wall	Mauer
go (went)	gehen (ging)

A fly drive holiday
Ein Urlaub mit Flugzeug und Auto

hire (hired)	mieten (mietete)
stay (stayed)	bleiben (blieb)
talk to (talked to)	sprechen (sprach) mit
visit (visited)	besuchen (besuchte)
want (wanted)	wollen (wollte)
watch (watched)	beobachten (beobachtete)
work (worked)	arbeiten (arbeitete)
buy (bought)	kaufen (kaufte)
come (came)	kommen (kam)
do (did)	tun (tat)
drive (drove)	fahren (fuhr)
fly (flew)	fliegen (flog)
find (found)	finden (fand)
have (had)	haben (hatte)
see (saw)	sehen (sah)
take (took)	nehmen (nahm)
go (went)	gehen (ging)
ago	vor *(zeitlich)*
alone	allein
last	letzte(r, -s)
lighthouse	Leuchtturm
magazine	Zeitschrift
map	Plan, Karte
plane	Flugzeug
route	Strecke
waterfall	Wasserfall
wonderful	wunderbar

How to talk about past holidays
Über vergangene Urlaube sprechen

Last (month) ...
Letzten (Monat) ...
(Two years) ago ...
Vor (zwei Jahren) ...
We went to ...
Wir fuhren nach ...
We flew / drove ...
Wir flogen / fuhren
We saw / bought / visited ...
Wir sahen / kauften / besuchten ...
The weather / hotel was ...
Das Wetter / Hotel war ...
The mountains / beaches were ...
Die Berge / Strände waren ...
There was a festival / market ...
Es gab ein Festival / einen Markt ...
There were a lot of tourists / restaurants ...
Es gab viele Touristen / Restaurants ...

Unit 8 Part A
Culture **Kultur**

A famous entertainer
Ein berühmter Unterhaltungskünstler

ballet	flamenco	jive	polka
Ballett	Flamenco	Jive	Polka
salsa	tango	twist	break-dancing
Salsa	Tango	Twist	Break-dancing

audience	Publikum
charisma	Ausstrahlung
Cuban	Kubaner(in), kubanisch
eleventh	elfte(r, -s)
entertainment	Unterhaltung
flair	Gespür, Atmosphäre
generation	Generation
homework	Hausaufgaben
kid	Kind
most popular	beliebteste(r, -s)
poor	arm
power	Macht, Kraft
primary school	Grundschule
prize	Preis
professional	professionell
project	Projekt
style	Stil
talent	Talent
truck driver	Lastwagenfahrer(in)
was born	wurde geboren
What's next?	Was kommt als Nächstes?
work hard	hart arbeiten
youngest	jüngste(r, -s)
dance (danced)	tanzen (tanzte)
die (died)	sterben (starb)
practise (practised)	üben (übte)
start (started)	beginnen (begann)
become (became)	werden (wurde)
forget (forgot)	vergessen (vergaß)
give (gave)	geben (gab)
leave (left)	verlassen (verließ)
run away (ran)	weglaufen (lief)
send away (sent)	wegschicken (schickte)
send back (sent)	zurückschicken (schickte)
sing (sang)	singen (sang)
win (won)	gewinnen (gewann)

didn't go	ging nicht
didn't like	mochte nicht
didn't want	wollte nicht

Music, films and literature
Musik, Film und Literatur

get married (got)	heiraten (heiratete)
star (starred)	die Hauptrolle spielen (spielte)
write (wrote)	schreiben (schrieb)
hundred	Hundert
initial	Anfangsbuchstabe
thousand	Tausend

How to say years Jahreszahlen sagen

1800: eighteen hundred
achtzehnhundert
1907: nineteen hundred and seven
neunzehnhundertundsieben
1963: nineteen sixty-three
neunzehnhundertunddrei
2000: two thousand
zweitausend
1009: two thousand and nine
zweitausendundneun
2024: two thousand and twenty-four
zweitausendundvierunzwanzig

How to give biographical information
Biografische Informationen geben

I was born in ...
Ich wurde in ... geboren.
I went to school / university in ...
Ich ging in ... zur Schule / auf die Universität.
I left school / university in ...
Ich ging (im Jahr) ... von der Schule / Universität ab.
I started my first job in ...
Ich begann (im Jahr) ... zu arbeiten.
I worked there from ... to ... / for ... years.
Ich arbeitete dort von ... bis ... / ... Jahre lang.
I met my (first) husband / wife in ...
Ich traf meinen (ersten) Mann / meine (erste) Frau (im Jahr)...
I got married / got divorced in ...
Ich heiratete / wurde geschieden (im Jahr)...
My first child was born in ...
Mein erstes Kind wurde (im Jahr) ... geboren.
Then I worked / went to / met ...
Dann arbeitete ich / ging nach / traf...

Unit 8 Part B
Staying in and going out
Zuhause bleiben und ausgehen

Staying in Zuhause bleiben

- ■ Did you go out?
  Bist du ausgegangen?
- ◆ Yes, I did. / No, I didn't.
  Ja, bin ich. / Nein, bin ich nicht.
- ■ When did you last go to the opera?
  Wann warst du das letzte Mal in der Oper?

average	durchschnittlich
bring into	hineinbringen
clean (cleaned)	putzen (putzte)
cup of coffee	Tasse Kaffee
game	Spiel
give (gave) flowers	Blumen schenken
high culture	Hochkultur
home entertainment	Heimunterhaltung
hour	Stunde
system	System
make (made)	machen (machte)
minute	Minute
more comfortable than	gemütlicher als
online	im Internet
spend (spent) time	Zeit verbringen
technology	Technologie
warmer	wärmer

An evening in front of the television
Ein Abend vor dem Fernseher

Word focus Adjectives Eigenschaftswörter

exciting	aufregend
frightening	furchteinflößend
funny	lustig
romantic	romantisch
sad	traurig
serious	ernst

action film	Actionfilm
comedy	Komödie
documentary	Dokumentation
horror film	Horrorfilm
love story	Liebesgeschichte
tragedy	Tragödie

How to talk about a film or TV programme
Über einen Film oder eine Fernsehsendung sprechen

I saw (title) on TV / at the cinema.
Ich habe (Titel) im Fernsehen / Kino gesehen.
It was a comedy / love story ...
Es war eine Komödie / Liebesgeschichte ...
It was boring / exciting ...
Es war langweilig / aufregend ...
It was with (name of actor)
Es war mit (Name des Schauspielers) ...

Going out – a day in London
Ausgehen – ein Tag in London

art and design	Kunst und Design
ceramics	Keramik
cheap	billig
child-centred	kinderorientiert
child-friendly	kinderfreundlich
childhood	Kindheit
doll	Puppe
east	Ost(en)
everything	alles
fashion	Mode
gift shop	Geschenkeladen
learn (learnt)	lernen (lernte)
sculpture	Skulptur
money	Geld
textiles	Stoffe
through	durch
toy	Spielzeug

File activity

detective series	Detektivserie
drama series	Dramaserie
other things	andere Dinge
reality show	Realityshow
talk show	Talkshow
the news	Nachrichten

taco	Taco
thank (thanked)	danken (dankte)
train (trained)	trainieren (trainierte)
world champion	Weltmeister(in)
world record	Weltrekord

Early or late? Früh oder spät?

assistant	Assistent
babysitter	Babysitter
boss	Chef
colleague	Kollege
to the doctor's	zum Arzt
handbag	Handtasche
late for work	spät für die Arbeit
lesson	(Unterrichts)Stunde
punctual	pünktlich
sleep well	gut schlafen
that sounds ...	das klingt ...
tram	Straßenbahn

How to apologise and give a reason, and how to react to apologies
Sich entschuldigen, Gründe nennen und auf Entschuldigungen reagieren

- ■ I'm sorry I'm late.
  Es tut mir leid, dass ich zu spät bin.
- ■ It was because ...
  Es war, weil ...
- ■ I had a problem with ...
  Ich hatte ein Problem mit ...
- ■ My train / bus / flight was late.
  Mein Zug / Bus / Flug war verspätet.
- ◆ That's alright.
  Das ist in Ordnung.
- ◆ No problem.
  Kein Problem.
- ◆ Don't worry.
  Machen Sie sich / Mach dir keine Sorgen.

Unit 9 Part A
Doing things differently
Etwas anders machen

Fast or slow? Schnell oder langsam?

Word focus Free time activities
Freizeitaktivitäten

How did he do that? – Wie hat er das gemacht?

badly	schlecht
beautifully	schön
clearly	klar
happily	glücklich
slowly	langsam
unclearly	unklar
unhappily	unglücklich
fast	schnell
hard	schwer
well	gut

African	Afrikaner(in), afrikanisch
all-you-can-eat buffet	*Büfett mit Einheitspreis, man isst soviel man will*
cheesecake	Käsekuchen
chicken wing	Hühnchenflügel
competition	Wettbewerb
competitive	Wettbewerbs-
enjoy (enjoyed)	genießen
everyone	jeder
fruit	Obst
hot dog	Hot Dog
kilo	Kilo
leukaemia	Leukämie
marathon	Marathon
only	nur
race	Rennen
rice	Reis
smile (smiled)	lächeln (lächelte)
snack	kleiner Imbiss
speed eating	Schnellessen (Wettbewerbsdisziplin)
sweet	Süßigkeit

Unit 9 Part B
Doing the right thing
Das Richtige tun

Life in Japan Leben in Japan

must	müssen
mustn't	nicht müssen

bath	Bad
conservative	konservativ

business card	Visitenkarte
business meeting	Geschäftstreffen
etiquette	Etiquette
hand	Hand
host	Gastgeber
immediately	sofort
important	wichtig
loudly	laut
mix (mixed)	mischen (mischte)
normal	normal
pocket	Tasche
politely	höflich
put (put)	stellen, legen, tun
respectfully	respektvoll
slippers	Hausschuhe
toilet	Toilette
wash	waschen

Saying the right thing Das Richtige sagen

Word focus Special days in the year
Besondere Tage im Jahr

birthday	Geburtstag
Christmas Day	1. Weihnachtstag
Easter Sunday	Ostersonntag
Father's Day	Vatertag
Mother's Day	Muttertag
New Year's Day	Neujahr(stag)
Valentine's Day	Valentinstag
wedding anniversary	Hochzeitstag

How to say the right thing in social situations
Das richtige in gesellschaftlichen Situationen sagen

Happy birthday.	Alles Gute zum Geburtstag.
Happy New Year.	Frohes neues Jahr.
Have a good trip.	Gute Reise.
Have a great day.	Schönen Tag.
Have a nice holiday.	Schöne Ferien.
I hope it goes well.	Ich hoffe, es geht alles gut.
Good luck with (your interview.)	Alles Gute für (dein Bewerbungsgespräch.)
I'm sorry I'm late.	Tut mir leid, dass ich zu spät bin.
Merry Christmas.	Fröhliche Weihnachten.
Oh dear.	Oh je.
Thanks very much.	Vielen Dank.
That's a pity.	Das ist schade.
Congratulations on (your test results!)	Glückwunsch zu (deinem Prüfungsergebnis!)
Well done.	Gut gemacht.

Unit 10 Part A
Houses and flats
Häuser und Wohnungen

Houses Häuser

Whose house is it? – It's Mozart's.
Wessen Haus ist das? – Es ist Mozarts Haus.

busy	beschäftigt
electrical	elektrisch
football stadium	Fußballstadion
garden	Garten
prime minister	Premierminister
quite	ziemlich
bigger than	größer als
cheaper than	billiger als
cleaner than	sauberer als
dirtier than	schmutziger als
older than	älter als
taller than	höher als
more beautiful than	schöner als
more comfortable than	gemütlicher als

Word focus Rooms and other parts of the house
Zimmer und andere Teile des Hauses

living room	bedroom	office	bathroom
Wohnzimmer	Schlafzimmer	Arbeitszimmer	Badezimmer
garage	balcony	kitchen	
Garage	Balkon	Küche	

Word focus Things in the home
Dinge zu Hause

bath	bookcase	chair
Bad	Bücherregal	Stuhl
cooker	dishwasher	fridge
Herd	Geschirrspüler	Kühlschrank
shower	sofa	toilet
Dusche	Couch	Toilette

How to describe a house or a flat
Ein Haus oder eine Wohnung beschreiben

(Flat) It's on the	*(Wohnung)* Sie ist im
first / second / third floor.	1. / 2. / 3. Stock.
It's old / modern / big.	Es ist alt / modern / groß.
It's in / near / ...	Es / Sie ist in / nahe ...
It's got ...	Es / Sie hat ...
There's a ...	Es gibt ein(e) ...
There are two ...	Es gibt zwei ...

Flats Wohnungen

cleaning	Putzen
couple	Paar
double / single bedroom	Doppel- / Einzelschlafzimmer
elegant	elegant
extra costs	Zusatzkosten
large	groß
lovely	reizend
nightclub	Nachtklub
per week	pro Woche
without	ohne
quieter	ruhiger
nearer	näher
friendlier	freundlicher
nicer	netter
better	besser
worse	schlechter

Unit 10 Part B
Hotels Hotels

Unusual hotels Ungewöhnliche Hotels

File activity

also	auch
astronomy	Astronomie
book (booked)	buchen (buchte)
conference facilities	Konferenzeinrichtungen
full breakfast	reichhaltiges Frühstück
hear (heard)	hören (hörte)
include	beinhalten
island	Insel
learn about (learnt)	über (etwas) erfahren
library	Bibliothek
lighthouse	Leuchtturm
maybe	vielleicht
popular	beliebt
sleeper car	Schlafwagen
special interest	besonderes Interesse
stay	Aufenthalt
still	noch
subject	Thema
take a chance (took)	die Chance nützen (nutzte)
tour	Rundfahrt
write (wrote)	schreiben (schrieb)
zoology	Zoologie

the cheapest	billigste(r, -s)
the easiest	einfachste(r, -s)
the biggest	größte(r, -s)
the quietest	ruhigste(r, -s)
the noisiest	lauteste(r, -s)
the most expensive	teuerste(r, -s)
the most romantic	romantischte(r, -s)
the best	beste(r, -s)
the worst	schlechteste(r, -s)

The biggest and the best
Das Größte und Beste

hotel reservation	Hotelreservierung
million	Million
passenger	Passagier
rich	reich
suite	Suite
sunshine	Sonnenschein
travel document	Reisedokument

Booking a hotel room
Ein Hotelzimmer buchen

Word focus Hotel services and facilities
Hoteldienstleistungen und -einrichtungen

babysitting service	Kleinkinderbetreuung
bar	Bar
car park	Parkplatz
children's play area	Kinderspielplatz
conference room	Konferenzraum
family room	Familienzimmer
Internet access	Internetzugang
lift	Aufzug
room service	Zimmerservice
swimming pool	Swimmingpool

anything	irgendetwas
arrival date	Anreisedatum
booking form	Buchungsformular
check out (checked)	auschecken
credit card	Kreditkarte
everything	alles
fine	in Ordnung

keycard	Chipkarte
minibar	Minibar
pay (paid)	zahlen (zahlte)

How to book a hotel room
Ein Hotelzimmer buchen

I'd like to book a double / single / family room with a bath / shower for (2) nights.
Ich möchte ein Doppel- / Einzel- / Familienzimmer mit Bad / Dusche für (2) Nächte buchen.
Is there a swimming pool / lift?
Gibt es einen Swimmingpool / Aufzug?
Is the price per person / per room?
Gilt der Preis pro Person / pro Zimmer?
Is breakfast included?
Ist das Frühstuck inbegriffen?
What time must I check out?
Wann muss ich auschecken?

Unit 11 Part A

Transport Verkehr

Different ways of travelling
Verschiedene Arten zu reisen

Word focus Methods of transport
Verkehrsmittel

bike	Fahrrad
bus	Bus
car	Auto
motorbike	Motorrad
plane	Flugzeug
by taxi	mit dem Taxi
by train	mit dem Zug
by tram	mit der Straßenbahn
by underground	mit der U-Bahn
on foot	zu Fuß

I cycle – I get around by bike.
Ich fahre Rad – Ich benutze das Rad.
I walk – I go on foot to keep fit.
Ich gehe – Ich gehe zu Fuß um fit zu bleiben.

Mum's taxi Mamas Taxi

calendar	Kalender
drama group	Theatergruppe
invite	einladen
kickboxing	Kickboxen
everywhere	überall
if you like	wenn du willst / Sie wollen

me	mich
you	dich
him	ihn
her	sie
it	es
us	uns
you	euch
them	sie

At the station Am Bahnhof

arr. (arrival)	Ankunft
departures board	Abfahrtstafel
expected	erwartet
on time	pünktlich
platform	Gleis
timetable	Fahrplan
zoo	Zoo

How to ask for train information and buy a ticket
Nach Zuginformationen fragen und eine Fahrkarte kaufen

When's the next train to ...?
Wann geht der nächste Zug nach ...?
Which platform?
Welches Gleis?
Is the train on time?
Ist der Zug pünktlich?
How much is a single / return?
Wieviel kostet eine einfache Fahrt / hin und zurück?
I'd like a single / return, please
Eine Einzelfahrkarte / Rückfahrkarte, bitte.

Unit 11 Part B

Going the right way
Den richtigen Weg nehmen

Warnings and instructions for travellers
Warnungen und Anweisungen für Reisende

along	entlang
directions	Wegbeschreibung
double yellow line	doppelte gelbe Linie
electronic	elektronisch
enter	betreten
get stuck (got)	stecken bleiben
head	Kopf
if	wenn

lane	kleine Straße
message	Nachricht
mistake	Fehler
narrow	eng
on the left	links
on the right	rechts
sat nav (satellite navigation system)	Satellitennavigation
stop (stopped)	anhalten (hielt an)
take a break	eine Pause machen
think (thought)	denken (dachte)
try (tried)	versuchen (versuchte)
village	Dorf
villager	Dorfbewohner(in)
warn (warned)	warnen (warnte)
warning sign	Warnschild
wide	breit
Follow your sat nav.	Folgen Sie Ihrem Navigationsgerät.
Don't follow your sat nav.	Folgen Sie Ihrem Navigationsgerät nicht.

Directions Wegbeschreibung

Word focus Things on a map
Dinge auf einem Plan

bus stop	Bushaltestellte
car park	Parkplatz
castle	Schloss
church	Kirche
football stadium	Fußballstadion
hospital	Krankenhaus
station	Bahnhof
taxi stand	Taxistand
theatre	Theater
tourist information office	Fremdenverkehrsamt
underground	U-Bahn
zoo	Zoo

How to ask for and give directions
Nach dem Weg fragen und den Weg beschreiben

- ■ Excuse me, can you tell me the way to (the station), please?
  Entschuldigung, können Sie / kannst du mir sagen, wie ich zum (Bahnhof) komme?
- ◆ Go along this street.
  Gehen Sie / Gehe diese Straße entlang.
- ◆ Go past the church.
  Gehen Sie / Gehe an der Kirche vorbei.
- ◆ Take the first / second / third street on the left.
  Nehmen Sie / Nimm die 1. / 2. / 3. Straße links.
- ◆ Go right into George Street.
  Biegen Sie / Biege in die George Street ein.
- ■ Can I repeat that, to check?
  Kann ich das wiederholen, um sicher zu gehen?

Unit 12 Part A

Plans for different seasons
Pläne für verschiedene Jahreszeiten

The seasons and the weather
Die Jahreszeiten und das Wetter

Word focus The seasons and the weather
Die Jahreszeiten und das Wetter

spring	summer	autumn	winter
Frühling	Sommer	Herbst	Winter

cloudy	bewölkt
sunny	sonnig
cold	kalt
warm	warm
hot	heiß
rain (rained)	regnen (regnete)
snow (snowed)	schneien (schneite)
windy	windig

How to talk about the weather and the seasons
Über das Wetter und die Jahreszeiten sprechen

- ■ What's the weather like in the (autumn)?
  Wie ist das Wetter im (Herbst)?
- ◆ It's often (cold).
  Es ist oft (kalt).
- ◆ It's sometimes (warm).
  Es ist manchmal (warm).
- ◆ It rains / snows a lot.
  Es regnet / schneit viel.

Plans for the weekend Wochenendpläne

cider	*engl. Apfelwein*
cinema page	Kinoseite
local newspaper	Lokalzeitung
shopping list	Einkaufsliste
tomorrow	morgen
tree	Baum
window	Fenster
I'm going to drink iced tea.	Ich werde Eistee trinken.
We're going to work in the garden.	Wir werden im Garten arbeiten.
He's going (to go) windsurfing.	Er wird windsurfen gehen.

Making small talk Smalltalk machen

How to make small talk Smalltalk machen

It's very warm / cold / hot today.
Es ist sehr warm / kalt / heiß heute.
I think we met ...
Ich glaube, wir haben (uns) ... getroffen.
I think you know my (colleague).
Ich glaube, Sie kennen / du kennst meinen (Kollegen).
It's a good conference / great party.
Es ist eine gute Konferenz / tolle Party.
Is this your first visit to (town)?
Ist das Ihr / dein erster Besuch in (Name der Stadt)?
Where are you from in (country)?
Von wo in (Ländername) sind Sie / bist du her?
Have you got any plans for the weekend / later?
Haben Sie / hast du schon Pläne für das Wochenende / später?

Unit 12 Part B

A weekend away
Eine Wochenendreise

Plans for a special weekend
Pläne für ein besonderes Wochenende

aromatherapy	Aromatherapie
free	gratis
golf	Golf
Indian head massage	indische Kopfmassage
indoor pool	Hallenbad
manicure	Maniküre
parkland	Grünland
reiki	Reiki (*jap. mediz. Behandlungsverfahren*)
sauna	Sauna
shiatsu	Shiatsu (*jap. Form der Körpertherapie*)
spa	Heilbad

What are you going to do?
Was wirst du tun?
I'm not going to have hot stone therapy.
Ich werde keine Therapie mit heißen Steinen machen.
They aren't going to celebrate.
Sie werden nicht feiern.
She isn't going to the beauty salon.
Sie wird nicht in den Schönheitssalon gehen.

A phone call Ein Telefonanruf

How to make an informal phone call
Einen privaten Telefonanruf machen

- ■ Hello, it's (name) here from (place).
  Hallo, hier spricht (Name) aus (Ort).
- ■ Is (name) there, please?
  Ist (Name) da?
- ◆ Just a minute, please.
  Einen Augenblicke, bitte.
- ● Thanks for phoning.
  Danke für Ihren / deinen Anruf.

Alphabetical word list

Phonetische Umschrift

englischer Laut		ähnlicher deutscher Laut	englischer Laut		ähnlicher deutscher Laut	englischer Laut		ähnlicher deutscher Laut
[ɪ]	in	*in*	[eɪ]	day	nicht wie deutsch *ei* sondern [e] + [ɪ]	[s]	seat	*Muße*
[e]	yes	*fett*				[z]	please	*Museum*
[æ]	thanks	zwischen *a* und *ä*	[aɪ]	nice	*Eile*	[ʃ]	she	*Schiff*
[ʌ]	come	*machen*	[ɔɪ]	boy	*heute*	[ʒ]	television	*Regie*
[ɒ]	coffee	*Motte*	[aʊ]	how	*Frau*	[tʃ]	cheers	*klatschen*
[ʊ]	look	*Butter*	[əʊ]	no	[ə] + [ʊ]	[dʒ]	German	[d] + [ʒ]
[ə]	number	*singe*	[ɪə]	here	*hier*	[ŋ]	song	*singen*
[iː]	meet	*Knie*	[eə]	where	*sehr*	[l]	old	hinten im Mund gesprochen
[ɑː]	father	*Bahn*	[ʊə]	tourist	[ʊ] + [ə]	[j]	unit	*ja*
[ɔː]	four	wie *o* in deutsch *Borke*	[v]	have	*Virus*	[w]	we	durch die Lippen gesprochen wie [uː]
[uː]	too	*Buch*	[θ]	thanks	wie ein gelispeltes *ss* in *Biss*			
[ɜː]	early	*Börse*	[ð]	this	wie ein gelispeltes *s* in *Sand*	[r]	repeat	vorn im Mund gesprochen

[ː] der vorangehende Laut wird lang gesprochen [ˈ] Hauptbetonung: die folgende Silbe wird stark betont [ˌ] Nebenbetonung: die folgende Silbe wird leicht betont

24 hour clock [ˈtwenti fɔː ˌaʊə ˈklɒk] 24-Stunden-Uhr 47
a, an [ə] [ən] ein(e) 10
about [əˈbaʊt] über 14
about [əˈbaʊt] ungefähr 30
above [əˈbʌv] oberhalb 146
accurate [ˈækjʊrət] genau 58
acting school [ˈæktɪŋ skuːl] Schauspielschule 101
action film [ˈækʃəŋ fɪlm] Actionfilm 103
active [ˈæktɪv] aktiv 59
activity, -ies [ækˈtɪvətɪ] Aktivität 59
actor [ˈæktə] Schauspieler 100
address, -es [əˈdres] Adresse, Anschrift 19
adopt [əˈdɒpt] adoptieren 35
adopted [əˈdɒptɪd] adoptiert 35
Advent [æˈdvent] Advent 76
aerobics [eəˈrəʊbɪks] Aerobic 67
afraid: be afraid of [əˈfreɪd] Angst haben vor 82
after [ˈɑːftə] nach 49
afternoon [ɑːftəˈnuːn] Nachmittag 48
again [əˈgen] wieder 25
aged [eɪdʒd] im Alter von 122
ago [əˈgəʊ] vor *(zeitlich)* 92
agree [əˈgriː] zustimmen 54
air con(ditioning) [eə kənˈdɪʃənɪŋ] Klimaanlage 93
airline spokesperson, -people [ˈeəlaɪn ˈspəʊks ˌpɜːsən -ˌpiːpl] Sprecher(in) einer Fluggesellschaft 158
airport [ˈeəpɔːt] Flughafen 26
alcohol [ˈælkəhɒl] Alkohol 65
all [ɔːl] alle, die ganzen 35
all-you-can-eat buffet [ɔːl juː ken ˈiːt ˌbʊfeɪ] *Buffetessen, bei dem man für denselben Preis so viel essen kann, wie man will* 109
alone [əˈləʊn] allein 92
along [əˈlɒŋ] entlang 140
alright [ɔːlraɪt] in Ordnung 111
alternative [ɔːlˈtɜːnətɪv] Alternativ- 67
always [ˈɔːlweɪz] immer 10
am [eɪ əm] vormittags, vor 12 Uhr 49
am *(I am)* [aɪ ˈəm] bin *(ich bin)* 9
America [əˈmerɪkə] Amerika 145
American [əˈmerɪkən] amerikanisch 11
an [ən] ein(e) 11
and [ənd] und 9
anniversary, -ies [ˌænɪˈvɜːsərɪ] Jahrestag 78
another [əˈnʌðə] ein anderer, eine andere, ein anderes 33
answer [ˈɑːnsə] Antwort 11
answer [ɑːnsə] beantworten 22
antique [ˌænˈtiːk] Antiquität 96
any [ˈenɪ] irgendein(e) 27
anything [ˈenɪθɪŋ] (irgend)etwas 41
apologise [əˈpɒlədʒaɪz] sich entschuldigen 111
appearance [əˈpɪərəns] Erscheinungsbild 40
apple [ˈæpl] Apfel 67
April [ˈeɪprəl] April 76
aquarobics [ˌækwəˈrəʊbɪks] Wassergymnastik 67
architect [ˈɑːkɪtekt] Architekt(in) 134
are *(to be)* [ɑːr] bist, seid, sind *(sein)* 9
aromatherapy [əˌrəʊməˈθerəpi] Aromatherapie 152
around 3,500 BC [əˈraʊnd θriː ˈθaʊzənd faɪv ˈhʌndrəd ˌbiː ˈsiː] um 3500 v. Chr. 58
around the world [əˈraʊnd ðə wɜːld] um die Welt 90
get around [get əˈraʊnd] herumkommen 135
arrival [əˈraɪvl] Ankunft 130
arrive [əˈraɪv] ankommen 54
art [ɑːt] Kunst 104
art gallery, -ies [ˈɑːt gæləri] Kunstgalerie 23
arthritis [ɑːˈθraɪtɪs] Arthritis, Gelenkentzündung 67
article [ˈɑːtɪkl] Artikel *(Zeitung)*, Geschlechtswort 61
artist [ˈɑːtɪst] Künstler(in) 134
as [əz] als, wie 113
as … as [əz] so … wie 190
Asian [ˈeɪʃən] asiatisch 40
ask [ɑːsk] fragen 23
ask for [ˈɑːsk fɔː] nach … fragen 85
assistant [əˈsɪstənt] Assistent(in) 111
astronaut [ˈæstrənɔːt] Astronaut(in) 52
astronomy [əˈstrɒnəmɪ] Astronomie 163
at (@) [ət] at (@) 15
at 9 o'clock [ət ˌnaɪn əˈklɒk] um 9 Uhr 44
at home [ət ˈhəʊm] zu Hause 48
at night [ət ˈnaɪt] abends 49
at the convention [ət ðə kənˈvenʃən] bei der Konferenz 20
at the end [ət ðɪ ˈend] am Ende 12
atmosphere [ˈætməsfɪə] Atmosphäre 71
attractive [əˈtræktɪv] attraktiv 96
au pair [əʊ ˈpeə] Aupair 120
audience [ˈɔːdɪəns] Publikum, Zuhörer 98
August [ˈɔːgəst] August 80
aunt [ɑːnt] Tante 33
Australia [ɒˈstreɪlɪə] Australien 11
Australian [ɒˈstreɪlɪən] australisch 11
Austria [ˈɒstrɪə] Österreich 10
Austrian [ˈɒstrɪən] österreichisch 11
author [ˈɔːθə] Schriftsteller(in), Autor(in) 67
automatic [ɔːtəˈmætɪk] automatisch 93
autumn [ˈɔːtəm] Herbst 147
average [ˈævərɪdʒ] durchschnittlich, Durchschnitts- 102
award [əˈwɔːd] Preis, Auszeichnung 131
away [əˈweɪ] weg 67
awful [ˈɔːfl] schrecklich 86
baby food [ˈbeɪbi fuːd] Babynahrung 17
baby, -ies [ˈbeɪbɪ] Baby 31
babysitter [ˈbeɪbisɪtə] Babysitter 111
babysitting service [ˈbeɪbisɪtɪŋ ˈsɜːvɪs] Kleinkinderbetreuung 129
back [bæk] zurück 17
bad [bæd] schlecht 86
badly [ˈbædlɪ] schlecht 110
bag [bæg] Tasche 85
baguette [bæˈget] Baguette *(frz. Weißbrot)* 71
baklava [bæˈklɑːə] Baklava *(oriental. Gebäck)* 71

balcony, -ies ['bælkənɪ] Balkon 124
ball [bɔːl] Ball 70
ballet ['bæleɪ] Ballett 97
bank [bæŋk] Bank *(Kreditinstitut)* 22
bar [bɑː(r)] Bar 71
Barbarian [bɑː'beəriən] Barbar 98
basic ['beɪsɪk] grundlegend 67
basketball ['bɑːskətbɔːl] Baketball 59
bath [bɑːθ] Bad(ewanne) 114
bathroom ['bɑːθruːm] Bad, Badezimmer 114
bathwater [bɑːθ'wɔːtə] Badewasser 114
BBC [biːbiː'siː] BBC (British Broadcasting Corporation: *staatl. brit. Rundfunkanstalt*) 57
be [biː] sein 11
beach volleyball [biːtʃ 'vɒlibɔːl] Strandvolleyball 122
beach, -es [biːtʃ] Strand 26
beard [bɪəd] Bart 40
beat (beat) [biːt, biːt] schlagen 70
beautiful ['bjuːtɪfʊl] schön 26
beauty salon ['bjuːtɪ sælɒn] Schönheitssalon 152
because [bɪ'kɒz] weil 41
become (became) [bɪ'kʌm] [-'keɪm] werden 97
bed [bed] Bett 48
bedroom ['bedruːm] Schlafzimmer 124
bedtime ['bedtaɪm] Schlafenszeit 96
beer [bɪə] Bier 61
before [bɪ'fɔː] vor, bevor 22
beginner [bɪ'gɪnə] Anfänger(in) 67
best [best] beste(r, -s) 29
best wishes [best 'wɪʃɪz] alles Gute 78
better ['betə] besser 41
between [bɪt'wiːn] zwischen 146
big [bɪg] groß 22
bike [baɪk] Fahrrad 135
biographical [baɪə'græfɪkəl] biografisch 99
biography [baɪ'ɒgrəfɪ] Biografie 105
birthday ['bɜːθdeɪ] Geburtstag 76
bit: a bit [bɪt] ein bisschen 14
black [blæk] schwarz 39
blind [blaɪnd] blind 55
blonde [blɒnd] blond 40
blouse [blaʊz] Bluse 39
blue [bluː] blau 39
boat [bəʊt] Boot 55
body ['bɒdɪ] Körper 67
book [bʊk] Buch 14
book [bʊk] buchen 130
booking ['bʊkɪŋ] Buchung 129
booking form ['bʊkɪŋ fɔːm] Buchungsformular 130
bookshop ['bʊkʃɒp] Buchhandlung 21
bored [bɔːd] gelangweilt 67
boring ['bɔːrɪŋ] langweilig 41
born [bɔːn] geboren 32
boss, -es [bɒs] Boss, Chef(in) 35
both [bəʊθ] beide 34
bottle ['bɒtl] Flasche 77
bought [bɔːt] kaufte, -est, -et,-en 91
boxer ['bɒksə] Boxer(in) 60
boxing ['bɒksɪŋ] Boxen 59
boy [bɔɪ] Junge 35
boyfriend ['bɔɪfrend] Freund 120
bread [bred] Brot 71

break [breɪk] Pause 141
break: city break [breɪk] Städtereise 26
break-dancing ['breɪk dɑːnsɪŋ] Breakdance machen 97
breakfast ['brekfəst] Frühstück 48
bridge [brɪdʒ] Brücke 26
Brie [briː] Brie *(frz. Käse)* 71
bring (brought) [brɪŋ, brɔːt] bringen 35
Britain ['brɪtn] Großbritannien 28
British ['brɪtɪʃ] britisch 72
brother ['brʌðə] Bruder 33
brown [braʊn] braun 39
budget ['bʌdʒɪt] Budget 77
buffet ['bʊfeɪ] Büfett 64
building ['bɪldɪŋ] Gebäude 26
Bulgaria [bʌl'geariə] Bulgarien 70
Bürli Bürli *(schweizer Gebäck aus Brotteig)* 71
bus stop ['bʌs stɒp] Bushaltestelle 111
bus, -es [bʌs] Bus 94
bush, -es [bʊʃ] Busch, Strauch 31
business card ['bɪznəs kɑːd] (Visiten)Karte 115
business contact ['bɪznəs ˌkɒntækt] Geschäftskontakt 120
business meeting ['bɪznəs ˌmiːtɪŋ] Geschäftstreffen 115
business partner ['bɪznəs ˌpɑːtnə] Geschäftspartner 117
business person, -people ['bɪznəs ˌpɜːsən], [ˌpiːpl] Geschäftsmann, -frau, -leute 29
busy ['bɪzɪ] beschäftigt 26
but [bət] aber 19
buy [baɪ] kaufen 40
by *(bus, train, plane, car)* [baɪ] mit *(dem Bus, dem Zug, dem Flugzeug, dem Auto)* 135
bye [baɪ] Auf Wiedersehen 11
café ['kæfeɪ] Café 23
cake [keɪk] Kuchen 38
call [kɔːl] (an)rufen 82
calling ['kɔːlɪŋ] Anrufen, Anruf 156
calorie ['kælərɪ] Kalorie 61
camera ['kæmərə] Kamera 85
can [kən] können 14
Canada ['kænədə] Kanada 90
candidate ['kændɪdət] Bewerber(in) 41
candlelit ['kændlɪt] ... bei Kerzenlicht 96
capital city ['kæptl 'sɪti] Hauptstadt 90
capital letter ['kæptl 'letə] Großbuchstabe 10
car [kɑː] Auto, Wagen 13
car crash ['kɑː ˌkræʃ] Autounfall 44
car park ['kɑː pɑːk] Parkplatz 21
card [kɑːd] (Glückwunsch)Karte 60
career [kə'rɪə] Laufbahn 38
careful ['keəfʊl] vorsichtig 93
carry ['kæri] Tragen 60
castle ['kɑːsl] Schloss, Burg 96
cat [kæt] Katze 35
Catholic ['kæθəlɪk] katholisch, Katholik(in) 46
celebrate ['selɪbreɪt] feiern 152
cell phone (AmE) ['selfəʊn] Handy 15
cellar ['selə] Keller 134
centimetre ['sentɪmiːtə] Zentimeter 134
central ['sentrəl] zentral 134
centre ['sentə] Mitte, Zentrum 27
ceramics [sɪ'ræmɪks] Keramik 67
chair [tʃeə] Stuhl 124

champagne [ʃæm'peɪn] Champagner 51
champion ['tʃæmpɪən] Meister(in) 70
championship ['tʃæmpɪənʃɪp] Meisterschaft 70
chance [tʃɑːns] Möglichkeit, Chance 168
change [tʃeɪndʒ] ändern, verändern 14
charisma [kə'rɪzmə] Charisma 98
cheap [tʃiːp] billig 58
check out [tʃek 'aʊt] auschecken *(Hotel)* 130
checkmate ['tʃekmeɪt] Schachmatt 70
Cheddar ['tʃedə] Cheddar *(engl. Käse)* 71
cheese [tʃiːz] Käse 60
cheesecake ['tʃiːzkeɪk] Käsekuchen 109
chef [ʃef] Küchenchef(in), Koch, Köchin 82
chess [tʃes] Schach 59
chicken ['tʃɪkɪn] Huhn 71
chicken wing ['tʃɪkɪn ˌwɪŋ] Hühnchenflügel 74
child, children [tʃaɪld], ['tʃɪldrən] Kind 33
child-centred [tʃaɪld 'sentəd] kinderorientiert 104
child-friendly [tʃaɪld 'frendli] kinderfreundlich 104
childhood ['tʃaɪldhʊd] Kindheit 104
children's play area [ˌtʃɪldrəns 'pleɪ eəriə] Kinderspielplatz 129
chilli ['tʃɪli] Chili 96
China ['tʃaɪnə] China 44
Chinese [tʃaɪ'niːz] chinesisch 22
chips [tʃɪp] Pommes frites 72
chocoholic [ˌtʃɒkə'hɒlɪk] schokoladensüchtig 96
chocolate ['tʃɒklət] Schokolade 17
choose (chose) [tʃuːz] (aus)wählen, (sich) aussuchen 33
Christ [kraɪst] Christus 58
Christmas ['krɪsməs] Weihnachten 116
church, -es [tʃɜːtʃ] Kirche 21
cider ['saɪdə] Cider *(engl. Apfelwein)* 148
cinema ['sɪnɪmə] Kino 22
city break [ˌsɪti 'breɪk] Städtereise 26
city, -ies ['sɪtɪ] Stadt, Großstadt 21
class clown [klɑːs 'klaʊn] Klassenclown 38
class, -es [klɑːs] Klasse 19
classical ['klæsɪkl] klassisch 61
clean [kliːn] reinigen 102
clean [kliːn] sauber 86
clear [klɪə(r)] deutlich, klar 113
clearly ['klɪəlɪ] deutlich, klar 110
climate ['klaɪmət] Klima 158
clock [klɒk] Uhr 46
clothes [kləʊðz] Kleidung, Kleider 39
cloudy ['klaʊdɪ] bewölkt 147
club [klʌb] Club, Verein 63
coat [kəʊt] Mantel 54
coffee ['kɒfɪ] Kaffee 46
cold [kəʊld] kalt 72
colleague ['kɒliːg] Kollege, Kollegin 83
college ['kɒlɪdʒ] *Teil einer Universität* 28
colonial [kə'ləʊnɪəl] Kolonial-, kolonial 164
colour ['kʌlə] Farbe 39
combine [kəm'baɪn] verbinden, kombinieren 70
come (came) [kʌm, keɪm] kommen 20
comedy, -ies ['kɒmədɪ] Komödie 103
comfortable ['kʌmftəbl] bequem 102
company, -ies ['kʌmpənɪ] Unternehmen 78
competition [kɒmpə'tɪʃn] Wettbewerb 109
competitive [kəm'petətɪv] Wettbewerbs- 109

compost [ˈkɒmpɒst] Kompost 67
computer [kəmˈpjuːtə] Computer, Rechner 38
computer expert [kəmˈpjuːtə ˌekspɜːt] Computerexperte 38
conference [ˈkɒnfərəns] Konferenz 129
confused [kənˈfjuːzd] verwirrt 158
congratulations [kənˌɡrætjʊˈleɪʃnz] Glückwünsche 116
conservative [kənˈsɜːvətɪv] konservativ 115
constable [ˈkʌnstəbl] brit. Polizist *(ehrenamtlich)* 55
contact [ˈkɒntækt] Kontakt 9
contact details [ˈkɒntækt ˌdiːteɪls] Kontaktdaten 14
control [kənˈtrəʊl] kontrollieren 161
convention [kənˈvenʃn] Konvention 20
conversation [kɒnvəˈseɪʃn] Gespräch, Unterhaltung 149
cook [kʊk] kochen 38
cook [kʊk] Koch, Köchin 113
cooker [ˈkʊkə] Herd 124
corner [ˈkɔːnə] Ecke 23
cost (cost) [kɒst] kosten 84
costume [ˈkɒstjuːm] Kostüm 87
could [kʊd] könnten 64
count [kaʊnt] zählen 28
country,-ies [ˈkʌntri] Land 11
countryside [ˈkʌntrisaɪd] Land(schaft) 60
couple [kʌpl] Paar 125
course [kɔːs] Kurs, Lehrgang 49
cousin [ˈkʌzn] Cousin, Kusine 33
craftsman, -men [ˈkrɑːftsmən], [-men] Handwerker 134
crash, -es [kræʃ] Unfall 44
cream [kriːm] Sahne 82
creative [kriˈːeɪtɪv] kreativ 29
credit card [ˈkredɪt kɑːd] Kreditkarte 130
criminal [ˈkrɪmɪnl] kriminell, verbrecherisch 55
Cuba [kjuːbə] Kuba 97
Cuban [ˈkjuːbən] kubanisch 97
cultural [ˈkʌltʃərəl] kulturell 120
culture [ˈkʌltʃə] Kultur 97
cup [kʌp] Tasse 75
customer [ˈkʌstəmə] Kunde, Kundin 72
cycle [ˈsaɪkl] Fahrrad fahren 135
dad [dæd] Papa, Vati 41
daily [ˈdeɪlɪ] täglich 47
dance [dɑːns] Tanz 97
dance [dɑːns] tanzen 38
dancer [ˈdɑːnsə] Tänzer(in) 87
danger [ˈdeɪndʒə] Gefahr 55
dangerous [ˈdeɪndʒərəs] gefährlich 54
date [deɪt] Datum 77
daughter [ˈdɔːtə] Tochter 33
day [deɪ] Tag 49
day return [deɪ rɪˈtɜːn] Tagesrückfahrkarte 137
daylight [ˈdeɪlaɪt] Tageslicht 58
dead [ded] tot 34
dear [dɪə] lieb(e, -er, -es) 29
debut [ˈdeɪbjuː] Debut 108
December [dɪˈsembə] Dezember 62
decor [ˈdeɪkɔː] Verzierung, Dekoration 164
decorate [ˈdekəreɪt] verzieren 38
degree [dɪˈgriː] Grad 146
demonstration [demənˈstreɪʃn] Demonstration 67
depart [dɪˈpɑːt] Abreise 93
department store [dɪˈpɑːtmənt stɔː] Kaufhaus 22
departure [dɪˈpɑːtʃə] Abfahrt 138
describe [dɪsˈkraɪb] beschreiben 38
design [dɪˈzaɪn] Design 104
design [dɪˈzaɪn] entwerfen 131
dessert [dɪˈzɜːt] Nachtisch, Dessert 73
detail [ˈdiːteɪl] Detail, Einzelheit 134
detective [dɪˈtektɪv] Kriminalbeamte, Kriminalbeamtin 93
detective series [dɪˈtektɪv ˌsɪəriːz] Detektivserie *(Fernsehen)* 165
dictionary, -ies [ˈdɪkʃənrɪ] Wörterbuch 144
did, *(past of* **do**) [dɪd] tat, -st, -et, -en 91
died, *(past of* **die**) [daɪd] hier: starb 97
different [ˈdɪfrənt] andere(r, -s), anders 67
digital [ˈdɪdʒɪtl] Digital-, digital 58
dinner [ˈdɪnə] Abendessen 48
dinnertime [ˈdɪnətaɪm] Abendessenszeit 49
direction [dɪˈrekʃn] Richtung 140
directly [dɪˈrektlɪ] direkt 115
dirty [ˈdɜːtɪ] schmutzig 86
disagree [dɪsəˈgriː] nicht einverstanden sein 54
dishwasher [ˈdɪʃˌwɒʃə] Geschirrspülmaschine 124
dislike [dɪsˈlaɪk] Abneigung 61
distance [ˈdɪstəns] Entfernung 28
district [ˈdɪstrɪkt] Bezirk 55
divorced [dɪˈvɔːst] geschieden 33
do (did) [duː, dɪd] tun, machen 15
doctor [ˈdɒktə] Arzt, Ärztin 44
documentary, -ies [dɒkjʊˈmentərɪ] Dokumentarfilm 103
does *(do)* [dəz] tut, macht 53
dog [dɒg] Hund 35
doing [ˈduːɪŋ] Tun 109
doll [dɒl] Puppe 104
dolls' house [ˈdɒlz haʊs] Puppenhaus 134
done: well done [dʌn] gut gemacht 116
door [dɔː] Tür 54
doorman, -men [ˈdɔːmən, -men] Portier 54
dot [dɒt] Punkt 15
double [ˈdʌbl] doppelt 141
double (room) [ˈdʌbl] Doppelzimmer 125
Down's syndrome [ˈdauns sɪnˈdrəʊm] Down-Syndrom 162
drama group [ˈdrɑːmə gruːp] Theatergruppe 136
drama series [ˈdrɑːmə sɪəˌriːz] Serie *(Fernsehen)* 165
dream [driːm] Traum 105
dream job [driːm ˈdʒɒb] Traumberuf 52
dress, -es [dres] Kleid 39
drink [drɪŋk] Getränk 71
drink (drank) [drɪŋk, dræŋk] trinken 64
drive (drove) [draɪv] (Auto) fahren 41
driver [ˈdraɪvə] Fahrer(in) 44
driving test [ˈdraɪvɪŋ test] Fahrprüfung 118
DVD [ˌdiː viː ˈdiː] DVD 68
dynamic [daɪˈnæmɪk] dynamisch 67
each [iːtʃ] jede(r, -s) 83
early [ˈɜːlɪ] früh 61
earn [ɜːn] verdienen 53
East [iːst] Ost 104
Easter [ˈiːstə] Ostern 76
eat (ate) [iːt, et] essen 64
eat out [iːt ˈaʊt] auswärts essen 73
eater [ˈiːtə] Esser(in) 109
egg [eg] Ei 71
Egyptian [ɪˈdʒɪpʃn] Äypter(in) 58
eight [eɪt] acht 15
eighteen [eɪˈtiːn] achtzehn 27
eighth [eɪtθ] achte(r, -s) 76
eighty [ˈeɪtɪ] achtzig 27
electrical [ɪˈlektrɪkl] elektrisch 124
electricity [ɪlekˈtrɪsətɪ] Elektrizität, Strom 125
electronic [ɪlekˈtrɒnɪk] elektronisch 140
elegant [ˈelɪgənt] elegant 125
elephant [ˈelɪfənt] Elefant 141
eleven [ɪˈlevn] elf 27
eleventh [ɪˈlevnθ] elfte(r, -s) 97
email [ˈiːmeɪl] E-Mail 16
email address, -es [ˈiːmeɪl əˌdres] E-Mail-Adresse 15
end [end] Ende 12
ending with [ˈendɪŋ wɪð] endend auf 124
energy, -ies [ˈenədʒɪ] Energie, Kraft 35
England [ˈɪŋglənd] England 12
English [ˈɪŋglɪʃ] englisch 9
enjoy [ɪnˈdʒɔɪ] genießen 67
enter [ˈentə] betreten, hineinfahren 140
entertainer [ˌentəˈteɪnə] Entertainer(in), Unterhaltungskünstler(in) 97
entertainment [ˌentəˈteɪnmənt] Unterhaltung 97
escalator [ˈeskəleɪtə] Rolltreppe 65
euro [ˈjʊərəʊ] Euro 81
Europe [ˈjʊərəp] Europa 128
European [ˌjʊərəˈpɪən] europäisch 70
evening [ˈiːvnɪŋ] Abend 48
event [ɪˈvent] Ereignis 70
every [ˈevrɪ] jede(r, -s) 44
everyday speech [ˈevrɪdeɪ ˌspiːtʃ] Alltagssprache 47
everyone [ˈevrɪwʌn] jeder, alle 110
everything [ˈevrɪθɪŋ] alles 86
everywhere [ˈevrɪweə] überall 136
example [ɪgˈzɑːmpl] Beispiel 58
excellent [ˈeksələnt] hervorragend 68
exciting [ɪkˈsaɪtɪŋ] aufregend, spannend 103
excuse me [ɪkˈskjuːz mi] Entschuldigung! 22
exercise [ˈeksəsaɪz] Übung 11
exercise [ˈeksəsaɪz] Bewegung 102
expected [ɪkˈspektɪd] erwartet 137
expensive [ɪkˈspensɪv] teuer 85
explain [ɪkˈspleɪn] erklären 44
express [ɪkˈspres] ausdrücken 54
extra [ˈekstrə] Zusatz-, zusätzlich 40
eye [aɪ] Auge 40
face [feɪs] Gesicht 42
facility, -ies [fəˈsɪlətɪ] Einrichtung 129
fact [fækt] Tatsache, Fakt 28
fact file [ˈfækt faɪl] Datenblatt 97
fair [feə] Jahrmarkt 96
family, -ies [ˌfæməlɪ] Familie 33
family member [ˌfæməlɪ ˈmembə] Familienmitglied 33
family-friendly [ˈfæməlɪ ˈfrendli] familienfreundlich 104

famous ['feɪməs] berühmt 27
fantastic [fæn'tæstɪk] fantastisch 67
fashion ['fæʃn] Mode 104
fast [fɑːst] schnell 109
fast food restaurant [fɑːst 'fuːd restrɒnt] Schnellrestaurant 27
fastest ['fɑːstəst] schnellste(r, -s) 135
father ['fɑːðə] Vater 33
faux pas [ˌfəʊ 'pɑː] Fehltritt 120
favourite ['feɪvərɪt] Lieblings- 41
February ['febrʊərɪ] Februar 44
female ['fiːmeɪl] weiblich 36
feminist ['femɪnɪst] Feministin 38
festival ['festɪvl] Festival, Festspiele 87
feta cheese [ˌfetə 'tʃiːz] Feta *(griech. Käse)* 71
fifteen [fɪf'tiːn] fünfzehn 27
fifth [fɪfθ] fünfte(r, -s) 76
fifty ['fɪftɪ] fünfzig 27
fight [faɪt] Kampf 20
fight [faɪt] kämpfen 20
fighting sport ['faɪtɪŋ spɔːt] Kampfsport 70
figure ['fɪgə] Zahl, Ziffer 28
file [faɪl] Ordner 97
film [fɪlm] Film 13
film star ['fɪlm stɑː] Filmstar 52
find (found) [faɪnd, faʊnd] finden 38
find out [faɪnd aʊt] herausfinden 49
fine [faɪn] schön, gut 9
finish ['fɪnɪʃ] beenden 48
fireworks ['faɪəwɜːks] Feuerwerk 87
first [fɜːst] erste(r, -s) 29
first class [fɜːst 'klɑːs] erstklassig 164
first floor [fɜːst 'flɔː] erster Stock 126
first name [fɜːst 'neɪm] Vorname 9
first time [fɜːst 'taɪm] erstes Mal 84
fish [fɪʃ] Fisch 43
fit [fɪt] fit 35
fitness ['fɪtnɪs] Kondition, Fitness 67
five [faɪv] fünf 15
flamenco [flə'meŋkəʊ] Flamenco *(span. Tanz)* 89
flat [flæt] Wohnung 125
flight [flaɪt] Flug 40
flirting ['flɜːtɪŋ] Flirten 161
floor [flɔː] Stockwerk 117
flower ['flaʊə] Blume 103
flush [flʌʃ] spülen 134
fly (flew) [flaɪ, fluː] fliegen 91
focus ['fəʊkəs] Fokus 11
foggy ['fɒgɪ] neb(e)lig 158
follow ['fɒləʊ] folgen 93
food [fuːd] Essen 64
foot, feet [fʊt, fiːt] Fuß 119
football ['fʊtbɔːl] Fußball 59
footballer ['fʊtbɔːlə] Fußballer(in) 52
for [fə] für 14
forget (forgot) [fə'get, fə'gɒt] vergessen 97
formal ['fɔːml] förmlich, formell 77
formally ['fɔːməlɪ] förmlich 119
formula one ['fɔːmjʊlə wʌn] Formel 1 52
forty ['fɔːtɪ] vierzig 27
four [fɔː] vier 15
fourteen [fɔː'tiːn] vierzehn 27
fourteenth [fɔː'tiːnθ] vierzehnte(r, -s) 80
fourth [fɔːθ] vierte(r, -s) 76
France [frɑːns] Frankreich 11
free [friː] frei 67
free time [friː 'taɪm] Freizeit 59
French [frentʃ] französisch 11
fresh [freʃ] frisch 64
Friday ['fraɪdeɪ] Freitag 49
fridge [frɪdʒ] Kühlschrank 124
friend [frend] Freund(in) 33
friendly ['frendlɪ] freundlich 83
frightening ['fraɪtnɪŋ] beängstigend, furchterregend 103
frogs' legs [frɒgs 'legz] Froschschenkel 82
from [frɒm] von, aus 10
fruit [fruːt] Obst, Frucht 72
full [fʊl] voll 96
fun [fʌn] Spaß 41
funny ['fʌnɪ] lustig, komisch 103
furniture ['fɜːnɪtʃə] Möbel 134
game [geɪm] Spiel 17
garage ['gærɑːʒ] Garage 124
garden ['gɑːdn] Garten 37
gastronomy [gæ'strɒnəmi] Gastronomie 163
gene [dʒiːn] Gen, Erbfaktor 64
general ['dʒenrəl] allgemein, generell 67
generation [dʒenə'reɪʃn] Generation 44
German ['dʒɜːmən] deutsch 11
Germany ['dʒɜːmənɪ] Deutschland 10
get (got) [get, gɒt] bekommen, kriegen 54
get married [get 'mærid] heiraten 99
get stuck [get 'stʌk] stecken bleiben 140
get up [get 'ʌp] aufstehen 48
getting around [get ə'raʊnd] Herumkommen 135
gift shop ['gɪft ʃɒp] Geschenkeladen 104
giraffe [dʒɪ'rɑːf] Giraffe 144
girl [gɜːl] Mädchen 52
give (gave) [gɪv, geɪv] geben 14
glass [glɑːs] Glas 78
glasses ['glɑːsɪz] Brille 40
go (went) [gəʊ, went] Versuch 38
go out [gəʊ 'aʊt] ausgehen 48
Golden Globe [gəʊldən 'gləʊb] *US-amerikanischer Filmpreis* 98
golf [gɒlf] Golf 62
good [gʊd] gut 22
good evening [gʊd 'iːvnɪŋ] guten Abend 74
good luck [gʊd 'lʌk] viel Glück! 116
good morning [gʊd 'mɔːnɪŋ] guten Morgen 130
goodbye [gʊd'baɪ] auf Wiedersehen! 11
good-looking [gʊd'lʊkɪŋ] gut aussehend 40
grammar ['græmə] Grammatik 11
grand [grænd] groß 31
grandchild, -ren ['grændʃaɪld, -tʃɪldrən] Enkelkind 33
granddaughter ['grænˌdɔːtə] Enkelin 33
grandfather ['grændˌfɑːðə] Großvater 33
grandma ['grænmɑː] Oma 35
grandmother ['grænˌmʌðə] Großmutter 33
grandparent ['grænˌpeərənt] Großelternteil 35
grandson ['grænsʌn] Enkel 33
great [greɪt] groß 35
great-grandchild, -ren [greɪt 'græntʃaɪld, -tʃɪldrən] Urenkel(in) 44
great-grandmother [greɪt 'grænˌmʌðə] Urgroßmutter 134
great-great-grandmother [greɪt greɪt 'grænˌmʌðə] Ururgroßmutter 134
great-great-grandson [greɪt greɪt 'grænsʌn] Ururenkel 44
Greece [griːs] Griechenland 11
Greek [griːk] griechisch 11
green [griːn] grün 39
grey [greɪ] grau 39
ground floor [graʊnd 'flɔː] Erdgeschoss 117
group [gruːp] Gruppe 67
grow (grew) [grəʊ, gruː] anbauen 67
guest [gest] Gast 54
guidebook ['gaɪdbʊk] Reiseführer 85
hair [heə] Haar 40
half [hɑːf] Hälfte 47
hall [hɔːl] Halle, Saal 59
ham [hæm] Schinken 71
hamburger ['hæmbɜːgə] Hamburger *(Nahrungsmittel)* 78
hand [hænd] Hand 115
handbag ['hændbæg] Handtasche 111
happen ['hæpn] passieren, geschehen 158
happily ['hæpɪlɪ] fröhlich, glücklich 110
happy ['hæpɪ] glücklich 35
harbour ['hɑːbə] Hafen 158
hard [hɑːd] hart 95
have (had) [hæv, həd] haben 14
have got [hæv 'gɒt] haben 33
he [hiː] er 10
head [hed] Kopf 67
headline ['hedlaɪn] Schlagzeile 106
healthy ['helθɪ] gesund 59
hear [hɪə] hören 167
heavy ['hevɪ] schwer 127
hello [hə'ləʊ] hallo 9
help [help] Hilfe 22
helpful ['helpfl] hilfreich, nützlich 55
her [hɜː] ihr(e) 10
here [hɪə] hier 22
hey [heɪ] he!, heda! 82
hi [haɪ] hallo 9
high [haɪ] hoch 102
highlight ['haɪlaɪt] Höhepunkt 158
him [hɪm] ihn, ihm 40
hire [haɪə] mieten 91
his [hɪz] sein(e) 10
history ['hɪstərɪ] Geschichte 32
hobby, -ies ['hɒbɪ] Hobby 38
hockey ['hɒki] Hockey (Sport) 60
holiday ['hɒlədeɪ] Urlaub 28
home [həʊm] Zuhause, Heim 29
homework ['həʊmwɜːk] Hausaufgaben 41
hope [həʊp] hoffen 116
horror ['hɒrə] Entsetzen, Grauen 103
hospital ['hɒspɪtl] Krankenhaus 44
host [həʊst] Gastgeber(in) 115
hostess, -es ['həʊstɪs] Gastgeberin 120
hot [hɒt] heiß 72
hotel [həʊ'tel] Hotel 19
hour [aʊə] Stunde 68
house [haʊs] Haus 22
househusband ['haʊs hʌzbənd] Hausmann 52
housewife, -wives ['haʊswaɪf, -waɪvz] Hausfrau 52
housework ['haʊswɜːk] Hausarbeit 41
how [haʊ] wie 9
how often [haʊ 'ɒfn] wie oft 60

hundred ['hʌndrəd] hundert 99
husband ['hʌzbənd] (Ehe)Mann 33
I [aɪ] ich 9
ice cream [aɪs 'kriːm] Eis, Eiscreme 22
iced tea [aɪst 'tiː] Eistee 148
Iceland ['aɪslænd] Island 61
Icelandic [aɪs'lændɪk] isländisch 61
idea [aɪ'dɪə] Idee 29
ideal [aɪ'dɪəl] ideal 67
if [ɪf] wenn, falls 53
ill [ɪl] krank 65
image ['ɪmɪdʒ] Bild 29
immediately [ɪ'miːdɪətlɪ] gleich, sofort 115
important [ɪm'pɔːtənt] wichtig 29
in [ɪn] in 23
in fact [ɪn 'fækt] tatsächlich 189
in front of [ɪn 'frʌnt əv] vor *(räumlich)* 103
include [ɪn'kluːd] einschließen 165
included [ɪn'kluːdɪd] inbegriffen 130
including [ɪn'kluːdɪŋ] einschließlich, inbegriffen 28
India ['ɪndɪə] Indien 90
Indian ['ɪndɪən] indisch 67
indoor pool [ɪndɔː 'puːl] Innenschwimmbad 152
info ['ɪnfəʊ] Info 19
informal [ɪnfɔː'məl] inoffiziell 77
informally [ɪn'fɔːməlɪ] 119
information [ˌɪnfə'meɪʃn] Informationen 40
initials [ɪ'nɪʃəlz] Initialen 99
initiative [ɪ'nɪʃətɪv] Initiative 162
instruction [ɪn'strʌkʃn] Anweisung 140
interest ['ɪntrəst] Interesse 166
interested ['ɪntrəstɪd] interessiert 35
interesting ['ɪntrəstɪŋ] interessant 32
international [ɪntə'næʃnl] international 26
Internet ['ɪntənet] Internet 84
Internet access ['ɪntənet ˌækses] Internetzugang 129
interview ['ɪntəvjuː] Interview 119
into ['ɪntʊ] in, hinein 102
introduce [ˌɪntrə'djuːs] vorstellen 10
invent [ɪn'vent] erfinden 58
invitation [ˌɪnvɪ'teɪʃn] Einladung 78
invite [ɪn'vaɪt] einladen 78
Ireland ['aɪələnd] Irland 11
Irish ['aɪərɪʃ] irisch 11
is *(to be)* [ɪz] ist *(sein)* 9
island ['aɪlənd] Insel 165
it [ɪt] es 11
IT technician [aɪ 'tiː tek'nɪʃn] IT-Techniker 52
Italian [ɪ'tæljən] italienisch 11
Italy ['ɪtəlɪ] Italien 11
item ['aɪtəm] Gegenstand 78
its [ɪts] sein(e) 108
jacket ['dʒækɪt] Jacke 39
January ['dʒænjʊərɪ] Januar 62
Japan [dʒə'pæn] Japan 114
Japanese [dʒæpə'niːz] japanisch 31
jazz [dʒæz] Jazz 78
jeans [dʒiːnz] Jeans 39
job [dʒɒb] Arbeitsplatz, Stelle 35
job interview ['dʒɒb ɪntəvjuː] Vorstellungsgespräch 116
jogging ['dʒɒgɪŋ] Joggen, Jogging 70
joke [dʒəʊk] Witz, Scherz 44
juice [dʒuːs] Saft 71
July [dʒʊ'laɪ] Juli 77
June [dʒuːn] Juni 89
just [dʒʌst] nur 67
keep (kept) [kiːp, kept] behalten 17
keep fit [kiːp 'fɪt] sich fit halten 135
key word [kiː 'wɜːd] Schlüsselwort 55
keycard ['kiːkɑːd] Chipkarte 130
kick away [kik ə'weɪ] wegtreten 67
kickboxing ['kikˌbɒksɪŋ] Kickboxen 67
kid [kɪd] Kind 97
kilo ['kiːləʊ] Kilo 127
kilometre [kɪ'lɒmɪtə] Kilometer 28
king [kɪŋ] König 32
kitchen ['kɪtʃɪn] Küche 124
knee [niː] Knie 67
knockout ['nɒk-aʊt] Knockout 70
know (knew) [nəʊ, njuː] wissen 26
land [lænd] landen 158
landmark ['lændmɑːk] Wahrzeichen 117
lane [leɪn] kleine Straße 22
language ['læŋgwɪdʒ] Sprache 67
language school ['læŋgwɪdʒ skuːl] Sprachschule 16
large [lɑːdʒ] groß 125
lark [lɑːk] Lerche 49
last [lɑːst] letzte(r, -s) 87
late [leɪt] spät, verspätet 65
late night [leɪt 'naɪt] am späten Abend 168
later ['leɪtə] später 120
Latin ['lætɪn] lateinisch 58
learn (learnt) [lɜːn, lɜːnt] lernen 32
learn about [lɜːn ə'baʊt] erfahren über 67
leave (left) [liːv, left] Urlaub 54
left [left] linke(r, -s), Links- 98
leisure centre ['leʒə ˌsentə] Freizeitzentrum 21
lesson ['lesn] (Unterrichts)Stunde 62
letter ['letə] Brief 124
leukaemia [luː'kiːmiə] Leukämie 110
library, -ies ['laɪbrərɪ] Bibliothek, Bücherei 134
life, lives [laɪf, laɪvz] Leben 47
lifeboat ['laɪfbəʊt] Rettungsbot 55
lifeboatwoman, -women ['laɪfbəʊt ˌwʊmən, -ˌwɪmɪn] Rettungsschwimmerin im Rettungsbot 55
lifestyle ['laɪfstaɪl] Lebensstil 64
lift [lɪft] (hoch)heben 17
lift [lɪft] Aufzug 65
light [laɪt] Licht 96
lighthouse ['laɪthaʊs] Leuchtturm 91
like [laɪk] wie 7
like [laɪk] mögen 54
line [laɪn] Linie, Reihe 77
list [lɪst] Liste 16
listen to ['lɪsn tə] (zu)hören 55
listening comprehension ['lɪsnɪŋ ˌkɒmprɪ'henʃn] Hörverständnis 45
literature ['lɪtrətʃə] Literatur 97
little ['lɪtl] klein 35
live [lɪv] leben 51
live music [laɪv 'mjuːzɪk] Livemusik 87
living room ['lɪvɪŋ ruːm] Wohnzimmer 124
local ['ləʊkl] örtlich 67
location [ləʊ'keɪʃn] Ort 93
logic ['lɒdʒɪk] Logik 70
long [lɒŋ] lang 40
look [lʊk] (an)sehen 9
look after [lʊk 'ɑːftə] sich kümmern um 53
look at ['lʊk ət] (an)sehen 9
lorry, -ies ['lɒrɪ] Lastwagen, Lkw 52
lot [lɒt] viel 26
loud [laʊd] laut 65
loudly [laʊdlɪ] laut 115
love [lʌv] Liebe 41
love [lʌv] lieben 54
lovely ['lʌvlɪ] wunderschön 125
loving ['lʌvɪŋ] liebevoll 33
low-impact [ləʊ 'ɪmpækt] sanft, schonend 67
lunch [lʌntʃ] Mittagessen 46
lunchtime ['lʌntʃtaɪm] Mittagszeit 49
macho ['mætʃəʊ] machohaft 38
magazine [ˌmægə'ziːn] Magazin, Zeitschrift 92
make (made) [meɪk, meɪd] machen 7
male [meɪl] männlich 36
man, men [mæn, men] Mann 12
manager ['mænɪdʒə] Manager(in), Geschäftsführer(in) 73
manicure ['mænɪkjʊə] Maniküre 152
many ['menɪ] viele 77
map [mæp] (Land)Karte 96
marathon ['mærəθən] Marathonlauf 110
March [mɑːtʃ] März 96
market ['mɑːkɪt] Markt 25
market place ['mɑːkɪt pleɪs] Marktplatz 21
marketing ['mɑːkɪtɪŋ] Marketing 29
married ['mærɪd] verheiratet 34
mass produce [mæs prə'djuːs] in großen Mengen produzieren 58
massage ['mæsɑːʒ] Massage 67
match [mætʃ] zuordnen 9
match, -es ['mætʃ] Spiel *(Sport)* 59
maximum ['mæksɪməm] Höchst-, maximal 70
May [meɪ] Mai 77
maybe ['meɪbiː] vielleicht 44
me [miː] mich, mir 14
meal [miːl] Mahlzeit, Essen 72
mean (meant) ['miːn, ment] bedeuten 54
medal ['medl] Medaille 61
medieval [medi'iːvəl] mittelalterlich 96
meet (met) [miːt, met] treffen 9
meeting ['miːtɪŋ] Treffen 53
meeting room ['miːtɪŋ ruːm] Versammlungsraum 167
member ['membə] Mitglied 35
memory, -ies ['memərɪ] Erinnerung 59
mentally ['mentəlɪ] geistig 70
menu ['menjuː] Speisekarte 72
merry ['merɪ] fröhlich, vergnügt 116
message ['mesɪdʒ] Mitteilung, Nachricht 140
method ['meθəd] Methode 67
metre ['miːtə] Meter 127
midday [ˌmɪd'deɪ] Mittag 49
midnight ['mɪdnaɪt] Mitternacht 49
mild [maɪld] mild 158
mile [maɪl] Meile 28
milk [mɪlk] Milch 71
million ['mɪljən] Million 58
mineral water ['mɪnrəl ˌwɔːtə] Mineralwasser 72
miniature ['mɪnətʃə] Mini(atur)-, Klein- 134
minibar ['mɪnibɑː] Minibar 130

minibus, -buses ['mɪnibʌs] Kleinbus 55
minimum ['mɪnɪməm] Mindest- 67
minute ['mɪnɪt] Minute 44
miss [mɪs] vermissen 120
mistake [mɪs'teɪk] Fehler 120
mix [mɪks] vermischen 115
mixed ['mɪkst] gemischt 84
mobile phone [məʊbaɪl 'fəʊn] Handy 15
model ['mɒdl] Modell, Fotomodell 41
modern ['mɒdn] modern 26
moment ['məʊmənt] Augenblick, Moment 98
Monday ['mʌndeɪ] Montag 49
money ['mʌnɪ] Geld 53
month [mʌnθ] Monat 59
more [mɔ:] mehr 14
morning ['mɔ:nɪŋ] Morgen 44
most [məʊst] meisten 17
mother ['mʌðə] Mutter 33
motorbike ['məʊtəbaɪk] Motorrad 140
mountain ['maʊntɪn] Berg 91
mouse [maʊs] Maus 146
moustache [mə'stɑ:ʃ] Schnurrbart 40
Mr ['mɪstə] Hr. 93
Mrs ['mɪsɪz] Fr. 44
much [mʌtʃ] viel 66
mum [mʌm] Mama 37
museum [mju:'zɪəm] Museum 21
music ['mju:zɪk] Musik 61
musical ['mju:zɪkl] Musical 141
must [mʌst] müssen 40
my [maɪ] mein(e) 9
name [neɪm] Name 9
name card ['neɪm kɑ:d] Namenschild 9
named [neɪmd] namens 20
narrow ['nærəʊ] schmal, eng 140
national ['næʃənl] national, National- 55
national park [næʃnəl 'pɑ:k] Nationalpark 94
nationality, -ies [,næʃə'nælətɪ] Nationalität, Staatsangehörigkeit 11
near [nɪə] nahe 10
need [ni:d] brauchen 29
negative ['negətɪv] negativ, verneinend 61
neighbour ['neɪbə] Nachbar(in) 60
nephew ['nevju:] Neffe 33
nervous ['nɜ:vəs] nervös 120
network [netwɜ:k] Netz(werk) 146
never ['nevə] nie(mals) 60
new [nju:] neu 29
New Zealand [nju: 'zi:lənd] Neuseeland 118
newspaper ['nju:s,peɪpə] Zeitung 60
next [nekst] nächste(r, -s) 11
nice [naɪs] nett 9
niece [ni:s] Nichte 33
night [naɪt] Nacht 49
nightclub ['naɪtklʌb] Nachtklub, Nachtlokal 125
nine [naɪn] neun 15
nineteen [naɪn'ti:n] neunzehn 27
ninety ['naɪntɪ] neunzig 27
ninth [naɪnθ] neunte(r, -s) 70
no [nəʊ] nein 11
Nobel Prize [nəʊ,bel 'praɪz] Nobelpreis 98
noisiest (noisy) ['nɔɪziəst] lauteste(r, -s) 128
normal ['nɔ:ml] normal 67
normally ['nɔ:məlɪ] normalerweise 9
north [nɔ:θ] Norden 155
not [nɒt] nicht 11
November [nəʊ'vembə] November 96
now [naʊ] nun, jetzt 17
number ['nʌmbə] Zahl 15
nurse [nɜ:s] Krankenschwester, Krankenpfleger 52
o'clock [ə'klɒk] Uhr *(Uhrzeit)* 47
October [ɒk'təʊbə] Oktober 70
of [əv] von 9
of course [əv 'kɔ:s] selbstverständlich 18
off: to be off to do [ɒf] unterwegs sein, etwas zu tun 160
offer ['ɒfə] anbieten 96
office ['ɒfɪs] Büro 51
often ['ɒfn] oft 54
oh [əʊ] null 15
OK [,əʊ'keɪ] OK 9
old [əʊld] alt 26
omelette ['ɒmlɪt] Omelett 72
on [ɒn] auf 23
on business [ɒn 'bɪznəs] geschäftlich 120
on time [ɒn 'taɪm] pünktlich 137
once [wʌns] einmal 59
one [wʌn] eins 15
one-way [wʌn 'weɪ] einseitig 164
online ['ɒnlaɪn] online, im Internet 102
only ['əʊnlɪ] nur, bloß 58
only child [əʊnlɪ 'tʃaɪld] Einzelkind 34
open ['əʊpən] offen, geöffnet 28
opening ['əʊpənɪŋ] Öffnung 78
opening hours ['əʊpənɪŋ aʊəs] Öffnungszeiten 84
opera ['ɒpərə] Oper 102
opera house ['ɒpərə haʊs] Opernhaus 26
opera singer ['ɒpərə sɪŋə] Opernsänger 54
opinion [ə'pɪnjən] Meinung 54
opposite ['ɒpəzɪt] gegenüberliegend 23
optimist ['ɒptɪmɪst] Optimist(in) 38
or [ɔ:] oder 22
orange ['ɒrɪndʒ] orange 39
orange ['ɒrɪndʒ] Orange 71
orange juice ['ɒrɪndʒ dʒu:s] Orangensaft 71
orchestra ['ɔ:kɪstrə] Orchester 87
order ['ɔ:də] Reihenfolge 10
order ['ɔ:də] bestellen 72
organisation [,ɔ:gənaɪ'zeɪʃən] Organisation 55
organise ['ɔ:gənaɪz] organisieren 77
Oscar ['ɒskə] *US-amerikanischer Filmpreis* 98
other ['ʌðə] andere(r, -s) 12
our [aʊə] unser(e) 16
out [aʊt] aus, heraus 27
outdoor [aʊt'dɔ:r] Außen- 61
outside [aʊt'saɪd] Außen- 53
over ['əʊvə] über 28
overpaid [,əʊvə'peɪd] überbezahlt 54
owl [aʊl] Eule 49
page [peɪdʒ] Seite 148
page number ['peɪdʒ nʌmbə] Seitenzahl 28
paint [peɪnt] malen 134
pair [peə] Paar 108
paper ['peɪpə] Papier 67
papermaking ['peɪpə,meɪkɪŋ] Papierherstellung 67
paradise ['pærədaɪs] Paradies 96
paragraph ['pærəgrɑ:f] Absatz, Abschnitt 106
parent ['peərənt] Elternteil 34
park [pɑ:k] Park 22
park [pɑ:k] parken 119
parkland ['pɑ:klænd] Parkgebiet 152
part [pɑ:t] Teil 22
partner ['pɑ:tnə] Partner(in) 67
party person, people ['pɑ:ti pɜ:sən, -pi:pəl] Partymensch 38
party, -ies ['pɑ:tɪ] Party 31
passenger ['pæsɪndʒə] Passagier(in) 137
past [pɑ:st] Vergangenhehit 92
past [pɑ:st] nach *(Uhrzeit)* 47
pasta ['pæstə] Teigwaren 17
patient ['peɪʃnt] Patient(in) 55
pay [peɪ] bezahlen 130
pence [pens] Pence 85
pendulum clock ['pendjʊləm ,klɒk] Pendeluhr 58
people ['pi:pl] Leute 19
per [pɜ:] pro 125
perfect ['pɜ:fɪkt] perfekt 54
performance [pə'fɔ:məns] Aufführung 108
person, people ['pɜ:sn, 'pi:pl] Person, Mensch 10
personal ['pɜ:sənl] persönlich 19
personal assistant (PA) [,pɜ:sənl ə'sɪstənt] persönliche(r) Mitarbeiter(in) 52
pessimist ['pesɪmɪst] Pessimist(in) 38
phone [fəʊn] Telefon 15
phone [fəʊn] anrufen 20
phone call ['fəʊn kɔ:l] Telefonanruf 153
phone number ['fəʊn nʌmbə] Telefonnummer 15
photo ['fəʊtəʊ] Foto, Aufnahme 29
phrase [freɪz] Wendung, Ausdruck 71
physically ['fɪzɪklɪ] körperlich 70
pick-up ['pɪk ʌp] Annahmestelle 93
picnic ['pɪknɪk] Picknick 144
picture ['pɪktʃə] Bild 106
pilot ['paɪlət] Pilot(in) 52
pink [pɪŋk] rosa, pink 39
pitta ['pɪtə] Pitta (griech. Brot) 71
pizza ['pi:tsə] Pizza 17
pizzeria [pi:tsə'ri:a] Pizzeria 89
place [pleɪs] Ort, Platz, Stelle 21
plan [plæn] Plan 23
plane [pleɪn] Flugzeug 92
platform ['plætfɔ:m] Bahnsteig 137
play [pleɪ] spielen 17
play area ['pleɪ eəriə] Spielplatz 132
player ['pleɪə] Spieler(in) 17
please [pli:z] bitte 14
pm [pi:'em] nachmittags, abends, nach 12 Uhr 49
pocket ['pɒkɪt] (Jacken)Tasche 115
point [pɔɪnt] Punkt 75
police [pə'li:s] Polizei 20
police officer [pə'li:s ,ɒfɪsə] Polizeibeamte, Polizeibeamtin 52
policeman, -men [pə'li:smən, -men] Polizist 20
polite [pə'laɪt] höflich 72
politics ['pɒlətɪks] Politik 147
poor [pʊə(r)] arm 97
pop star ['pɒp stɑ:] Popstar 41
popular ['pɒpjʊlə] populär, beliebt 58
population [,pɒpjʊ'leɪʃn] Bevölkerung, Einwohner 158

portrait ['pɔ:treɪt] Porträt 134
positive ['pɒzətɪv] positiv 29
post office ['pəʊst ˌɒfɪs] Post 21
postcard ['pəʊstkɑ:d] Postkarte 85
poster ['pəʊstə] Plakat 29
pot [pɒt] Topf 67
pound [paʊnd] Pfund 81
power ['paʊə] Macht, Gewalt 98
practical ['præktɪkl] praktisch 38
practise ['præktɪs] üben 98
pregnant ['pregnənt] schwanger 44
present ['prɪ'zent] vorstellen, präsentieren 55
present ['preznt] Geschenk 86
president ['prezɪdnt] Präsident(in) 146
price [praɪs] Preis 71
primary school ['praɪmərɪ sku:l] Grundschule 98
prime minister [praɪm 'mɪnɪstə] Premierminister(in) 123
prize [praɪz] (Sieges)Preis 97
probably ['prɒbəblɪ] wahrscheinlich 134
problem ['prɒbləm] Problem 35
product ['prɒdʌkt] Produkt, Erzeugnis 17
professional [prə'feʃnl] professionell, fachmännisch 97
programme ['prəʊgræm] Programm 103
project ['prɒdʒekt] Projekt 98
pub [pʌb] Kneipe 22
public ['pʌblɪk] öffentlich 28
public transport [ˌpʌblɪk 'trænspɔ:t] Öffentliche Personenbeförderung 135
pullover ['pʊləʊvə] Pullover 17
punctual ['pʌŋktjʊəl] pünktlich 58
put (put) [pʊt] stellen, legen, tun 10
puzzle ['pʌzl] Rätsel 20
quality, -ies ['kwɒlətɪ] Qualität 162
quarter ['kwɔ:tə] Viertel 47
queen [kwi:n] Königin 134
question ['kwestʃn] Frage 67
questionnaire [ˌkwestʃə'neə] Fragebogen 143
quicker (quick) ['kwɪkə] schneller 146
quiet ['kwaɪət] leise 26
quite [kwaɪt] ziemlich 123
quiz [kwɪz] Quiz 146
race [reɪs] Rennen 110
radio controlled ['reɪdiəʊ kən'trəʊld] funkgesteuert 58
rain [reɪn] Regen 54
rain [reɪn] regnen 151
react to [ri'ækt tə] reagieren auf 66
read (read) [ri:d, red] lesen 9
reading ['ri:dɪŋ] Lesen 20
reading comprehension ['ri:dɪŋ ˌkɒmprɪhenʃn] Leseverständnis 46
real [ri:l] echt, wirklich 105
realise ['rɪəlaɪz] erkennen 158
really ['rɪəlɪ] wirklich 35
reason ['ri:zn] Grund 111
reception [rɪ'sepʃn] Empfang 159
record ['rekɔ:d] (Schall)Platte 113
red [red] rot 39
reiki ['raɪkɪ] Reiki *(jap. medizinisches Behandlungsverfahren)* 152
relatively ['relətɪvlɪ] relativ 58
relax [rɪ'læks] sich entspannen 48
relaxed [rɪ'lækst] entspannt 67
relaxing [rɪ'læksɪŋ] entspannend 148
religion [rɪ'lɪdʒən] Religion 147
remember [rɪ'membə] sich erinnern 53
repair [rɪ'peə] reparieren 38
repeat [rɪ'pi:t] wiederholen 15
report back to [rɪˌpɔ:t 'bæk tə] berichten an 93
rescue ['reskju:] retten 55
reservation [rezə'veɪʃn] Reservierung 93
respectfully [rɪ'spektfəlɪ] mit Respekt 115
respond to [rɪ'spɒnd tə] reagieren auf, begegnen 66
restaurant ['restrɒnt] Restaurant, Gaststätte 21
result [rɪ'zʌlt] Ergebnis 116
retired [rɪ'taɪəd] im Ruhestand 55
return [rɪ'tɜ:n] *hier:* Rückfahrkarte 137
return [rɪ'tɜ:n] *hier:* Rückgabe 93
rice [raɪs] Reis 109
rich [rɪtʃ] reich 129
right [raɪt] richtig 114
right [raɪt] rechts 142
river ['rɪvə] Fluss 26
road [rəʊd] Straße 23
rolling ['rəʊlɪŋ] rollend 60
Roman ['rəʊmən] römisch 32
romantic [rəʊ'mæntɪk] romantisch 26
room [ru:m] Zimmer 16
rose [rəʊz] Rose 120
round [raʊnd] rundherum 14
round up ['raʊnd ʌp] Abrundung 13
route [ru:t] Strecke, Route 91
routine [ru:'ti:n] Routine 47
royal ['rɔɪəl] königlich 134
Royal National Lifeboat Institution ['rɔɪəl 'næʃnəl 'laɪfbəʊt ˌɪnstɪ'tju:ʃn] *brit. Lebensrettungsgesellschaft* 55
rucksack ['rʌksæk] Rucksack 90
run (ran) [rʌn] laufen, rennen 38
runner ['rʌnə] Läufer(in) 60
running ['rʌnɪŋ] Laufen, Rennen 68
Russian ['rʌʃən] russisch 40
sad [sæd] traurig 103
safari [sə'fɑ:ri] Safari 90
salad ['sæləd] Salat 64
sales manager ['seɪlz mænɪdʒə] Verkaufsleiter(in) 52
salesperson, -people ['seɪlz ˌpɜ:sən, -ˌpi:pl] Verkäufer(in) 55
same [seɪm] der/die/das gleiche 44
sandwich, -es ['sænwɪdʒ] Sandwich, Butterbrot 21
satellite navigation (sat nav) ['sætəlaɪt ˌnævɪ'geɪtʃn 'sæt næv] Satellitennavigation 140
Saturday ['sætədeɪ] Sonnabend, Samstag 49
sauna ['sɔ:nə] Sauna 152
save [seɪv] retten 55
say [seɪ] sagen 10
scheme [ski:m] Plan, Einrichtung 35
school [sku:l] Schule 23
schoolwork ['sku:lwɜ:k] Schulaufgaben 98
Scotland ['skɒtlənd] Schottland 57
Scrabble ['skræbl] *Brettspiel* 61
screen [skri:n] Bildschirm 161
sculpture ['skʌlptʃə] Skulptur 104
sea [si:] Meer, See 55
season ['si:zn] Jahreszeit 147
seat [si:t] (Sitz)Platz 119
second ['sekənd] zweite(r, -s) 58
see (saw) [si:, sɔ:] sehen 11
seminar ['semɪnɑ:] Seminar, Kurs 67
send (sent) [send, sent] schicken 29
sentence ['sentəns] Satz 29
September [sep'tembə] September 77
series ['sɪəri:z] (Fernseh)Serie 165
serious ['sɪərɪəs] ernst 103
service ['sɜ:vɪs] Service, Dienstleistung 54
seven ['sevn] sieben 15
seventeen [sevn'ti:n] siebzehn 27
seventh ['sevnθ] siebente(r, -s) 76
seventy ['sevntɪ] siebzig 27
shake hands (shook) [ʃeɪk, ʃʊk] Hände schütteln 120
she [ʃi:] sie 10
shiatsu [ʃi'ætsu:] Shiatsu *(jap. Form der Körpertherapie)* 152
shirt [ʃɜ:t] Hemd 39
shocked [ʃɒkt] schockiert 120
shoe [ʃu:] Schuh 39
shop [ʃɒp] Geschäft, Laden 21
shop assistant ['ʃɒp əˌsɪstənt] Verkäufer(in) 52
shopping ['ʃɒpɪŋ] Einkaufen 85
shopping list ['ʃɒpɪŋ lɪst] Einkaufszettel 148
short [ʃɔ:t] kurz 40
shorts [ʃɔ:ts] kurze Hose 39
show [ʃəʊ] zeigen 28
show [ʃəʊ] Vorführung 87
shower ['ʃaʊə] Dusche 124
Sicilian [sɪ'sɪlɪən] sizilianisch 87
side [saɪd] Seite 148
sign [saɪn] Zeichen 140
silly ['sɪlɪ] albern 60
sing (sang) [sɪŋ, sæŋ] singen 38
singer ['sɪŋə] Sänger(in) 74
single ['sɪŋgl] *hier:* Einzelzimmer 125
single ['sɪŋgl] *hier:* Einzelfahrkarte 137
sir [sɜ:] *höfliche Anrede für einen Herrn* 82
sister ['sɪstə] Schwester 33
sit (sat) [sɪt, sæt] sitzen 64
situation [sɪtjʊ'eɪʃn] Situation, Lage 116
situational response [sɪtʃu'eɪʃənəl rɪ'spɒns] situationsbedingte Reaktion 46
six [sɪks] sechs 15
sixteen [sɪks'ti:n] sechzehn 27
sixth [sɪksθ] sechste(r, -s) 76
sixty ['sɪkstɪ] sechzig 27
skiing ['ski:ɪŋ] Skifahren 59
skirt [skɜ:t] Rock 39
sky [skaɪ] Himmel 163
sleep [sli:p] Schlaf 66
sleeper car [sli:pə kɑ:] Schlafwagen 167
slippers ['slipəs] Hausschuhe 114
slogan ['sləʊgən] Werbespruch 29
slow [sləʊ] langsam 109
slowly ['sləʊlɪ] langsam 110
small [smɔ:l] klein 17
small talk ['smɔ:l tɔ:k] Geplauder 149
smart [smɑ:t] schick 54
smile [smaɪl] Lächeln 22
smoke [sməʊk] rauchen 64
snack ['snæk] Imbiss 109

snack bar ['snæk bɑː] Imbiss(restaurant) 46
snow [snəʊ] Schnee 54
so [səʊ] so 54
social ['səʊʃl] sozial 116
society, -ies [sə'saɪətɪ] Gesellschaft 55
sock [sɒk] Socke 108
sofa ['səʊfə] Sofa, Couch 41
soft [sɒft] weich 96
some [sʌm] einige 26
someone ['sʌmwʌn] jemand 15
something ['sʌmtaɪmz] etwas 64
sometimes ['sʌmθɪŋ] manchmal 64
son [sʌn] Sohn 33
song [sɒŋ] Lied 41
soon [suːn] bald 87
sorry ['sɒrɪ] traurig 19
sort: a sort of ['sɔːt əv] eine Art von 33
sort out [sɔːt 'aʊt] lösen 53
sound [saʊnd] Laut, Geräusch 98
soup [suːp] Suppe 72
sour milk [saʊə 'mɪlk] Sauermilch 61
south [saʊθ] Süd- 155
South Africa [saʊθ 'æfrɪka] Südafrika 163
South African [saʊθ 'æfrɪkan] südafrikanisch 163
south-west [saʊθ 'west] Südwest 158
spa [spɑː] Kurort 152
Spain [speɪn] Spanien 11
Spanish ['spænɪʃ] spanisch 11
speak (spoke) [spiːk, spəʊk] sprechen, reden 38
speaker ['spiːkə] Sprecher(in) 9
special ['speʃl] besondere(r, -s), speziell 55
speciality, -ies [ˌspeʃɪ'ælətɪ] Spezialität 96
speed [spiːd] Geschwindigkeit 109
spell (spelt) [spel, spelt] buchstabieren 14
spend (spent) [spend, spent] verbringen, ausgeben 104
spider ['spaɪdə] Spinne 82
spokesperson, -people ['spəʊksˌpɜːsən, -ˌpiːpl] Sprecher(in) 70
sport [spɔːt] Sport 41
sports centre ['spɔːts sentə] Sportzentrum 29
sports fan ['spɔːts fæn] Sportfan 38
sportsperson, -people ['spɔːtsˌpɜːsən, -piːpl] sportlicher Mensch 61
sporty ['spɔːtɪ] sportlich 38
spring [sprɪŋ] Frühling 147
stadium ['steɪdɪəm] Stadion 124
stage [steɪdʒ] Bühne 108
stairs [steəz] Treppe 68
stamp [stæmp] (Brief)Marke 11
stand (stood) [stænd, stʊd] stehen 54
stand up [stænd 'ʌp] aufstehen 111
star [stɑː] Stern 31
star in a film [stɑː] in einem Film eine Hauptrolle spielen 98
start [stɑːt] anfangen 20
station ['steɪʃn] Bahnhof 23
stay [steɪ] bleiben, sich aufhalten 48
steak [steɪk] Steak 73
still [stɪl] noch 58
stone [stəʊn] Stein 108
stop [stɒp] anhalten, aufhören 20
store [stɔː] Geschäft 22
story, -ies ['stɔːrɪ] Geschichte 44
strange [streɪndʒ] seltsam, merkwürdig 120
street [striːt] Straße 22
street plan ['striːt plæn] Straßenplan 23
stress [stres] Stress 67
stressful ['stresfl] stressig 54
strong [strɒŋ] stark 167
student ['stjuːdnt] Student(in) 31
study ['stʌdi] studieren 120
style [staɪl] Stil 97
subject ['sʌbdʒɪkt] Thema 29
subway (AmE) ['sʌbweɪ] U-Bahn 146
suggestion [sə'dʒestʃən] Vorschlag 66
suitcase ['suːtkeɪs] Koffer 85
suite [swiːt] Suite, Zimmerflucht 129
summer ['sʌmə] Sommer 54
suncream ['sʌnkriːm] Sonnencreme 85
Sunday ['sʌndeɪ] Sonntag 49
sundial ['sʌndaɪəl] Sonnenuhr 58
sunglasses ['sʌnglɑːsɪs] Sonnenbrille 85
sunny ['sʌnɪ] sonnig 86
sunshine ['sʌnʃaɪn] Sonnenschein 129
superdad ['suːpə dæd] Superpapa 38
super-fast ['suːpə fɑːst] sehr schnell 117
supermarket ['suːpəˌmɑːkɪt] Supermarkt 23
supermum ['suːpə mʌm] Supermamma 38
sure [ʃʊə] sicher 108
surname ['sɜːneɪm] Familienname, Nachname 13
sushi ['suːʃɪ] Sushi *(jap. Speise)* 79
Sweden ['swiːdn] Schweden 146
sweet [swiːt] süß 109
swim (swam) [swɪm, swæm] schwimmen 38
swimmer ['swɪmə] Schwimmer(in) 59
swimming pool ['swɪmɪŋ puːl] Swimmingpool 25
Swiss [swɪs] Schweizer, schweizerisch 11
Switzerland ['swɪtsələnd] die Schweiz 11
system ['sɪstəm] System 102
table ['teɪbl] Tisch 63
taco ['tækəʊ] Taco *(mex. Speise)* 109
take (took) [teɪk, tʊk] nehmen 38
talent ['tælənt] Begabung, Talent 98
talk [tɔːk] sprechen, reden 26
talk show ['tɔːk ʃəʊ] Talkshow 165
tall [tɔːl] groß 40
task [tɑːsk] Aufgabe 29
taxi ['tæksɪ] Taxi 54
tea [tiː] Tee 55
teacher ['tiːtʃə] Lehrer(in) 11
team [tiːm] Team 29
technique [tek'niːk] Technik 67
technology, -ies [tek'nɒlədʒɪ] Technologie, Technik 102
teddy bear ['tedi beə] Teddybär 17
telephone ['telɪfəʊn] Telefon 44
telescope ['telɪskəʊp] Teleskop, Fernrohr 163
television ['telɪˌvɪʒn] Fernsehen 54
tell (told) [tel, təʊld] erzählen 41
temperature ['temprətʃə] Temperatur 158
ten [ten] zehn 27
tennis ['tenɪs] Tennis 38
tenth [tenθ] zehnte(r, -s) 76
terminal ['tɜːmɪnl] Terminal 93
test [test] Test 33
textile ['tekstaɪl] Stoff 104
Thai [taɪ] thailändisch 21
than [ðæn] als 44
thank [θæŋk] danken 110
thank you ['θæŋk jʊ] danke 9
thanks [θæŋks] danke 9
that [ðæt] der/die/das, jene(r, -s), diese(r, -s) 10
that's a pity ['pɪtɪ] das ist schade 116
the [ðə, ðɪ before vowels] der/die/das 12
theatre ['θɪətə] Theater 28
their [ðeə] ihr(e) 16
them [ðem] sie, ihnen 54
theme [θiːm] Thema 96
then [ðen] da, damals 70
therapy, -ies ['θerəpɪ] Therapie 152
there [ðeə(r)] dort, da 21
these [ðiːz] diese 70
they [ðeɪ] sie 16
thing [θɪŋ] Ding 22
think (thought) [θɪŋk, θɔːt] denken 11
thinking sport ['θɪŋkɪŋ spɔːt] Denksport 70
third [θɜːd] dritte(r, -s) 76
thirteen [θɜː'tiːn] dreizehn 27
thirtieth ['θɜːtɪɪθ] dreißigste(r, -s) 76
thirty ['θɜːtɪ] dreißig 27
this [ðɪs] dieser/diese/dieses 9
thousand ['θaʊznd] tausend 99
three [θriː] drei 15
through [θruː] durch 104
thumb [θʌm] Daumen 82
Thursday ['θɜːzdeɪ] Donnerstag 49
ticket ['tɪkɪt] Fahrkarte, Fahrschein 40
time [taɪm] Zeit 32
timetable ['taɪmˌteɪbl] Fahrplan 137
tip [tɪp] Spitze 54
tired ['taɪəd] müde 66
title ['taɪtl] Titel 70
to [tuː] zu 9
today [tə'deɪ] heute 44
together [tə'geðə] zusammen 29
toilet ['tɔɪlɪt] Toilette 114
tomato, -oes [tə'mɑːtəʊ] Tomate 72
tomorrow [tə'mɒrəʊ] morgen 83
tonight [tə'naɪt] heute Abend 73
too [tuː] auch 9
top [tɒp] oberer Teil, Spitze 117
top floor [ˌtɒp 'flɔː] oberstes Stockwerk 117
total ['təʊtl] Gesamtmenge 46
tour [tʊə(r)] Tour 96
tourist ['tʊərɪst] Tourist(in) 26
tourist attraction ['tʊərɪst ə'trækʃn] Touristenattraktion 90
towel ['taʊəl] Handtuch 85
tower ['taʊə] Turm 94
town [taʊn] Stadt 13
toy [tɔɪ] Spielzeug 104
track [træk] Gleis 146
traditional [trə'dɪʃnl] traditionell 54
tragedy, -ies ['trædʒədɪ] Tragödie 103
train [treɪn] Zug 22
train [treɪn] trainieren 109
train driver ['treɪn ˌdraɪvə] Zugführer 52
training ['treɪnɪŋ] Ausbildung, Schulung 61
tram [træm] Straßenbahn 111
tramcar ['træmkɑː] Straßenbahnwagen 164
transport ['trænspɔːt] Beförderung 135
travel ['trævl] Reisen 128

travel agent ['trævl ˌeɪdʒənt] Reisebürokaufmann, Reisebürokauffrau, Reisebüro 158
travel document ['trævl ˌdɒkjuːmɛnt] Reisedokument 129
traveller ['trævələ] Reisende(r) 140
tree [triː] Baum 148
trip [trɪp] Ausflug, Trip 116
trousers ['traʊzəz] Hose 39
truck [trʌk] Lastwagen 97
try [traɪ] versuchen 20
t-shirt ['tiː ʃɜːt] T-Shirt 60
tube [tjuːb] *Londoner U-Bahn* 146
Tuesday ['tjuːzdeɪ] Dienstag 49
tuna ['tjuːnə] Thunfisch 72
Turkey ['tɜːkɪ] die Türkei 11
Turkish ['tɜːkɪʃ] türkisch 11
TV [ˌtiː'viː] Fernsehen 101
TV presenter [ˌtiː'viː prɪ'zentə] Fernsehmoderator 52
twelfth [twelfθ] zwölfte(r, -s) 76
twelve [twelv] zwölf 27
twentieth ['twentɪɪθ] zwanzigste(r, -s) 76
twenty ['twentɪ] zwanzig 27
twenty-six-year-old [ˌtwentɪ 'sɪks jɪə əʊld] 26-Jährige(r) 70
twice [twaɪs] zweimal 59
twin city, -ies/town [twɪn 'sɪti/taʊn] Partnerstadt 28
two [tuː] zwei 15
two-minute [tuː'mɪnɪt] zweiminütig 70
type [taɪp] Typ, Art 39
typical ['tɪpɪkl] typisch 72
uncle ['ʌŋkl] Onkel 33
unclearly [ˌʌn'klɪə] unklar 110
under ['ʌndə] unter 73
underground ['ʌndəgraʊnd] unterirdisch 134
underpaid [ˌʌndə'peɪd] unterbezahlt 54
understand (understood) [ˌʌndə'stænd, -stʊd] verstehen 15
underwater [ˌʌndə'wɔːtə] unter Wasser 60
unfriendly [ʌn'frendlɪ] unfreundlich 86
unhappy [ʌn'hæpɪ] unglücklich 151
unhealthy [ʌn'helθɪ] nicht gesund 64
uniform ['juːnɪfɔːm] Uniform 53
Union Station ['juːnjən 'steɪʃn] *Bahnhofsname* 167
university, -ies [juːni'vɜːsətɪ] Universität 28
unusual [ʌn'juːʒʊəl] ungewöhnlich 73
up [ʌp] oben 68
upstairs [ˌʌp'steəz] oben 65
us [ʌs] uns 64
USA (United States of America) [ˌjuːes'eɪ] USA (Vereinigte Staaten von Amerika) 12
use [juːz] benutzen, gebrauchen 9
useful ['juːsfʊl] nützlich 54
usually ['juːʒʊəlɪ] meistens, normalerweise 64
Valentine's Day ['væləntaɪnz deɪ] Valentinstag (14. Februar) 76
vase [vɑːz] Vase 67
vegetable ['vedʒtəbl] Gemüse 71
vegetarian [ˌvedʒɪ'teərɪən] Vegetarier(in) 82
very ['verɪ] sehr 9
Victoria and Albert Museum (V&A) [vɪkˌtɔːriə ənd ˌælbət mjuː'ziːəm] *Museum in London* 104
video camera ['vɪdiəʊ ˌkæmərə] Videokamera 161
view [vjuː] Aussicht 117
village ['vɪlɪdʒ] Dorf 140
villager ['vɪlɪdʒə] Dorfbewohner(in) 140
visit ['vɪzɪt] besuchen 91
visit ['vɪzɪt] Besuch 149
visitor ['vɪzɪtə] Gast, Besucher 29
voluntary ['vɒləntrɪ] freiwillig 55
volunteer [vɒlən'tɪə] Freiwillige 55
waiter ['weɪtə] Kellner 82
wake up (woke) [weɪk ʌp, wəʊk] aufwachen 167
Wales [weɪlz] Wales 148
walk [wɔːk] spazieren gehen,wandern 38
walker ['wɔːkə] Wanderer(in), Spaziergänger(in) 59
wall [wɔːl] Mauer 90
want [wɒnt] wollen 26
warm [wɔːm] warm 33
warn [wɔːn] warnen 140
warning ['wɔːnɪŋ] Warnung 140
was *(to be)* [wɒz] war 32
wash [wɒʃ] waschen 114
washing machine ['wɒʃɪŋ mə'ʃiːn] Waschmaschine 38
watch [wɒtʃ] ansehen, beobachten 59
watch, -es [wɒtʃ] (Armband)Uhr 47
water ['wɔːtə] Wasser 58
waterfall ['wɔːtəfɔːl] Wasserfall 91
way [weɪ] Art, Weise 109
way [weɪ] Weg 140
we [wiː] wir 16
wear (wore) [weə, wɔː] tragen 53
weather ['weðə] Wetter 86
wedding ['wedɪŋ] Hochzeit 152
Wednesday ['wenzdeɪ] Mittwoch 49
week [wiːk] Woche 11
weekend [ˌwiːk'end] Wochenende 60
weekend break [ˌwiːk'end 'breɪk] Wochenendreise 96
welcome ['welkəm] willkommen 16
well [wel] nun, gut 9
were [wɜː(r)] warst, -t, -en 86
West [west] Westen 148
what [wɒt] was 15
what about ... [wɒt ə'baʊt] wie wäre es mit ... 54
when [wen] wann 15
where [weə] wo 10
which [wɪtʃ] welche(r, -s) 63
white [waɪt] weiß 39
who [huː] wer 37
whose [huːz] wessen 123
why [waɪ] warum 66
wide [waɪd] breit 140
wife, wives [waɪf, waɪvz] (Ehe)Frau 33
will [wɪl] wird 140
win (won) [wɪn, wʌn] gewinnen 97
window ['wɪndəʊ] Fenster 148
windy ['wɪndɪ] windig 147
wine [waɪn] Wein 71
wine-cellar ['waɪn selə] Weinkeller 134
winter ['wɪntə] Winter 54
with [wɪð] mit 20
without [wɪð'aʊt] ohne 125
woman, women ['wʊmən, wɪmɪn] Frau 12
won [wʌn] gewonnen 70
wonderful ['wʌndəfʊl] wunderbar, wundervoll 91
word [wɜːd] Wort 11
work [wɜːk] Arbeit 48
work [wɜːk] arbeiten 41
worker ['wɜːkə] Arbeiter(in) 113
world [wɜːld] Welt 26
worry ['wʌrɪ] sich sorgen 111
worse [wɜːs] schlechter 125
worst [wɜːst] schlechteste(r, -s) 54
would like a [wʊd 'laɪk ə] hätte gern 75
would like to [wʊd 'laɪk tuː] würde gern 75
write (wrote) [raɪt, rəʊt] schreiben 77
writer ['raɪtə] Verfasser(in) 100
writing ['raɪtɪŋ] Schreiben 67
wrong [rɒŋ] falsch 158
year [jɪə] Jahr 44
yellow ['jeləʊ] gelb 39
yes [jes] ja 11
yesterday ['jestədeɪ] gestern 101
you [juː] du 9
young [jʌŋ] jung 44
your [jɔː] dein(e) 9
your turn ['jə, tɜːn] du bist / Sie sind an der Reihe 12
you're welcome [jə, 'welkəm] gern geschehen 22
yourself [jɔː'self] dich 45
zero ['zɪərəʊ] null 15
zone [zəʊn] Zone 132
zoo [zuː] Zoo 137
zoology [zuː'ɒlədʒɪ] Zoologie 168

Can do list A1

Hören

• Ich kann verstehen, wenn jemand sehr langsam und deutlich mit mir spricht und wenn lange Pausen mir Zeit lassen, den Sinn zu erfassen.	**Unit:** 1A **CD-R:** 1/7, 1/52, 2/32 **www:** U10B1
• Ich kann eine einfache Wegerklärung, wie man zu Fuß oder mit einem öffentlichen Verkehrsmittel von A nach B kommt, verstehen.	**Unit:** 2A, 11B **CD-R:** 1/18 **www:** U2A2, U11B1
• Ich kann Fragen und Aufforderungen verstehen, mit denen man sich langsam und sorgfältig an mich wendet, und ich kann kurzen einfachen Anweisungen folgen.	**Unit:** 11B **CD-R:** 1/14, 1/42
• Ich kann Zahlen, Preisangaben und Uhrzeiten verstehen.	**Unit:** 1B, 7A, 4A **CD-R:** 1/11, 2/1, 1/38 **www:** U1B4, U7A1, U4A2

Lesen

• Ich kann in Zeitungsartikeln Angaben zu Personen (Wohnort, Alter usw.) verstehen.	**Unit:** 5A, 8A
• Ich kann einen Fragebogen (bei der Einreise oder bei der Anmeldung im Hotel) so weit verstehen, dass ich die wichtigsten Angaben zu meiner Person machen kann (z. B. Name, Vorname, Geburtsdatum, Nationalität).	**Unit:** 1B **www:** U1B3
• Ich kann Wörter und Ausdrücke auf Schildern verstehen, denen man im Alltag oft begegnet (wie z. B. „Bahnhof", „Parkplatz", „Rauchen verboten", „rechts bleiben").	**Unit:** 2A, 4A, 11B **www:** U9B3
• Ich kann kurze, einfache schriftliche Wegerklärungen verstehen.	**Unit:** 2A, 11B **www:** U11B2
• Ich kann kurze, einfache Mitteilungen auf Postkarten verstehen, z. B. Feriengrüße.	**Unit:** 7A **www:** U7A3

Strategien

• Ich kann sagen, dass ich nicht verstehe.	**Unit:** 4A
• Ich kann mit ganz einfachen Worten darum bitten, etwas zu wiederholen.	**Unit:** 1B, 2A

Schreiben

• Ich kann eine Glückwunschkarte schreiben, zum Beispiel zum Geburtstag.	**Unit:** 9B **www:** U9B1
• Ich kann eine einfache Postkarte (z. B. mit Feriengrüßen) schreiben.	**Unit:** 7A **www:** U7A3
• Ich kann einen Notizzettel schreiben, um jemanden zu informieren, wo ich bin oder wo wir uns treffen.	**Unit:** 6B **www:** U6B1

• Ich kann in einfachen Sätzen über mich schreiben, z. B. wo ich wohne und was ich mache.	**Unit:** 1B, 3B

Zusammenhängend sprechen

• Ich kann Angaben zu meiner Person machen (z. B. Adresse, Telefonnummer, Alter, Herkunftsland, Familie, Hobbys).	**Unit:** 1A, 1B, 3A, 5A **CD-R:** 1/4, 1/12, 1/27, 1/50 **www:** U1A4, U1B1, U1B3, U1B4, U3A2, U5A3
• Ich kann beschreiben, wo ich wohne.	**Unit:** 2B, 10A **CD-R:** 1/16, 1/17, 2/29, 2/30 **www:** U2B3, U10A2

An Gesprächen teilnehmen

• Ich kann jemanden vorstellen und einfache Gruß- und Abschiedsformeln gebrauchen.	**Unit:** 1A **CD-R:** 1/2, 1/3 **www:** U1A1, U1A3
• Ich kann einfache Fragen stellen und beantworten, einfache Aussagen machen oder auf einfache Aussagen von anderen reagieren, sofern es um ganz vertraute oder unmittelbar notwendige Dinge geht.	**Unit:** 9A, 10A **CD-R:** 1/14, 1/29, 1/42 **www:** U6A1, U8B1, U8B2, U9A1, U9A2, U12A3
• Ich kann mich auf einfache Art verständigen, bin aber darauf angewiesen, dass die Gesprächspartnerin / der Gesprächspartner bereit ist, etwas langsamer zu wiederholen oder anders zu sagen, und mir dabei hilft zu formulieren, was ich sagen möchte.	**CD-R:** 1/46, 1/48, 1/67
• Ich kann einfache Einkäufe machen, wenn es möglich ist, durch Zeigen oder Gesten zu verdeutlichen, was ich meine.	**Unit:** 7A **CD-R:** 2/1 **www:** U7A1
• Ich komme mit Zahlen, Mengenangaben, Preisen und Uhrzeiten zurecht.	**Unit:** 1B, 6B, 7A, 4A **CD-R:** 1/11, 1/66, 2/1, 1/38 **www:** U1B4, U6B4, U7A1, U4A1, U4A2
• Ich kann andere um etwas bitten und anderen etwas geben.	**Unit:** 6A **CD-R:** 1/60, 1/61 **www:** U6A3
• Ich kann Leuten Fragen zu ihrer Person stellen – z. B. wo sie wohnen, was für Leute sie kennen oder was für Dinge sie haben – und ich kann auf Fragen dieser Art Antwort geben, wenn die Fragen langsam und deutlich formuliert werden.	**Unit:** 1B, 3A, 10A **CD-R:** 1/1, 1/3, 1/4, 1/27, 1/28, 2/29, 2/30 **www:** U1B3, U3A3, U10A1, U10A2
• Ich kann Angaben zur Zeit machen mit Hilfe von Wendungen wie „nächste Woche", „letzten Freitag", „im November", „um drei Uhr".	**Unit:** 4A, 5A, 6B, 7B **CD-R:** 1/38-41, 1/51, 1/52, 2/8, 2/9 **www:** U4A2, U4A4, U5A1, U5A2, U6B3, U7B1, U8A1, U12A2

Acknowledgements

The material reproduced in this book has been taken from the following sources:

Photographs:

Action Press, Hamburg: page 60 (middle) – Associated Newspapers Ltd.: page 140 (top) – Associated Press GmbH, Frankfurt a. M.: page 163 (top) – BBC Worldwide, London: page 14 (BBC) – www.britainonview.com: page 60 (left) – CINETEXT, Frankfurt: page 123 (5) – Vanessa Clark, Abingdon: pages 21, 32, 49, 55 (top right + left), 67 (middle left), 85 (5), 136 (top), 140 (8–10), 163 (bottom), 164 (bottom) – Consignia plc. Reproduced by kind permission of Consignia. All Rights Reserved.: page 11 (2) – Corbis GmbH, Düsseldorf: pages 16 (right), 17 (background), 19, 52 (2), 54, 56 (9), 70 (middle), 98, 104 (middle, top), 114 (top middle, top right, bottom left), 123 (top), 134 (top), 135 (middle), 137, 154 (middle right) – picture–alliance/dpa: page 59 (right) – Mary Evans Picture Library, London: page 58 (middle) – Fotolia Deutschland, Berlin: pages 11 (top 1), 24 (1), 14 (sms), 99 (left), 118 (6), 163 (bottom), 164 (bottom) – Getty Images: pages 60 (right), 109, 154 (top left), 158 (bottom), 161 (bottom) – Gray Line New York Sightseeing: page 31 – HiPP GmbH & Co. Vertrieb KG: page 17 – The Historic Union Station Hotel, Indianapolis: page 167 – Lynda Hübner, München: pages 22, 65 – IFA Bilderteam GmbH, München: page 123 (Barbie) – InterContinental Hotels Group 2008: page 128 (middle) – iStock International Inc., Calgary: cover, pages 3, 11 (5, 8), 14 (bottom), 35, 40 (a–c), 52 (8), 58 (bottom right), 61 (left, right), 79 (bottom left), 102, 104 (middle right, left), 114 (bottom, middle), 119 (8), 131, 136 (bottom), 152 (middle, left), 154 (bottom left), 155, 161 (top), 162 (top) – Jay Bietz: page 165 – Jerry: page 164 (top) – laif, Köln: pages 59 (middle right), 162 (bottom) – Langenscheidt Archiv: pages 13 (top left), 101, 116 (right) – Tricia Lewis: page 128 (left) – Library Hotel, New York: page 128 (right), 168 – Bildarchiv Mauritius, Mittenwald: pages 16 (left), 130 – Dieter Mayr, München: cover (inserts), pages 9, 21 (top), 32 (top left), 34, 48, 51, 64, 77, 78, 93, 153, 154 (middle left, top right, bottom right) – MTV Networks Germany GmbH: page 14 (MTV) – www.nearthecoast.com: page 55 (bottom right) – Österreichische Post AG: page 11 (3) – PA Photos Ltd., London: pages 73, 108, 110 – pixelio: pages 92 (middle left, top left, bottom left + right), 163 (bottom), 164 (bottom) – Polyglott Verlag, München: page 146 (top) – Sabine Reiter, München: page 47 – The Ritz, London: page 133 – RNLI: page 55 (left) – Rough Guides Ltd.: page 85 (6) – shutterstock.com: pages 10 (right, left), 11 (middle 1, 2, 4, 6, 7), 12, 13 (bottom left, right), 15, 24 (2–16), 25 (left), 26, 27, 28, 29, 33, 37, 39, 40 (bottom), 41 (bottom right, middle right, 2nd from top right, bottom left, top left, top middle, middle left), 44, 52 (3, 4, 5, 6, 7, 9), 53, 56 (1–8), 58, 59 (left, middle left), 61 (middle), 62, 63, 64, 66, 67, 68, 69, 70 (left, right), 74 (1–16), 76, 79, 80 (1–6), 81, 85 (1, 2, 3, 4, 7, 8), 86 (bottom, top), 87, 88, 89, 90, 91 (right), 92, 94 (top, bottom), 96, 97, 99 (middle, right), 100 (middle, right), 105, 111, 114 (middle left), 116 (left, bottom, top middle), 117, 118 (1–5), 119 (1–7), 120, 123 (1, 2, 3, 4), 125, 126, 129, 131 (2nd from top right), 134 (bottom), 135 (left, right), 138, 140 (1–7), 143, 146 (bottom), 147 (bottom, top), 149, 151, 152 (right), 158 (top), 161 middle), 162 (middle), 163 (bottom), 164 (bottom), 166 – Margarete Steiff GmbH: page 17 – Stockfood, München: page 79 (top left) – Tips Images: page 41 (top right) – Transport for London: page 141 – Ullstein Bilderdienst, Berlin: pages 17 (pasta, W. Porsche, A. Oetker, G. Barilla), 100 (left) – Time Warner Inc.: page 14 (CNN)

Illustrations:

Grafik Design Jürgen Bartz, München: page 91
Gerlinde Keller Illustration, München: pages 25, 42, 48, 49, 60, 65, 71, 88, 106, 119, 139, 145, 167, 168, 180
Graham Round (Linda Rogers Associates, London): pages 20, 82

Text:

schulverlag blmv AG, Bern: pages 222, 223

We should be very grateful for any information which might assist us in tracing the copyright owners of sources we have been unable to acknowledge.

Learner CD/CD-ROMs:

Weitere Informationen zu den beigelegten CDs finden Sie unter www.langenscheidt.de/englishcompass.